WOMEN AND RETIREMENT

In the last century, changes to the nature and patterns of women's working lives have been vast. Notably, the huge increase in women's participation in the paid workforce means that today women are retiring in unprecedented numbers. How do they cope with this lifestyle transition? What major difficulties do they face? How do they process the problems associated with managing this transition in fulfilling ways while juggling family, financial, friendship, ageing and health issues? To date, most retirement studies have focused on men, and therefore gender-specific issues relating to post-work life, such as the pay gap, the double shift, women's longer lifespans and their traditional roles as carers and social nurturers, have been afforded far less attention.

Women and Retirement: Challenges of a New Life Stage is the first book of its kind to examine women's retirement using a lifespan perspective. Based on the authors' extensive study of over 1,000 retired Australian women as well as current research, the book presents models of various retirement trajectories and compares women's experiences with the more widely researched retirement experiences of men. Moore and Rosenthal consider the nature of the transition from full-time work to retirement and the many different pathways and factors influencing this journey: women's financial status in the retirement years; their health changes; and the varied activity patterns they adopt.

Women and Retirement is a comprehensive, up-to-date and evidence-based review of the female retirement experience. It will be invaluable for courses on ageing and health within psychology, women's studies, social work and sociology, and for use by practitioners in these fields.

Susan Moore is a researcher in social and developmental psychology, with over 40 years' experience in academic and professional environments. Now retired, she was the inaugural research professor in psychology at both Victoria University of Technology and Swinburne University in Australia, and is a Fellow of the Australian Psychological Society.

Doreen Rosenthal is a developmental psychologist and public health researcher, and an international expert in the field of adolescence. She was Professor of Women's Health and Director, Key Centre for Women's Health in Society in the Melbourne School of Population Health at The University of Melbourne until her retirement in February 2008. Doreen is a Fellow of the Academy of Social Sciences in Australia and an Officer in the Order of Australia.

WOMEN AND RETIREMENT

Challenges of a New Life Stage

Susan Moore and Doreen Rosenthal

LONDON AND NEW YORK

First published 2019
by Routledge
2 Park Square, Milton Park, Abingdon, Oxon OX14 4RN

and by Routledge
711 Third Avenue, New York, NY 10017

Routledge is an imprint of the Taylor & Francis Group, an informa business

© 2019 Susan Moore and Doreen Rosenthal

The right of Susan Moore and Doreen Rosenthal to be identified as the authors of this work has been asserted by them in accordance with sections 77 and 78 of the Copyright, Designs and Patents Act 1988.

All rights reserved. No part of this book may be reprinted or reproduced or utilised in any form or by any electronic, mechanical, or other means, now known or hereafter invented, including photocopying and recording, or in any information storage or retrieval system, without permission in writing from the publishers.

Trademark notice: Product or corporate names may be trademarks or registered trademarks, and are used only for identification and explanation without intent to infringe.

British Library Cataloguing in Publication Data
A catalogue record for this book is available from the British Library

Library of Congress Cataloging in Publication Data
Names: Moore, Susan, 1945- author. | Rosenthal, Doreen, 1938- author.
Title: Women and retirement: challenges of a new life stage / Susan Moore and Doreen Rosenthal.
Description: Abingdon, Oxon ; New York, NY : Routledge, 2019. | Includes bibliographical references and index. | Description based on print version record and CIP data provided by publisher; resource not viewed.
Identifiers: LCCN 2018023123 (print) | LCCN 2018026195 (ebook) | ISBN 9781351696715 (Adobe) | ISBN 9781351696692 (Mobipocket) | ISBN 9781351696708 (ePub) | ISBN 9781138045217 (hardback) | ISBN 9781138045231 (pbk.) | ISBN 9781315172057 (ebook)
Subjects: LCSH: Retired women. | Retirement.
Classification: LCC HQ1062 (ebook) | LCC HQ1062 .M635 2019 (print) | DDC 306.3/8082--dc23
LC record available at https://lccn.loc.gov/2018023123

ISBN: 978-1-138-04521-7 (hbk)
ISBN: 978-1-138-04523-1 (pbk)
ISBN: 978-1-315-17205-7 (ebk)

Typeset in Bembo
by Taylor & Francis Books

Printed and bound in Great Britain by
TJ International Ltd, Padstow, Cornwall

CONTENTS

Acknowledgements		*vi*
1	Retirement: then and now	1
2	Women at work	16
3	Financial security in retirement	31
4	Planning and decision-making	50
5	The psychosocial journey: from worker to retiree	67
6	Retirement and health	83
7	What next?	97
8	Accentuate the positive	112
References		*123*
Index		*142*

ACKNOWLEDGEMENTS

We would like to thank our colleagues and institutions (the Department of Psychological Sciences, Faculty of Health, Arts and Design at Swinburne University of Technology and the Centre for Women's Health, Gender and Society, Melbourne School of Population Health at The University of Melbourne) for providing the resources that enabled us to complete this book. Thanks also to research assistants Alex Poll and Kerrie Shandley who assisted us with their careful work. Special acknowledgement and thanks are due to the women who generously gave their time and considered thoughts as part of our studies and to the various organisations and individuals who helped us to recruit participants for our study of retired women.

We thank our publisher for continuing support and encouragement and our husbands for helping us to enjoy our own retirements.

1

RETIREMENT

Then and now

Man may work from sun to sun,
but woman's work is never done.

(Proverb)

Women, retirement and social change

The old adage sets the scene for our book on women's retirement. It needs some deconstructing in this modern era, but it puts the history of women's (mostly unpaid) work in context. It suggests that women never retire, but also implies continuity in a woman's working life that does not recognise the transition (or transitions) from paid employment to domestic work, and back again. In the last 100 years or so, changes to the nature and patterns of women's working lives have been vast. Accordingly, their lifespan developmental journey needs re-examining. In this book, we review the research and theory relating to one part of that journey – the retirement years.

Of course, women have always worked. They have carted and carried, gathered and collected, toiled in the fields, gardens and kitchens, spun and sewn, laboured to bear, nurture and raise children, and acted as teachers and moral instructors in households and communities. Women's work was mostly done in exchange for food and shelter, or to contribute to a household or farm's self-sufficiency, or to produce goods to sell at markets. Salaried work developed as nations industrialised, but until 50 years ago 'going to work' was far less common for women – especially married women – than for men. During the first half of the twentieth century in the western world, relatively few women worked outside the home after marriage. Some occupations were banned to married women by law, and when women were employed they were paid a fraction of men's salaries. Educational

2 Retirement

opportunities were also limited, further reducing salaried job options. In the nineteenth and twentieth centuries there were several periods during which working women were stigmatised, the attitude being that a woman worth her salt should be able to find a man to support her. The expected gender roles in society were for males to be the breadwinners while women stayed at home, looked after children, and attended to the domestic chores. Some went back to work when the children became adults but this was relatively uncommon.

How things have changed, at least in industrialised countries where women have the right and opportunity to work outside the home. In the UK, the US, Australia and other developed nations, female participation in the workforce more than doubled – in some cases tripled – during the twentieth century (Australian Bureau of Statistics (ABS), 2012; United States Department of Labor, 2000; Lindsay, 2003). Increases in female work participation rates are particularly striking among older age groups. In Australia, more than twice the number of women in the 45–55 year age group were in paid employment in 2011 (around 80 per cent) compared to 1961 (ABS, 2012). Significantly for our population group of interest, between 2001/2002 and 2014/2015 the participation rate for women aged 55–64 years rose from 38.3 per cent to 56.5 per cent, an increase of 18.2 per cent: the highest increase in all age groups for both men and women during this period (ibid., 2016). Similar trends are evident in the UK (Office for National Statistics, 2013) and the US (United States Department of Labor, 2016).

Major world and local events, alterations to the law, and different attitudes have all contributed to this massive social change. Two world wars brought many women into the workforce to fulfil essential services while the male population was fighting. Although most were summarily sent back home when the soldiers returned, their experiences of workplace collegiality and financial independence got many women thinking about life beyond the confines of hearth and home.

Legal changes facilitating women's work began with the suffragettes and votes for women, and continued as the barriers to education for women and girls were gradually stripped away. The Equal Pay Act was passed in America in 1963 (Snow and Snow, 2016), with Australia and the UK following suit in 1969 and 1970, respectively (Commonwealth of Australia, 1998; Office for National Statistics, 2013), thus removing many (but certainly not all) pay differentials between the sexes.

Other examples of systemic facilitation of women's working conditions included the passing in 1975 of both the Sex Discrimination Act and the Employment Protection Act (which made it illegal to dismiss women because of pregnancy and introduced mandatory maternity provisions) in the UK, and the repeal of laws preventing married women from working. For example, in Australia, although women were eligible to vote from 1910 onwards, it was not until 1966 that married women were legally permitted to work in the Commonwealth Public Service (Gibbins, 1996).

Social changes that have markedly influenced women's patterns of work outside the home include later age of marriage, fewer children and longer lifespans. In 1961, the median age for first-time brides in Australia, the US and the UK was 21 years or younger; the majority of women married and had a first child while they were in their 20s (ABS, 2012; Briggs, 2014; Centers for Disease Control and Prevention, 2015). Today, the average age of first marriage for women is 27 years in the US, 30 in the UK, Canada and Australia, and 31 in New Zealand (ABS, 2017a; Office for National Statistics, 2016; Statistics Canada, 2013; Stats NZ, 2017; Stritof, 2017). Similarly, the median age of women on the birth of their first child is around ten years older than it was in the mid-twentieth century. Furthermore, women's lifespans have increased markedly – by more than 30 years over the past century – rising from late 50s to early- to mid-80s in developed countries (World Health Organization (WHO), 2011, 2012). Thus, for women, the years spent bearing and nurturing young children comprise a far smaller percentage of the typical lifespan than they once did. There are more years available for education, work and, of course, retirement activities.

As an aside, it is of interest that an index entitled Healthy Working Life Expectancy (originally developed by Lievre *et al.* (2007) to compare life expectancy in European countries) is now used more broadly to determine the potential of older workers to remain in paid employment for longer. The index has been used by some researchers and policy makers to argue that both mandatory retirement and access to social security/pension benefits could occur at older ages without compromising employee health and wellbeing (e.g. Cutler *et al.* 2011; Forette *et al.* n.d.). These arguments raise many questions about retirement expectations, for nations and for individuals. Issues include, for example, the cost of social security and old age pensions, the impact on the labour market of keeping seniors at work longer, and the role of personal preferences to retire while still healthy enough to enjoy leisure and community activities.

Returning to the discussion of the influence of social context on women's lives, we note that over the last century there has been a huge change in public attitudes to female roles, a change that has in turn led to altered expectations and practical action. In the 1960s and 1970s second-wave feminism accelerated the movement towards gender equality. Real world outcomes of this movement, including more readily available childcare, better pay rates and more generous leave benefits for women workers, meant that longer stretches in the paid workforce became a more realistic possibility for women. Because working women have traditionally worked a 'double shift', doing the lion's share of domestic work, developments such as extended shopping hours, labour-saving devices in the home, and take-away food all facilitated their participation in the paid workforce by reducing the burden of household chores.

The outcome is that baby-boomers (those born in the decade that followed the end of World War II) and subsequent generations of women are far more likely than their mothers to remain in the paid workforce after having children, and to still be there in their 50s and 60s. Although their employment patterns may have included time out while their children were young and also significant periods of part-time work, today's older women have a real presence in the paid labour force. Their identities are not solely based around *Kinder, Kuche, Kirche* (children, kitchen, church); they have work-related and social interests and responsibilities outside of the family as well as the potential for financial independence.

To summarise, in the first half of the twentieth century we saw a situation in which a relatively small proportion of women, especially middle-aged and older women, were in the paid workforce. Those who did work outside the home tended to 'retire' on marriage or when their first child was born, and then did not re-enter the workforce for another twenty or so years – if at all. Those who spent longer periods in the paid workforce – single women, professionals, women in poverty – before retiring in their 50s, 60s or later, were far less likely than today to continue living for many healthy years post-retirement. Since the middle of the last century, this has changed. Now, the expectation is that women will work outside the home for significantly long periods of their lives. They will retire, not at the age of 21 to have children, but in their late 50s, 60s, or even 70s – similarly to men.

This is happening now. Many of those women who went back to work in the 1960s, 1970s or later have recently retired, or will soon do so. It has been suggested that we are 'at a unique point in history when an unprecedented number of women are beginning to retire' (van den Hounaard, 2015, p. 40). Thus, a new social phenomenon has arisen – a large cohort of healthy women living 30 years or more post-retirement. What are these women doing with themselves and how are they faring? How do they face this life transition?

Past research on retirement has mostly been about men (Matlin, 2011). Studies suggest that the major issues faced are perceived loss of status and role, financial stress, boredom and health problems (Wang and Shi, 2014). Do these issues also affect retiring women, and to the same degree? Are there some specific problems that women face? Borrero and Kruger argue that 'male models' of the retirement experience can be ill-suited to apply to women, given 'the unique work histories, institutional barriers, and social inequalities that women have faced in the labor force' (2015, p. 310). Simmons and Betschild (2001) note that those few pre-twenty-first-century studies that were female-focused tended to conclude that women's retirement decisions were largely based around their husbands' work patterns and that women adjusted to retirement more easily than men because their primary role, and sense of self, was tied to home duties and caring for the family. Is this still the case?

In recent years, research groups like Everingham *et al.* (2007) and Duberley *et al.* (2014) have used empirical data to describe a range of more typically female models of work/retirement. Examples include 'downshifting' through an extended period of part-time work before finally retiring, or periodically leaving then re-entering the workforce as a way of managing family responsibilities. An approach that recognises inequalities and differences between men and women's working lives is important, yet a feminist viewpoint in the retirement literature has been 'largely absent as a model to understanding women's experiences' (Simmons and Betschild, 2001, p. 56).

In the following sections of this chapter, we present the generic models or frameworks that have been used by psychologists and other social scientists to study retirement. A brief description of our own study of retired women follows. Throughout the book we have used these data to illustrate and extend our analysis of the published literature. Finally, we present an analysis of the different ways in which 'retirement' is defined, including the difficulties researchers encounter when attempting to pin down this slippery concept.

Retirement frameworks

Several different models or frameworks have shaped psychosocial research into retirement. Wang and Shi (2014) classify these into three overarching approaches (lifespan development models; multilevel models; and outcome focus models) that can also be applied to retirement research within other social science disciplines.

Lifespan development models. These models consider retirement to be a process occurring over time and comprising different stages. These might include a pre-retirement phase of imagining/fantasising, collecting information and making concrete plans. Then might follow a decision-making phase in which pros and cons of different retirement possibilities are weighed up, pressures responded to, intentions formed and eventually resolutions made about when and how to retire. The transition to retirement – a subsequent phase – could involve either a lengthy staged withdrawal from the workforce or a quick departure – at work one day, at home the next. The early years of retirement comprise another phase that may possibly be construed as a 'honeymoon' or as a very difficult adjustment period. Medium- and long-term outcomes are also of interest to researchers, as retirees build up new roles for themselves but also face issues of ageing and often financial constraints. This lifespan perspective on retirement lends itself to research framed in a range of biopsychosocial theories, such as decision-making models, role theory and continuity theory.

One lifespan model often used to frame studies that focus on life transitions is Erikson's (1963) theory of ages and stages. For Erikson, each life stage is characterised by a major crisis or conflict to be worked through and resolved. Probably the most well-known stage is the adolescent identity crisis, in which a young person struggles to find a sense of who she is, where she is going in life and what sort of person she wants to become. While a basic sense of identity may be established in adolescence, a questioning and changing of identity can also occur later in life when an individual's situation alters in some crucial way, for example through parenting, divorce, moving to a new country or – of relevance to our discussion – retirement. The extent to which women have shaped their sense of identity through work roles will influence their approach to retirement and how they cope with the transition, as we see in subsequent chapters in this volume.

In Erikson's theory, a crucial aspect of psychosocial maturity from mid-life onwards is a sense of generativity. This refers to concern for, and the nurture and guidance of, the next and future generations, usually but not exclusively through parenting and grandparenting. It involves making a contribution to society rather than focusing only on self-related concerns. Work can contribute to one's sense of

6 Retirement

generativity through productive efforts and mentoring in the workforce. Mor-Barak, for example, studied a sample of job seekers and noted, but only among older adults, the tendency to view work generatively, 'as a way to teach, train and share skills with younger generations' ((1995, p. 325).

Retirement has the potential to lead to a generativity 'crisis' unless other significant activities and goals can be substituted for those provided in the work environment. Post-retirement, some may feel they are 'on the scrap heap', bitter that their work contributions have been undervalued, or 'useless' as they contemplate the difficulties of meaningful goal-setting in an unstructured non-work environment. Particularly for retirees who were 'workaholics', the challenge to find new goals and activities and avoid self-absorption is one of the early tasks of the transition out of the paid workforce.

Carstensen's Socioemotional Selectivity Theory (2006) is a different kind of lifespan model from Erikson's but it is nevertheless of relevance to the study of ageing and retirement. According to this theory, an individual's perceived time horizon will have a powerful influence on their motivational priorities. When we are young, time seems open-ended, leading to strong motives to 'optimise the future' via meeting new people, extending experiences and learning new things. As we age, the theory predicts that we will instead seek to optimise the present, by spending time with those to whom we are closest and seeking out emotional rewards. Reaching retirement age, or retirement per se, has the potential to narrow our perceived time horizons as we ponder on 'what's left?' rather than 'what's next?' Lockenhoff (2012) postulates that wellbeing outcomes are likely to be suboptimal unless a post-retirement broadening follows this narrowing of time horizons. In order to adjust to life post-retirement, we will need to set new goals that are much less attached to workplace identities. Research to date has been ambiguous, with Lockenhoff noting that time horizons have not been adequately studied over the full course of the retirement years.

Multilevel models. A second overarching model for the examination of the phenomenon of retirement is categorised as 'multilevel' by Wang and Shi. This type of framework emphasises the range of factors that influence adjustment to retirement, from broad national and cultural factors like laws about retiring age, pension provisions and population health, through to social and individual variables such as one's temperament, interests and strength of family and friendship networks. This approach focuses most strongly on the different sets of antecedents to retirement and their effects on coping, adjustment and wellbeing.

Bronfenbrenner's ecological systems theory (1979) is an old but still influential example of the multilevel approach, in which an individual is viewed as being influenced by increasingly distal factors, usually depicted as a series of concentric circles. The inner circle of factors, the microsystem, includes an individual's biological and temperamental disposition as well as the proximal effects of family, peers and immediate neighbourhood. The outer circle is the macrosystem, the broad set of influences on individual behaviour and psychosocial development including cultural attitudes and ideologies, economic and political circumstances of a nation, ethnicity, race and the law.

Between micro- and macrosystems are the mesosystem and the exosystem. The first of these refers to interactions *between* microsystems. In the case of women at, or close to, retiring age, this could include conflicts (or harmonies) between immediate and extended family members. For example, should she retire to spend more time with grandchildren or stay at work in order to more satisfactorily fund retirement? It could also include interactions between home life and work life, for example a woman's partner may wish her to retire to keep him company but her workplace may wish her to stay on longer to manage new developments.

Finally, the exosystem refers to interactions between an individual's immediate context (microsystem influences) and the broader macrosystem factors. For example, a woman may wish to continue in the paid workforce and these wishes may be in harmony with those of her family, peer group and even her workplace, but compulsory retirement age laws may prevent this from happening.

Duberley *et al.* draw on Bronfenbrenner's approach in collecting and analysing their data – one of the few retirement studies to do so. These researchers suggest that in order to understand women's retirement experiences we need to view them within a social context that incorporates 'micro, meso and macro levels of analysis and the relationships between them' (2014, p. 86). They point out the extent to which the retirement experience for women is changing as organisations (and, we might add, government policies) change in terms of, for example, acceptance of part-time work, flexible hours, pay rates for women workers, and respect for older workers.

Focus on outcomes. Wang and Shi call their final model an outcomes framework. Studies using this framework emphasise the many different dimensions relating to the way in which individuals cope with retirement. Financial wellbeing among retired women has been the focus of a number of major studies and reports (e.g. Collinson, 2015; Commonwealth of Australia, 2016), but health/physical wellbeing and mental health are also the subject of a significant amount of research (e.g. Fondow and Emery, 2008; Zhu, 2016). These topics are covered in detail in Chapters 3 and 6.

Carol Ryff's multidimensional model takes a eudemonic approach to wellbeing, that is, the model focuses on meaning and self-realisation as the key to happiness and fulfilment, rather than the pursuit of pleasure. This model can be productively applied to the study of retirement outcomes (Ryff and Keyes, 1995). Ryff delineates six wellbeing dimensions: autonomy; environmental mastery; personal growth; positive relations with others; purpose in life; and self-acceptance. In doing so, she broadens those narrow conceptions of wellbeing as equivalent to either happiness or absence of mental illness, thus allowing for a more nuanced approach to describing adjustment and coping. To give one example, Kubicek *et al.* (2011) used Ryff's model of wellbeing to examine the retirement process, employing large sample data from the Wisconsin Longitudinal Study. The results were complex. Interestingly, Kubicek *et al.* found that both feelings of wellbeing *and* depressive symptoms declined during the transition to retirement. Furthermore, men and women reacted differently to a post-retirement decrease in financial resources and perceived status,

8 Retirement

with men experiencing a greater reduction than women in most aspects of well-being. In our own study of retired women (described in the next section), we used ratings of 14 different types of life satisfaction as well as the concept of generativity in order to pinpoint specific areas in which adjustment has been smooth or rocky, and to relate these areas to a range of potential predictor variables. It was interesting to note that generativity – a developmental maturity/adjustment indicator – was associated with different predictor variables from retirement satisfaction. As well, overall life satisfaction, retirement satisfaction and satisfaction with social life each had different demographic and behavioural predictors. Conceptualising retirement outcomes more broadly enriches our understanding of the psychosocial and behavioural changes that retirement brings, and highlights specific needs and challenges for retirees.

The three frameworks proposed by Wang and Shi are overlapping and can be used in conjunction with one another. Lifespan development during pre- and post-retirement periods can be considered in terms of a changing series of multilevel influences and multidimensional outcomes. Results of studies that use observations, individual and focus group interviews, surveys or case studies can yield quantitative and qualitative data that shed light on the many aspects of the retirement experiences of women. Throughout this book, our aim is to draw together information from all these sources to triangulate current knowledge and delineate still-to-be-resolved questions about women's retirement experiences.

Our study

To enrich this review of the literature and make it as current as possible, in 2016 we conducted an online survey of Australian women aged 55 years and above who self-selected on the basis of being 'substantially retired from the paid workforce'. The survey included many 'tick the box' items about women's working lives, their pre-retirement years and their post-retirement activities, challenges, pleasures and problems. In addition, we included open-ended questions to provide women with the opportunity to write about their experiences in more detail, and to use their own words to communicate their feelings and attitudes.

Our broad research aim was to assess how today's women are managing the transition to retirement, and evaluate what factors are associated with more and less successful retirement experiences. We accessed a sample of 939 women aged 55–94 years, with the average age being 67.4 years. Nearly half had been retired for between two and ten years; one-third were more recent retirees and 20 per cent had been retired for a long time (more than ten years). The sample comprised a mix of partnered (57 per cent), single (never married, 15 per cent), divorced (17 per cent) and widowed (11 per cent) women. Despite a bias towards well-educated women who have had professional and managerial careers, the sample was large and varied enough to enable comparisons to be made between those with almost the full range of educational backgrounds and job status levels. We have used data from our study judiciously throughout the book, both to extend what is known from the published literature and to provide examples of women's points of view and attitudes to retirement issues. Quotes used throughout the book, unless otherwise indicated, are drawn (anonymously) from our study.

What is retirement?

They are interesting words, 'retiring' and 'retirement'. Dictionary definitions stress the cessation of work, sometimes noting that the term is usually applied to paid work. The word can carry the implication that cessation is due to age or infirmity; 'retiring' is also a term associated with going to bed for the night, or being a shy person who avoids the social demands of daily life. On the other hand, Ekerdt (2010) referred to retirement as 'pensioned leisure' and noted that given our increased longevity, it could be seen historically as a new stage of the life course – possibly even 'the crown of life' (Wink and James, 2006). But as with any new life stage, there will be challenges. How can we fill in time, how can we find meaning and purpose? Is there anything left to do?

The 'winding down and opting out' aspect of retirement is represented – somewhat too dramatically for modern sensibilities – in a quotation by the ageing king from Shakespeare's *King Lear*:

> ... and 'tis our fast intent
> To shake all cares and business from our age,
> Conferring them on younger strengths, while we
> Unburdened crawl towards death.
> *(Act 1, Scene 1)*

No doubt because of these negative overtones, Ernest Hemingway was reputed to have called retirement the ugliest word in the language. Many of the women in our study also told us they hated the term and did not want to be defined by it. Several qualitative researchers have noted similar tendencies of retirees to reject the label (e.g. Duberley *et al.*, 2014; Onyx and Benton, 1996). Some saw it as reflecting the stereotype of a woman with her feet up on the couch, watching daytime television, or sitting in a rocking chair, knitting and dozing – a stereotype at odds with the active lives led by so many of today's retired women.

The following quotations from our study participants illustrate some of the complexities that researchers have to face in deciding who is and who is not retired. It is worth reminding the reader that despite their discomfort with the word 'retirement' (and their penchant for writing it in quotation marks), all these women had self-selected into the study of 'women in retirement'.

> I don't believe in retirement as such. ... In more traditional societies, everyone had value from birth to death. Let's get our act together.

> I am enjoying 'retirement' – if you can call it that. I am now putting in more unpaid hours doing voluntary work than when I was in paid work. ... If it

10 Retirement

> was not for the countless hours of unpaid volunteer work carried out by the elder 'retired' members of the community, I think [our country] would grind to a halt.

> I hate the words 'retired' and 'retirement'. I don't see them as referring to me. My life is simply different, less pre-determined and more free-form on a daily basis. I no longer have any formal role so all that I do is totally voluntary.

> I don't like the word 'retirement'. Redefining the whole paradigm around 'work' needs to occur so that women are better represented in Government and business policy and practice conversations. ... I'm an ecological feminist and have very different notions of 'retirement' and 'community' than the patriarchal world we are expected to live in.

Wang and Shi (2014) note that researchers have operationalised the notion of retirement in many different ways, making it difficult at times to compare findings. They quote Ekerdt, who comments on the ambiguity of this concept, 'because there are multiple overlapping criteria by which someone might be called retired, including career cessation, reduced work effort, pension receipt, or self-report' (2010, p. 70).

Retirement also cannot be assumed because someone is older and not working. For example, a woman who is unemployed at the age of 55 years could be retired, or she could be looking for work, 'trying out' retirement but keeping her options open, or training for a new career. Defining when someone is retired tends to be more difficult in a female sample simply because of the greater flexibility and change in women's work histories. We know of women who were not working in their mid-50s owing to redundancy, ill health or family issues, but who later rejoined the paid workforce, some continuing in full-time positions for more than ten years before they finally retired.

To give some idea of the range of definitions used, consider the study by Svensson *et al.* (2015) in comparison with the many pieces of research (including our own) that rely on women's self-report as to when they considered that they had retired. Svensson *et al.*'s longitudinal study of all women born in Sweden in 1935 used a strict definition of retirement age as 'the individual's age the first year the annual income from pensions exceeds the income from annual labour earnings' (ibid., p. 861). While such a definition appears to have a high level of objectivity, the data required to classify retirement in this way are likely to be very difficult to access. Additionally, such 'objective', economic-based assessments of when someone is retired may not always align with their own subjective assessments, nor with their actual source of income; for example, some retired women rely entirely on a husband's income. Nevertheless, each type of definition has its place.

The ambiguities of 'retirement' are even greater when women's work histories are considered. Usually, a distinction is made between paid work and domestic work, with retirement only referring to the former. One could raise the question as to whether most women ever retire from domestic work! Furthermore, Borrero and Kruger (2015) argue that retirement is often an individualised and subjective phenomenon, and that models of retirement should consequently adopt more fluid definitions. But even self-definition is not that easy. Clearly, some of the women in our study saw themselves as both retired and not retired – they volunteered to be in a study of retirees but they also wanted to change the thinking about what that meant. Suffice to say here that throughout this book we take a flexible approach to the meaning of retirement, as recommended by so many commentators.

Retirement pathways

The way individuals define their retirement may relate to their workforce exit strategies (or constraints). A study by Everingham *et al.* (2007) illustrates this. These researchers conducted 28 individual interviews and seven focus groups with women aged 65–70 years and 20 individual interviews and four focus groups with women aged 53–58 years. The first group comprised some recently retired women and the second was a cohort facing retirement in the near future. Discussions ranged around work and family histories, as well as the expectations, preparations and concerns prior to retirement and indeed the actual experiences of retirement.

Focusing on retirement as a process rather than an end state, three models of retirement emerged. 'Gateway model' women retired in the traditional manner, ceasing paid work 'cold turkey' as it were. After retirement, they moved on to different pursuits, often to do with family, volunteer work or hobbies. For these women, retirement could be defined simply as the end of their (paid) working life outside the home. A woman from our research study described her own retirement this way:

> What is retirement? I have three volunteer workplaces, several elderly relatives and a grandchild to care for, a home and garden to keep, gym classes and more activities on offer than can be managed. What is quiet and retired about that?

For 'transitional model' women, there was no clear moment when they defined themselves as 'retired'. These women gradually slowed down their work commitments, moving to part-time and casual positions. They eased out of their paid work lives and gradually spent more time on family and leisure pursuits. One woman put it this way:

> I wound down over about five years, going from full-time to four days a week, then three days, then two. This way I was able to complete projects at work and hand over some of my responsibilities gradually. It also meant that over those five years I had a clear day each week to devote to my two pre-school grandchildren, but I also had excuses not to be too over-committed to babysitting! Now there's more time for travel and interests, but I still occasionally take on some casual work to keep the mind ticking over.

12 Retirement

The third group were described as fitting into a 'transformative model' of retirement in which '[r]etirement is a lifestyle which may include paid work, but *the nature of work is transformed*' (Everingham *et al.* 2007, p. 518; emphasis in the original). These women left their (usually) long-term workplace, viewed themselves as retired, yet either worked on a casual basis to supplement their incomes or, in some cases, developed a whole new career, one that was more likely to be centred on personal interests and a flexible lifestyle. One of our research participants summed up this approach:

> I don't see retirement as clear-cut any more. For me and many others 'retirement' has meant a move into my own business and I see a lot of that – Airbnb hosting, blogging, etc. etc.

Reasons for this particular pattern of moving in and out of the workforce could include boredom with the retired lifestyle, desire to follow a new work-related interest, or the need to boost finances. Interestingly, it is a pattern that appears to be quite common for women, with recent data from the Australian Bureau of Statistics (2017b) indicating that in the year prior to their report, the bulk of Australians who had retired and then rejoined the workforce were female (61 per cent).

Byles *et al.* (2013) found further support for Everingham *et al.*'s models of retirement in a large sample quantitative study of retired and retiring women. They noted that '[f]or many women retirement is seen as a continuation of previous roles, commitments, and household activities', a process rather than a one-off event. They further commented that 'traditional models of retirement are becoming increasingly irrelevant, particularly for those of the baby boomer generation' (ibid., p. 40), and particularly, it seems, for women.

Retirement types

Based on a study of 100 retired American men and women, psychologist Nancy Schlossberg (2004) developed a typology of retirees according to their psychological and behavioural characteristics rather than their work patterns. Her focus was less on gender differences than on counselling individuals of both sexes to be flexible in retirement and to recognise that it involves more than one transition. For example, as well as the change to working intensity, there may be changes to family and social relationships, health, fitness, finances and interests. Not all expectations will be met and unexpected twists and turns may occur during the course of the journey. Schlossberg hypothesised that there were six general patterns of behaviour evident in the way people dealt with the vagaries of this process.

She designated the various types as continuers, adventurers, searchers, easy gliders, retreaters and involved spectators. *Continuers* are retirees who keep alive their pre-retirement interests and skills, using them in further work, volunteer or hobby situations. *Adventurers* begin new activities post-retirement, often taking up pursuits they had wishfully imagined but not had time for during their working lives, such as artistic endeavours or travel. *Searchers* experiment with a range of new activities, exploring many interests through trial and error, keeping busy but not necessarily focusing on a goal-directed pathway. *Easy gliders* are even less purposeful, taking time to enjoy the freedom and flexibility of retirement and letting each day unfold without any fixed goals. *Retreaters* are a group who disengage from many former work-based pursuits, expressing the desire to wind down and reduce life stress. *Involved spectators*, while less active than continuers, adventurers and searchers, maintain a higher level of interest in the world around them than retreaters. For example, they are less likely than retreaters to discontinue work-based relationships when they retire.

A retiree's type may be partly associated with personality characteristics, but as Schlossberg points out, it is also likely to be dependent on many other factors such as age and length of retirement, mental and physical health, financial and family circumstances. One's 'type' may also change as retirement (and age) progress, so that these should not be considered as fixed categories. For example, an individual could begin retirement as a searcher or continuer, fix on some new goals and develop into an adventurer then, with age, settle into becoming an involved spectator. Phases of easy gliding and retreat may well be interspersed throughout this period of lifespan development.

Another typology comes from our study of nearly 1,000 women retirees. We grouped women into five 'clusters' based on their life satisfaction ratings, activity levels and demographic variables. We do not present this grouping as a fixed set of stable types, but it does demonstrate the range of ways in which women respond to retirement – ways that may be partly dependent on their circumstances and partly on personality and other individual differences.

Socially active/generative women retirees (30 per cent of the sample) were highly engaged in social and domestic activities, and were generally in good health and financially comfortable. They had the highest rates of church attendance and volunteer work, and the second highest rate of caring for grandchildren and family engagement. Their levels of satisfaction with retirement and in most life areas were high and they were significantly more generative than other groups, that is, they rated their lifetime levels of contribution to work, family and community very positively.

Also well adapted to their retirement years were the *physically active* women (15 per cent). They were healthy, energetic, participated in get-fit activities and/or played sport. Although no younger than those in other groups, these active women were the most satisfied with their health, exercise regimes, finances and standards of living, and in fact expressed high levels of satisfaction across most life domains. They were also active in social and domestic spheres.

Family-focused grandmas (20 per cent) stood out from those in any other group because they spent more time with their families, particularly in caring for grandchildren. This was possibly to the detriment of other social interactions, hobbies and volunteer work, in which they had lower levels of participation, although domestic activity, cooking, gardening and social media/internet use were frequent pursuits.

They were satisfied with most life domains, especially their close family relationships, and were more likely to be partnered than women in the other groups.

Two quite similar groups expressed lower levels of satisfaction with retirement and with life in general than the majority of the sample. *Unsatisfied* women (17 per cent) were the least financially secure and the least contented across nearly all of the 14 life domains that we measured. They were also more likely to have retired for health reasons or before they felt ready to do so. These women spent less time than others socializing, travelling, exercising or participating in hobbies, but they were reasonably active domestically; for example, they cooked, gardened and did housework. *Passive disconnected* women (19 per cent) were also somewhat dissatisfied with life in retirement, and more likely to be in poor health and financially insecure than all except the *unsatisfied* group, with whom they showed similarly low levels of involvement in most activities. The difference was that *passive disconnected* women showed the lowest levels of domestic activity and family engagement. Women in both the *passive disconnected* and *unsatisfied* groups were more likely to be single than those in the other categories.

Overall, the groups did not differ in terms of their current age, retirement age or length of retirement, but differences in life satisfaction were clear. Key factors contributing to dissatisfaction were poorer health, less secure finances, lower activity levels and to some extent, single status. We take up the issues of financial security, health in retirement, and retirement activity level in more detail in subsequent chapters.

The scope of the book

Most studies of retirement have been conducted in westernised, first world countries, and for that reason we have focused on research mainly from these nations, adding cross-cultural data where it is available. Given that lifespans are increasing in almost all nations, it is expected that the issues we discuss will eventually have worldwide relevance, although of course this will be tempered by the cultural context. It is also possible that as the nature of work changes – for example with more people working from home and increasing options to work flexible hours – that the nature of retirement will also change. Key issues for today's retiring women differ from those faced by their mothers and grandmothers; they are bound to be different again for their daughters and granddaughters. Only time (and more research) will tell!

In the following chapters we discuss the processes of retirement for women, examining research relating to women's work trajectories, retirement decision making and planning, and the 'journey' transitioning out of the workforce through to full retirement. We consider the pleasures and problems of retirement, particularly the thorny issue of financial security. The health and wellbeing of retired women is discussed, as is the diversity of outcomes among partnered, single and divorced women. We describe the ways in which women reshape their identities post-retirement and the kinds of activities in which they participate, and then consider how these relate to life satisfaction and psychosocial growth. Finally, we draw conclusions about adaptive ways for women to approach and enjoy their retirement years, in the hope that more might be able to say, like one of our research participants, 'I always knew it would be the best time of my life'.

2

WOMEN AT WORK

If any would not work, neither should he eat.

2 Thessalonians 3:10

Each morning sees some task begun,
Each evening sees it close;
Something attempted, something done,
Has earned a night's repose.

Longfellow, 1840, 'The Village Blacksmith'

Work banishes those three evils, boredom, vice and poverty.

Voltaire, 1759, Candide

In this chapter we consider the function that work plays in our lives, the reasons women work, their work/life patterns and how these relate to retirement decisions and outcomes. The recognition that women's work trajectories are often markedly different from those of men is important in understanding women's planning for, and reaction to, retirement.

Functions of work

Why does anyone work? The biblical answer is simple. Basically, we work to eat, clothe ourselves, pay the rent or mortgage, educate the children, and fund our health care, holidays and leisure activities. This is the 'manifest function' of work – to earn a living (Jahoda, 1997; Paul and Batinic, 2010). But there's more to it than that, as the lines from 'The Village Blacksmith' remind us. Work can provide a sense of satisfaction that comes from a job well done; it can help to create meaning in our lives. As Voltaire points out, it can keep us out of trouble in more ways than one. Jahoda *et al.* (2002) analysed some of these functions of work in their groundbreaking 1930 study of widespread unemployment in the Austrian village of Marienthal. They showed that work has 'latent functions', in the sense that participation in the paid workforce satisfies more than just survival needs. Those who are unemployed (or retired), it is argued, must find other ways to satisfy these needs in order to maintain wellbeing.

Jahoda *et al.* (2002) proposed five major latent functions of work. First, work helps to *structure time*. There is a rhythm to the day – getting up at a certain hour, making preparations, performing the workday tasks, returning home and participating in relaxation and leisure activities for which there are only limited periods available. We may wish for more 'free' time, but too much of this without clear time structures can be boring and disheartening. As one woman from our research study said about her recent retirement:

> It's a much bigger change of life than I expected. It's a big struggle to get motivated every day … My week had some order to it when I worked.

Most work also provides *social contact*, regular shared experiences with those outside the family. These contacts do not have to be 'arranged' but occur as a natural part of the day without particular effort. They can be enriching, interesting and broadening, giving the worker food for thought and conversational topics to share at home and with friends and family. Some of these contacts may grow into important friendships. The unemployed can too readily become socially isolated and lonely, especially when most of their peers are working. In our study, many retired women said they missed the social aspects of work, such as the camaraderie, incidental socialising and friendship. It was not uncommon for them to talk of loneliness and even depression as an outcome of social isolation.

> I became severely depressed within six months of retiring, and I am sure the reason was social isolation. Antidepressants helped and I am now working on increasing my social contacts. I live alone and have no children, and all my siblings are interstate. So, work and recreation have always been my source of social contacts. Despite only working one day per week in the year before retiring, this was enough to keep me in regular contact with colleagues/ friends, and I did not expect the cessation of work to have such a drastic impact, but it did!

There is an increasing tendency these days for workers to operate from home-based offices; for example, many IT professionals work from home. It will be interesting for social scientists to explore whether these arrangements also lead to social isolation or whether home-based workers develop protective strategies (such as regular café meet-ups) to ensure that they maintain social connections. If they do, the impact of retirement on this aspect of life is likely to be far less noticeable.

18 Women at work

The third latent function of work is the sense of *collective purpose* that one's occupation can provide. This is the sense of feeling part of a team that is doing something useful, and of contributing to communal goals. For example, many occupations involve helping people in some way, or producing goods that others need or enjoy. It is of course possible to find such purpose through volunteering or unpaid creative work, but to do so requires a degree of self-motivation that can be difficult to sustain without support and feedback from others. These retired women from our study summarised what many felt:

> I miss the intellectual stimulation, the sense of achievement, the feeling of being valued and the thanks and praise you never receive as a volunteer or unpaid worker or even a family member.

> I miss the sense of purpose. While it was hugely stressful, I felt useful. Now I feel at a loss. Doing housework is absolutely unsatisfying and I loathe it.

Status provision is the fourth latent function of work postulated by Jahoda *et al.* (2002). Status is associated with being in an occupation that is valued, or in managing others. While professional jobs may attract greater status than, say, manual labour, there is prestige in employment itself. The unemployed, for whatever reason, often feel stigmatised, and are rated very low in the hierarchy of who is a valued person. In our study, many retired women missed their workplace status, a situation sometimes exacerbated by the lack of prestige also associated both with ageing and with domestic work. One put it this way:

> [I miss] the sense of status – that your opinion is worth something and you're not just a silly old lady.

> I miss the feeling of being appreciated for achieving something, and of being considered a competent person.

Finally, jobs provide *activity*; they keep us moving and doing, not just physically but mentally. This is the fifth latent function of work, to get us out in the world, interacting, exercising the mind and the body. To avoid sinking into the apathetic and unhealthy 'couch potato' role, the unemployed, including retired people, need interests and activities that stimulate, engage and keep them connected with others. To illustrate this, when asked an open-ended question about what they missed most about work, 10 per cent of the retired women in our sample said 'stimulation' and 8 per cent wrote 'challenge'.

Jahoda *et al.*'s (2002) major observation at Marienthal was that prolonged unemployment leads to apathy, reduced aspirations and a sense of hopelessness that goes beyond the deprivations associated with financial hardship. The researchers argued that this was because the latent functions that work provided were not being fulfilled. Even although there was more time to socialise, study, start new ventures or make domestic improvements, the unemployed fell into patterns of inactivity and depression. There is ample evidence that such outcomes of unemployment are still prevalent today and that paid work remains a key source of the 'latent functions' (e.g. Paul and Batinic, 2010).

Interestingly, the ill effects of forced unemployment in the Marienthal study appeared less extreme among women. Why might this be the case? Particularly for women with dependent children, an inbuilt time structure to the day remains, whether they are in paid work or not. Children must be fed, bathed, entertained, sent to school, put to bed. Jahoda *et al.* (2002) found that unemployed women, who continued 'as usual' with household and childcare routines, had a considerably less disrupted sense of time compared to men. Furthermore, for some women, a sense of collective purpose may be found in child rearing and through domestic activities, and these activities certainly have the capacity to stimulate activity. Nevertheless, they are often viewed as low status and can be socially isolating.

Of course, retirement is different from the forced unemployment that characterised the Marienthal study. On the positive side, retirement can be viewed as a reward for many years of hard work, a chance to wind down and focus on leisure and activities of choice. On the negative side, retirement does not always occur at a time of one's choosing, and it can be associated with ageing or with a lower standard of living. In modern-day tests of the Jahoda work functions, Paul and Batinic (2010) and Selenka *et al.* (2011) showed that both full-time and part-time employees reported higher levels of time structure, social contact, collective purpose, and activity than unemployed persons and those who were not working for other reasons, such as retirement. Gender was not a key factor in the strength of the work functions; lower levels of work functions were associated with higher levels of distress, for both men and women.

The question arises as to whether women's common patterns of moving in and out of the workforce, discussed below, could act as a buffer against the debilitating aspects of unemployment (and potentially, retirement) – boredom, inactivity, social isolation, loss of purpose and reduction of status. Women may be more used to 'switching gears' between paid and unpaid work, for example through having put more effort into maintaining non-work friendships and interests. Early researchers tended towards the consensus that retirement was unlikely to pose many adjustment problems for women because they were more invested in home duties (Simmons and Betschild, 2001), but this is a conclusion that needs re-examination in the light of changes in women's roles over the past 50 years or so. Before we discuss this more recent research on retirement adjustment among women, however, we need to consider more thoroughly the typical patterns of participation in paid and unpaid work among women today, particularly women of, or close to, retirement age.

Issues affecting women's work

In the next section, we discuss four major issues that affect women's working lives: the 'second shift' of domestic activities; the prevalence of part-time work among women;

20 Women at work

occupational segregation by gender; and women's lifetime work history disruptions. Each of these has potential implications for how retirement will be experienced by women, particularly in relation to their financial position as retirees.

The second shift

Working women have often been described as having to negotiate the 'second shift' or the 'double shift' (Hochschild, 1989), fulfilling the requirements of paid work while also managing the lion's share of unpaid household chores and child-care. Sullivan (2000) presents data from a longitudinal study of work patterns among British couples carried out between 1975 and 1997 showing that women performed the majority of unpaid domestic labour. This was regardless of whether the partners were in paid full-time work, or the husband was full-time and the wife part-time, or the wife was not working outside the home. However, over 20 years of the study, the contribution of the male partner to unpaid domestic work had increased markedly. Among couples both working full-time, for example, women did 77 per cent of domestic unpaid work (on average) in 1977, 62 per cent in 1987 and 60 per cent in 1997. The imbalance may have decreased but it has not yet disappeared, even in studies conducted more recently. For example, among a large group of professional couples with children, Jolly *et al.* (2014) found, after adjusting for work hours, spousal employment and other factors, that women spent 8.5 more hours per week on domestic activities than men and were far more likely than their partners to take time off work if childcare arrangements were disrupted.

Yet some observers argue that the second shift may have become less onerous for women, for a range of reasons. Bianchi *et al.* (2000) present time-diary data from representative samples of American adults showing that the number of hours spent on domestic labour has declined steadily since 1965, mainly due to a dramatic decrease in the amount of housework done by women. In short, the discrepancy between the amount of domestic work performed by men and women is decreasing partly because men's contribution to housework has increased, but also because there is less domestic work *to do* as couples partner later, have fewer children and, even among the less affluent, have access to more labour-saving and outsourcing options. For example, in the 1950s, 1960s and 1970s mothers typically knitted full wardrobes for their new babies, sewed, altered and mended clothing for children (and sometimes themselves), hand-washed many items, and used cloth diapers which had to be laundered. Today, babies wear disposable diapers and grow-suits that are machine washable and cheap enough to be thrown away once they are no longer in pristine condition. Food preparation and household maintenance have undergone similar revolutions in today's world of 'fast, easy-care and disposable' options.

Nevertheless, other observers contend that today the reduction in the gender gap in domestic work has stalled, with women still bearing the major burden of household chores and family maintenance tasks (Blair-Loy *et al.*, 2015; Miller and Sassler, 2010; Young *et al.*, 2015). This appears to be particularly the case in certain cultural and national groups (e.g. Carriero, 2011; Davaki, 2016) and, not surprisingly, when children are younger (Buhlmann *et al.*, 2010; Miller and Sassler, 2010; Newkirk *et al.*, 2017). Blair-Loy *et al.* (2015) acknowledge that although the leisure gap between men and women who cohabit may have been reduced (e.g. Craig, 2007; Gershuny and Sullivan, 2014), it is not because women do a smaller share of the housework but because they are more likely to be part-time in the paid workforce than men. Furthermore, what is not usually included in surveys of who does the household chores is the mental workload that women still carry in terms of being the ones who notice, organise and manage what needs to be done around the home. This 'invisible' work includes activities like meal planning, writing shopping lists and sorting out children's school requirements, not to mention the emotional work of noticing and organising family relationship maintenance such as remembering birthdays and keeping in touch with in-laws and grandparents (Wade, 2016; Walzer, 1998).

Part-time work

Part-time work is certainly more prevalent among women than men. The UK Office for National Statistics reports that in 2013 67 per cent of women aged between 16 and 64 years were working; 42 per cent of them part-time. The comparative figures for men were 76 per cent in paid work, of whom only 12 per cent were part-timers. Data from the US and Australia are very similar (Workplace Gender Equality Agency, 2017; US Department of Labor, 2016). A report commissioned by the European Parliament's Committee on Women's Rights and Gender Equality (Davaki, 2016) states that in all the member nations of the European Union women are far more likely than men to work part-time. Why is this the case?

The major reason is that women have to fit work in with childcare and other family duties, a finding that suggests that these duties and responsibilities are still not shared equally between the sexes. The European Institute for Gender Equality (2014) survey conducted in 2012 showed that 55 per cent of women in the 25–49 year age group said that they chose to work part-time work *because of family care responsibilities* whereas 12 per cent of men in that age group cited this reason. Among those aged 50–64 years, who are more likely to be caring for a grandchild or aged parent, the percentages were again much higher for women than men (37 per cent and 20 per cent, respectively). By contrast, only one-quarter of these women said that they chose to work part-time because no full-time option was available, while this was the case for just over one-half of the men.

The expectations and negotiations between couples regarding the domestic workload are variables that clearly influence women's work choices. At a broader 'macro' level of influence, government and workplace policies, along with welfare provisions, are also likely to have an effect. Would women choose full-time work over part-time work if work-place policies were more family-friendly? Does the provision of parental leave entitlements, public childcare services, flexible hours,

22 Women at work

work-at-home options and the like change the job choices and career patterns for women? Research suggests that they do, but the situation is complex, as we shall see.

Some studies have compared whole nations in terms of the effect of policies on women's work patterns. Using data collected from the European Social Survey in 2004, Buhlmann *et al.* (2010) classified 14 European countries in terms of their relevant work and family policies. The groups included (1) liberal nations, described as providing only minimal government support for families (Switzerland, the UK, Ireland, the Netherlands); (2) conservative nations, described as supporting families but without explicitly promoting the occupational reinsertion of women in the workforce after childbirth (Germany, Spain, France, Greece, Austria, Belgium, Luxembourg, Portugal); and (3) socio-democratic nations, described as supporting double earners by promoting women's participation in the labour market through both family-friendly and insertion policies (Denmark, Finland, Norway, Sweden). Buhlmann *et al.* compared the extent to which the work practices of couples, aged between 18 and 45 years, living in these countries were more or less 'egalitarian' or 'gendered'. They found that in the liberal nations, childless couples shared work equally, but strongly gendered work patterns emerged among couples with one or more dependent children. Women in these situations were more likely to stay at home or undertake casual or part-time work than were their partners. Couples living in conservative nations showed similar patterns, although these were somewhat less pronounced and had greater variability, especially when children reached school age. At this stage of family development, 'the frequency of couples with egalitarian occupational practices is 44 per cent in conservative countries as opposed to 25 per cent in liberal ones' (ibid., p. 57).

In socio-democratic countries, egalitarian work patterns were more common than 'traditional' gendered patterns among couples across all family development stages (apart from when children were in their first year of life). The division of work among couples with school-age children, for example, was equivalent to that among childless couples. We can conclude then, at the broad national level, that government interventions and welfare policies do indeed make a difference to the extent to which women with children participate in the paid workforce on a full-time basis.

There is a strong implication in Buhlmann *et al.*'s 2010 study, and in European Union (EU) policies and principles, that women's more frequent engagement in part-time rather than full-time work is not beneficial and ought to be overcome by more legislation. This idea echoes feminist contentions that male-female differences in work outcomes are a result of both overt and subtle sex discrimination that acts against women's interests. Is this a valid argument? Data such as that from Eurofound (2013) indicates that men in EU countries spend on average over 37 years in the labour market compared with 29 years for women. Clearly, this eight-year gap has negative implications for women's career opportunities, their pay packets and their retirement pension savings and entitlements. On the other hand, the gap may have positive implications for women's potential for self-development through non-paid work activities, for example through having more time for family life, home-oriented interests and social groups based around children's activities. We might ask the question whether women's preponderance in part-time work can be viewed as a constraint brought about by social inequity and social conditioning or as a preferred choice, one that might be welcomed by many males if it were more readily available and an accepted practice.

Choice or constraint? The debate is intense. Catherine Hakim (1995, 2005, 2006, 2011) is an oft-quoted and controversial sociologist who strongly maintains that most women want to achieve flexibility in their work/home life balance. Specifically, her thesis is that there are stages in life when the majority of women favour staying at home or engaging in part-time work, even if policies described as 'family friendly' that encourage full-time work are in place. She argues that there will always be limits to the effectiveness of social engineering in providing equal workplace participation for both sexes, because women's greater commitment to family life will lead many of them to choose reduced hours in the paid workforce.

Preference Theory

In her Preference Theory, Hakim (2006) claims that western societies offer women many more lifestyle options than were once possible. This is due to social changes such as the ready availability of contraception, the equal opportunities revolution and increased affluence. It is Hakim's contention that genuine choice is now available, with the consequence that western women will opt into one of three lifestyles: home-centred, work-centred or 'adaptive'. In countries such as the UK and the US, 'where public policy does not bias the distribution' (ibid., p. 287), about 20 per cent of women will choose the home-centred option, making family life and children their main priority to the extent of preferring not to enter the paid workforce. These are the 'stay-at-home' mums. At the other end of the scale, about 20 per cent of women will be work-centred. These women's primary focus in life is their careers. They are likely to have made a large investment in training/education and will expend considerable effort on working towards promotion and climbing the professional or corporate ladder. Childless women or those with small families will be more prevalent in this group. Neither home- or work-centred women will be particularly affected by employment policies that favour or encourage women; their choices are based more on personal interests and preferences.

The majority of women, about 60 per cent, form the adaptive group, so named because they will adapt or change the key focus of their orientation depending on circumstances. This is a diverse group of women who want to combine work and family life. They will probably stay at home or work part-time when their children are young, moving in and out of full-time or part-time work depending on family and economic circumstances. Hakim argues that this group is the most responsive to social policies such as the availability of family welfare benefits, economic prosperity, workplace flexibility, and the like. For example, if governments pay a family allowance or benefit to non-working mothers, or offer 'baby bonuses', only women in this adaptive group are likely to calculate whether it is economically worth going

24 Women at work

back to work while their children are young, thus losing this benefit. On the other hand, if subsidies for childcare are available, the economic/lifestyle balance perceived by adaptive women may tip in the other direction, leading them back into the paid workplace while their children are still of pre-school age. Hakim contends that neither the home- or work-centred women will find these incentives or dis-incentives to work or stay at home strong enough to overcome their lifestyle preferences.

In a study that could be interpreted as supporting Hakim's position, Baxter and Chesters (2011) examined perceptions of work/family balance in relation to institutional family-friendly work entitlements among a sample of more than 1,600 women working in the public sector in Queensland, Australia. One of the few policies that consistently related to positive perceptions of work/family balance was access to the option of part-time work. Less favourable perceptions of work/family balance were linked to longer work hours and being asked to do extra work at short notice – features of work that wreak havoc with family care needs such as picking up children from school or crèche.

One important criticism of Hakim's Preference Theory is that women in lower socio-economic groups do not have the same degree of choice over the nature of their working lives as do more affluent women (Procter and Padfield, 1999). For example, women from higher socio-economic groups have greater access to educational and career opportunities and are therefore more likely to be in higher-paid, more satisfying jobs and in a position to afford acceptable childcare and home help. These factors could bias the work-centred group towards women of higher socio-economic status. Johnstone and Lee (2009) set out to test the extent to which the three lifestyle groups were distributed across socio-economic categories, among a large sample (>6,000) of women aged 25–29 years who were part of the Australian Longitudinal Study on Women's Health. They concluded that lifestyle grouping and socio-economic status were not independent of one another. Home-oriented women in their sample were more likely to be ranked lower than other groups on an index of socio-economic status. However, some points concerning the methodology of this study are worth noting here. First, the measure of socio-economic status used was not based on income. It was developed from a complex of variables, some of which overlap with the definitional descriptions of the lifestyle groups, such as level of education. Second, the age range of the sample was younger than the average age at the birth of a first child among Australian women (30 years), probably accounting for the very low number of home-centred participants. A truer test of the hypothesis would be to assess women in the 30–45 year age group.

Other criticisms of Hakim's theory include (1) that the 'adaptive' group is too heterogeneous and probably comprises several categories; (2) that single (unpartnered) workers are not adequately considered in the theory; and (3) that women's lifestyle orientations change according to their circumstances (e.g. Johnstone and Lee, 2009; Procter and Padfield, 1999). From a feminist viewpoint, the strongest critique is that structural and attitudinal discrimination against women in the workplace still exists and has either not yet been recognised or attempts to remedy it have been inadequate. This is the argument put forward by Damaske and Frech (2016) whose research followed up participants in the US-based National Longitudinal Survey of Youth. These individuals, born between 1957 and 1964, were retested at periods between 1982 and 2010. Findings indicate that women with the greatest financial needs (poor when they were young, less well-educated, unpartnered and lacking a second income) appeared to face the greatest barriers to finding full-time work. The argument that women only work full-time if they financially need to was not supported by their US data, with the authors claiming that stable full-time work 'is an accrued advantage' to which not all women have access. In other words, the opportunity to work full-time for longer periods is not a choice freely open to all women, even in first world countries.

Constraints on choice are not always related to gender-based discrimination as it is normally conceived, such as barriers to women working in certain occupations, lack of flexible hours or leave arrangements. Choice is influenced through public attitudes to women's roles – attitudes that are transmitted to girls and women through their families, friends and the media. Previously, mothers were exhorted to stay at home with their children, to not take men's jobs, to not expect equal pay, because they were not the breadwinners. In some quarters, a sense of shame was attached to being a woman in the paid workforce. Today, the pressure may be in the opposite direction. An article entitled 'Housewives are a drain on the economy, new research claims' (*Herald Sun*, 10 March 2017) reported on a study conducted by the Organisation for Economic Co-operation and Development (OECD, 2017a) which concluded that 'stay-at-home' mothers represented the greatest untapped potential for Australia's workforce. These young women, who tend to be better educated than their young male counterparts, were described as not contributing to national prosperity – because they were not in the paid workforce. Many young mothers who did have jobs were also considered as not pulling their weight for the nation because nearly half were 'only' working part-time. Never mind that they were nurturing the next generation. Women could be forgiven for thinking 'you can't win'. To be fair, the key thrust of the OECD report was a discussion of barriers to maternal employment and how these could be overcome, the implication being that full-time work for mothers would be better for their own, as well as the nation's, wellbeing. Not all would agree.

Not surprisingly, the debate about women and part-time work continues. More broadly speaking, however, as the nature of work changes rapidly in this technological era, the gender differences in preponderance of part-time work (and the resulting pay gap) may disappear, not necessarily because women work more but because men work less.

Pink-collar work and the gender occupational divide

Women's working lives differ from men's not just in terms of extent of part-time work or frequency of disruptions. Workplaces are 'gendered' because certain occupations are male dominated and others female dominated. The term 'pink

26 Women at work

collar' has sometimes been used to describe occupations predominantly staffed by women workers, such as elementary school teaching and nursing. It has also been applied to non-professional female-dominated jobs such as routine office work, cleaning and sales-cashier jobs that are contrasted with male-dominated 'blue-collar' manual work yet do not qualify as 'white collar'. A feature of pink-collar occupations, however they are defined, is that they tend to attract lower pay rates than 'masculine' occupations requiring a similar skill set or level of education (Cohen and Blanchi, 1999). Not only that, there is evidence that once women enter an occupation in significant numbers, it becomes 'feminised' and tends to attract lower wages (Pocock and Alexander, 1999). A US study gives the striking example of outdoor workers in national parks, for example camp leaders and park rangers. Prior to 1950 men dominated these occupations; by 2000 they were pre-dominantly held by women. Median hourly wages across that time declined by 57 percentage points (in relation to national wage trends). The opposite pattern occurred for computer programmers once this profession became more masculinised (Levanon et al., 2009).

Occupational segregation can be horizontal (as in male-dominated and female-dominated jobs) but it can also be vertical, in the sense that men tend to dominate higher-status positions in both traditionally male and traditionally female occupa-tions (Charles, 2003). Thus, as well as being more likely to run major corporations or govern nations, men are also more likely to assume leading roles in feminised occupations, for example to manage domestic cleaning businesses or be the principal of a primary school (OECD, 2014).

One widely discussed feature of the vertical occupational divide between the sexes is called the 'glass ceiling'. This term refers to the obstacles women face in attaining positions that appear to be within their reach, but which are made inac-cessible by unspecified barriers. A US politician, Anna Belle Clement O'Brien, used a campaign slogan that cleverly drew attention to an attitude that may con-tribute to these barriers: 'A woman's place is in the house … and in the senate'. The slogan was extended to include '… and in the Oval Office' during Hillary Clinton's (unsuccessful) 2016 candidature for the US presidency. The slogan causes us to reflect on social attitudes to 'a woman's place', and why it should be any different from a man's.

Hakim, whose Preference Theory we discussed above, does not accept that it is institutional barriers or discriminatory attitudes that keep women from high-status jobs; rather it is their own preferences to avoid these positions. This is because, she argues, some careers – particularly those that attract very high salaries, status, or power – 'cannot be domesticated'. In other words, they require '24/7'-type time commitments that are not compatible with family life. She argues that, on the whole, women with children will not choose these careers because of this incompatibility. Those who do are more likely to encounter the glass ceiling because such jobs require 'a high level of dedication, virtually to the exclusion of a major investment in family work and family life' (2006, p. 281).

As if to drive home Hakim's point, Kate Ellis, a senior Australian federal politician, handed in her resignation on the day we were revising this chapter. This is what she wrote in a letter to her constituents:

> This has been a really hard decision for me. In the end it is a decision that I have made for only one simple reason. Whilst my son could travel with me as a baby, during the next term of parliament he will start school and have to stay in Adelaide. The simple truth is that I just cannot bear the thought of spending at least 20 weeks of every year away from him and the rest of the family.
>
> *(March 2017)*

Was this a free choice, or was it constrained by aspects of the job that were amenable to change without affecting quality of performance? Hakim's idea that such decisions do represent a free choice is at odds with the feminist argument that discrimination, both direct and structural, is the major reason that men and women differ in labour market outcomes such as pay, promotion and job status.

Whatever the reasons behind the horizontal and vertical segregation of occupations, both of these phenomena contribute to the pay gap between men and women. This gap is cumulative across working life and is a major contributor to differences between men and women's retirement savings and incomes. We discuss this further in Chapter 3.

Work disruptions and trajectories

A topic relevant to occupational choices is the extent to which women typically experience disruptions in their working lives, taking time off to bear and nurture children, manage families, care for other relatives such as ageing parents, fit in with a partner's job demands, study, travel, or experience non-voluntary periods of unemployment. Among the retired women we studied, for example, nearly three-quarters had experienced significant breaks of more than a year in their working lives, mostly for child rearing but also for reasons such as those listed above.

We have noted several different patterns in the work trajectories of retired women, evidenced as they reflect back on their working lives. Some, especially childless single women, show similar work patterns to the majority of men, that is, full-time for all or most of their working lives. Some take significant breaks to study and retrain for more interesting and/or lucrative jobs than those chosen in their youth – jobs which were often constrained by the sex-role stereotyping and limited educational opportunities available to women in the first 50 or so years of the twentieth century. A common pattern for baby boomer and older women was to work for a couple of years post-school or university then 'retire' on marriage if they belonged to the pre-oral contraceptive generation (prior to the 1960s), or a few years after marriage for those who had the advantage of being able to plan their families. Many of these women did not return to the workforce at all; some did – often part-time – when the youngest child went to school. Working women with school-age children often chose employment that fitted in with school hours, after school care options, flexible leave possibilities and shorter travel times from home, rather than employment that was best suited to their interests, qualifications and experience.

On the other hand, some women did not return to work until their children were teenagers or adults. Such a long break in one's working life could often mean acceptance of low-paid positions owing to a lack of training and experience and/or not being up to date with advancements in their field, particularly given the speed of technological change. Retraining through further study was not always a realistic or simple option, not just because of the expense, but because many women reported low self-esteem and a lack of confidence after many years of being 'just a housewife'. A well-known novel from the 1970s, *The Woman's Room* by feminist Marilyn French, famously portrays the key character having a panic attack in a university toilet before going to her first class, such is her fear on beginning the journey from financially dependent housewife to independent career woman.

Some women give up work (permanently or temporarily) well before retirement age for potentially 'benign' reasons such as fitting in with the requirements of their partner's job (usually travel), or for more stressful reasons such as their own health, or the need to care for a sick relative or dependent grandchild. Some who planned their work patterns and retirement finances with a partner find a marriage break-up or widowhood later in life sends them back into the workforce or keeps them working longer than planned to shore up their savings or pension entitlements.

How do women's work histories affect their retirement decisions? This is not an easy question for researchers to answer. Retrospective studies in which retired women reflect on their work histories across a lifetime are open to many biases, especially the distortions and failures of memory. Retired women reading this: how difficult is it to calculate how many years of full-time work would equate to the total sum of work you did pre-retirement? The details of work patterns across forty or more years, especially for those who have had many different jobs, some casual, some full-time and some part-time, are not easy to recall. Longitudinal studies may be more reliable, but these are expensive, especially considering the timespans needed to adequately study this phenomenon. Another issue is deciding on a definition of retirement, as we saw in Chapter 1. Yet a further complexity is attempting to create some measure or categorisation of work history variability, given that there is such variety in these patterns.

In our study of nearly 1000 retired Australian women, one measure we used was 'number of breaks of one or more years in your working life'. About 27 per cent reported no breaks prior to retirement; of the rest (73 per cent), 36 per cent had one, 29 per cent had two or three and 8 per cent had more than three. The number of breaks was significantly and positively related to economic insecurity, with those women who had taken three or more breaks being particularly likely to assess themselves as being 'very insecure' financially.

Apart from showing that financial resources upon retirement will, not surprisingly, tend to be less for those who have worked fewer years, not much is known about how different work histories affect retirement decisions. A related, overlapping issue that has been researched is how women's family structures influence retirement. Family characteristics such as number of children, their ages, responsibilities in caring for older relatives, and financial contributions of a partner are all likely to influence a woman's work history and possibly affect when she retires. We found women who had more children, or more grandchildren, tended to retire later but we were unable to establish the reasons for this. Two extensive longitudinal studies, one carried out in Sweden and the other in the Netherlands, considered this topic in more detail.

First, Svensson *et al.* (2015) examined the effects of women's different family configurations on their retirement decisions. Between 1990 and 2006 they collected longitudinal data on the full cohort of Swedish women born in 1935. During this period, most of the participants had retired at some time between the ages of 55 and 71 years. Sequence analysis was employed to predict the characteristics of those women who retired comparatively early or late.

Women who retired earlier tended to belong to one of two groups. The first were more likely to live alone and/or have few relatives living either with them or close by – they were mostly childless and single women. This was contrary to Svensson *et al.*'s (2015) hypothesis that early retirement is likely to be triggered by the presence of family members needing care-based support, but was certainly consistent with our study findings that those with fewer children retired earlier. Svensson *et al.* speculatively suggested several explanations for their findings. One was that less family-connected individuals are able retire early because they have no economic responsibility for their relatives. Another was that they could have been propelled into retirement through ill-health, given that having a partner is associated with better health (e.g. Lui and Umberson, 2008). It is also possible that because this group is less likely to have disrupted work histories (for example they will not have taken time off for childbirth or childcare), they have been able to save more money for their own retirement needs. As we described earlier, this was the case in our Australian study where fewer breaks in a woman's work history were associated with greater financial security.

The second group of earlier retirees mostly comprised women who had two younger generations 'present' in their lives, that is, living with them or nearby. These women may be using their freed-up time to care for grandchildren, consistent with Svensson *et al.*'s (2015) hypothesis that women who retire early often do so in order to help to care for family members.

Later retirement was associated with late family formation and having children still living at home. Women in this situation may keep working during their late 50s, 60s and even 70s because they have greater economic responsibilities for the younger generation. Interestingly, Svensson *et al.* found no relationship between retirement age and caring for elderly relatives, a finding that did not support the researchers' expectations. Because this study comprised a large sample of women, the researchers were able to control for many variables in their sophisticated analyses; nevertheless, while some associations between

30 Women at work

women's work trajectories and their retirement ages were found, the data were far from straightforward.

Another major study of relevance examined the role of women's childbearing and marital histories on retirement intentions and behaviours (Damman *et al.*, 2015). The researchers used longitudinal data collected in 2001, 2006–2007 and 2011 from Dutch female older workers (N=420) and, if applicable, their partners. The results showed that women who postponed childbearing and still had children living with them in their pre-retirement years intended to retire relatively late (as was seen in Svensson *et al.*'s 2015 study). However, although there was a trend for these women to carry out their intentions and *actually* retire later, it was not statistically significant. Another group of women who both intended to, and did retire relatively late, included those who had divorced and had not re-partnered. No other family constellation variables were linked with retirement age, which was most strongly predicted by pre-retirement financial situation, health and work type. Women in this study stayed in work longer when they found their work more stimulating, when they were healthier, or when their financial situations were less beneficial.

In summary, women's work histories affect their retirement decisions and their lifestyle management during the retirement years. Critically, women's greater share of domestic chores and their need to take time out from full-time work for childbirth, childcare and other family responsibilities are likely to impact on their retirement savings and employer-sponsored pension entitlements, as is the tendency for women to work in lower-paid jobs than men. This pay gap and its implications are discussed in detail in the next chapter. Women's more varied work histories are also associated with other retirement-related factors, such as when they retire and how they cope with this life change. The variables affecting retirement decisions are discussed in Chapter 4, and while financial security is clearly important, it is only one of many influencing factors. Finally, women's non-linear work histories may help them to build up a greater array of strategies to deal with the transition to retirement, for example through time spent establishing close relationships and non-work interests. The characteristics of this transitional journey are considered in Chapter 5.

3

FINANCIAL SECURITY IN RETIREMENT

> Girls in my year were not told about government superannuation back in the mid-1960s. Boys were. Male teachers of my age retired in their mid to late 50s on 60 per cent salary for life ... Because I took eight years off for childrearing in two lots (which I don't regret), I never heard about this until government had stopped it. [I] took out private superannuation (of which I lost a lot in [the] financial crash). [I] tried to salary sacrifice, but couldn't afford it as well as [a] mortgage. [I] brought up two children alone without maintenance, so no savings.

This complex story of one woman's struggle highlights some of the problems that women face in the effort to plan for adequate finances post-retirement. As we saw in the previous chapter, women are typically in lower-paid jobs and so earn less than men. They take breaks in their employment for childrearing or as carers for others. These factors and the nature of pension/superannuation systems all play a role in ensuring that many women enter retirement with insufficient funds to support themselves over what is now an extended 'post-work' period in western countries, with women's life expectancy being, on average, above 83 years of age. As women also typically live longer than men, their retirement savings and benefits need to last longer yet are typically less robust.

It is clear that the risk of poverty is much greater for people past retirement age than for younger people. For example, the Australian Human Rights Commission (2014), reporting on different indices of poverty in Australia, concluded that one-quarter of people over the age of 65 years experience poverty. In this chapter we examine the various factors that impact on retirement finances, concentrating on the differential between women and men.

Generally, retirement financial resources are described as deriving from three 'pillars': personal superannuation contributions by employers and employees while working; state pensions; and savings. We discuss each of these within the

32 Financial security in retirement

context of gender differences. Superannuation is designed to ensure that funds are available for a comfortable retirement, but as we describe in the chapter typically the balances available on retirement suggest that this is unlikely, especially for women whose funds, on average, amount to half those of men (Workplace Gender Equality Agency, 2016). Low wealth, little or no retirement savings and longer life expectancy result in many having to rely on state pensions as their main or only source of retirement income. And even in wealthy western countries pensions are often barely adequate to sustain a modest post-retirement lifestyle.

Gender pay gap

One key driver in women's poorer resources on retirement is the gender wage gap (Even and Macpherson, 2009; Leith, 2014; World Development Report, 2012). Most retirement income systems fail to take into account the different work patterns of women and men and structurally favour higher-income earners who work full-time without breaks for their entire work life. Those who do not fit this pattern are significantly handicapped when saving for their retirement. Women are clearly disadvantaged in this regard.

There are a number of interrelated work, family and societal factors that influence the pay gap. First, women and men typically work in different industries or professions and historically female-dominated industries and jobs have attracted lower wages than male-dominated industries and jobs.

As demonstrated in Chapter 2, women are more likely than men to work part-time or flexibly because they still undertake most of society's unpaid domestic and caring work and thus may find it difficult to climb the career or occupational path and to access senior roles. Largely because of their childrearing and other caring responsibilities, women often work in casual jobs. Additionally, discrimination, both direct and indirect, still means that women have only recently being accepted in roles that previously were the exclusive purview of men. For example, there are substantial gender differences in the number of men and women occupying the most senior roles in major public companies. This is salutary, given that the occupants of these roles are held responsible for company equity policies and have potential influence on government policy.

In all countries where senior executives' salaries are examined, women are hardly represented. In the US, the Standard & Poor's 500 Index comprises 500 stocks and is seen as a leading indicator of equities. Women currently hold only 26 (5.2 per cent) CEO positions in these companies (Catalyst, 2017). Similar data are available for Australia and the European Union (EU). In the latter, the proportion of women among Company Board chairs is very low – around one in 14 – and just 3.6 per cent of the largest listed companies in Europe have a female CEO. There are only eight countries – France, Latvia, Finland, Sweden, the UK, Denmark, Italy and Germany – in which women account for at least one-quarter of board members (European Institute for Gender Equality, 2015).

Looking more broadly at the gender differential in pay, an Organisation for Economic Co-operation and Development (OECD, 2017b) report showed in 2014 that the difference between women's and men's median wages varied dramatically from 3.3 per cent in Belgium, to just over 6 per cent in New Zealand, Norway and Denmark, 36.7 per cent in the Republic of Korea. Most western countries, including the UK, the US, Australia and Germany, had a gap of around 17–19 per cent. The average for the 28 EU member countries was 19.1 per cent. In no country did women earn more than men.

In Australia the gender pay gap increases to 23.9 per cent for full-time workers when taking into account total remuneration, which includes superannuation, overtime, bonus payments and other discretionary pay. Moreover, the gap is greater in higher-level, executive and managerial roles (Vu and Doughney, 2009).

While the gender pay gap exists across all age groups, the divergence between male and female earnings increases after women reach 25–34 years of age, reflecting a reduction in workforce participation by women when they have children.

The gender wealth gap

Women also fare badly in relation to men in terms of their lifetime accumulation of assets (the gender wealth gap). Australian data (Economics References Committee, 2016) showed that in 2006

> the accumulated wealth of single adult men was, on average, 14.4 per cent higher than that of single women. Although female labour market participation has increased, the rate of wealth accumulation by single women to finance retirement needs has been slower than that of single men's. The gender wealth gap among single men and women more than doubled from 10.4 per cent to 22.8 per cent between 2002 and 2010.
>
> *(Section 2.19)*

Research reported by Ong and Austen (2017) shows that Australian women have less diversified assets and are more likely than men to have their assets in a family home. Data from the 2016 Household, Income and Labour Dynamics in Australia (HILDA) Survey (Wilkins, 2016) show that the family home accounts for close to one-half of the total assets held by single women, and only 39 per cent of the total assets held by single men. This means that they have less saved for retirement and, in the absence of significant other assets, the family home has become the key form of wealth for many Australian women. Relying on this form of wealth comes with relatively high risks. For example, women are particularly vulnerable to the way housing is treated in the Australian age pension asset test. Including the family home in this test would have consequences for pension eligibility and may force many retirees to draw down their home equity to fund their retirement at earlier life stages. There is also the uncertainty of future price and interest rate movements – risks that cannot be defended against. Most tellingly for retirees, to have

34 Financial security in retirement

major assets tied up in the family home significantly reduces resources that can be used as income.

Women's earlier retirement from the workforce further contributes to the gender wealth gap. In Australia, for example, Australian Bureau of Statistics (ABS) data for 2012–2013 show that 21.6 per cent and 44.3 per cent of women aged 55–59 years and 60–64 years, respectively, were retired, compared to 11.0 per cent and 27.6 per cent, respectively, of men (Martin and Xiang, 2015). As Fisher *et al.* (2016) note, early retirement is likely to lead to the use of existing financial resources, while retiring later has economic benefits, including earned wages, and possibly those accruing from employer-provided health insurance and retirement plan contributions. In one American study, working for an additional two years was shown to have a significant impact on the preservation of retirement wealth (Munnell and Sass, 2008).

In short, the gender pay gap and choices about work careers lead women to be financially disadvantaged when they retire, compared to men.

Retirement income

There is not enough space in a single chapter to describe the range of retirement income systems among the western countries; however, most accept the 'three pillars' approach that includes social security pensions, employer contributions, and savings (Ekerdt, 2010). We have chosen to use the Australian model to illustrate how these systems typically disadvantage women. (For a detailed discussion of the US system, see ibid.)

In Australia, employer-contributed superannuation was uncommon until the 1970s, when it began to be included in industrial awards. Three decades ago, only 24 per cent of women and 50 per cent of men had access to superannuation. In 1992, superannuation became a major element of Australia's retirement system when employers were required to contribute a percentage of an employee's earnings into a superannuation pension fund. By the following year, the gender gap in superannuation coverage had narrowed, with 82 per cent of employed men and 78 per cent of employed women covered by superannuation. Subsequently, a co-contribution scheme was introduced whereby employees also made contributions. However, the gender gap in superannuation balances remains (Economics References Committee, 2016).

A government report (Workplace Gender Equality Agency, 2016) revealed that the average man's superannuation balance was nearly twice that of the average woman at retirement. While compulsory superannuation is based on income, the superannuation savings gap will continue to exist for many retired women and men. However, state pensions and allowances remain the main source of income for over three-quarters of women and three-quarters of men (see Table 1.24, Economics References Committee, 2016).

In Australia, 44 per cent of retired women list their partner's income as their main financial support (Australian Bureau of Statistics, 2016). But, as one report puts it, 'A husband is not a retirement plan' (Economics Reference Committee, 2016). Difficulties can arise when a relationship ends or when a partner dies. Single-person households, particularly those of single women, have the lowest capacity for self-funding and are most likely to rely almost entirely on government aged pensions as their main source of retirement income.

Analysis by the Australian Institute of Family Studies (Warren, 2015a, 2015b) shows that, based on household disposable incomes in 2012–2013 and taking household expenses into account, about two-thirds of partnered retirees had a modest but reasonable standard of living. However, among single retired women, two-thirds of those aged 65–79 years were not able to afford at least a modest lifestyle compared to just over half of single male retirees. As one woman told us:

> My husband passed away. I had co-signed loans for his business, so had to sell my house and pay off all the debts for his business. I was left with nothing and now live in a tiny Government unit.

The 'Economic Security for Women in Retirement' report also examined retirement savings and superannuation, comparing who is better off among separated men and women. Not surprisingly, they found separated women have much lower retirement incomes and superannuation than separated men (Economics References Committee, 2016).

Americans, like Australians, rely on multiple sources of income later in life. These include Social Security benefits, based on lifetime earnings, and defined benefit pension distributions. Once again, the gender pay gap leaves women with less income from these sources than men. Incomes from public and private pensions based on women's own work were just 60 per cent and 48 per cent of men's pension incomes, respectively (US Bureau of Labor Statistics, 2014).

In the UK, a briefing report by the Pension Policy Institute provided details from the Wellbeing, Health, Retirement and the Lifecourse project (WHERL). This project partially focuses on how women's life courses affect their retirement incomes (Ewert et al., 2016). The projected retirement incomes of women who have worked full-time throughout their lives but who had children showed that the 'Motherhood Penalty' has substantially affected retirement incomes. Women's different life courses result in substantial variations of projected pension outcomes when compared to men whose life courses are less diverse. Moreover, the Motherhood Penalty increases with additional children, from 2 per cent for a mother who has one child, to 12 per cent for a mother with two children, and to 15 per cent for a mother with three children.

Savings

Other financial assets such as shares, managed funds and cash in bank accounts make up a (typically) small proportion of household wealth and less so for women than men, for obvious reasons.

36 Financial security in retirement

In our study, 34.9 per cent of women reported that at least part of their post-retirement income came from their own private resources. A partner's income was a source for 23.4 per cent of women and 72.6 per cent from superannuation pensions. The 2016 Scottish Widows study conducted in the UK, a large annual research programme assessing the challenges facing women as they prepare for retirement, found that many of the women interviewed were relying on their partners to support them in retirement and that, although record numbers of women were saving for retirement (53 per cent), more men were doing this (60 per cent). However, one-quarter of women, compared with only 14 per cent of men, were not saving anything for retirement. Those who were saving still trailed their male counterparts by £50 a month on average and in many cases by much more. In addition, and discouragingly, the age at which women started saving for retirement had increased over the past decade – up from 28 years in 2006 to 32 years in 2016.

Even among those who have carefully put money aside for their retirement, various factors can diminish their nest egg. Taxation may reduce savings income and savings are not protected from inflation unless wisely invested (which requires effort and knowledge). Savings may have been sufficient when people did not live as long as they do now, but they would need to be very high to provide an income stream for 20–30 years as is now required.

The issues discussed above, together with the other retirement income data, suggest that retirement may be a financially bleak (and lengthy) period for many women. To what extent do women worry about their financial security in retirement? How confident do they feel about their capacity to live comfortably after they leave paid work?

Retirement financial security

> I am a grasshopper. I lived from pay to pay. I did not save or plan.

While this respondent in our survey may not be typical, her comment raises questions about how financially secure women believe themselves to be on retiring. Retirement financial security will partly depend on women's assessment of changes in their finances since their retirement. For the majority of women in our sample, retirement resulted in no reduction (58 per cent) or an improvement (15 per cent) in their financial circumstances. That most were managing may be because our sample of women were well educated and, in general, occupied relatively high-level and well-paid positions before retiring. It is also interesting that, for most women, their financial resources were self-generated and less than one-quarter cited contributions from a partner. Good investing/financial planning, having no debts or mortgage, and being beneficiaries of inheritance were the most frequently given reasons offered by those whose financial circumstances had improved.

> Our super fund has maintained a fairly consistent level so even though we dropped income from not working full-time we have still managed to lead much the same lifestyle by being a little more careful.

On the other hand, more than one-quarter (27 per cent) stated that their finances had worsened since retirement. Most commonly they blamed low or inadequate superannuation and volatility in the share market. Family-related issues such as death or illness of a partner were also regarded by some as a cause of decline in finances, as were unanticipated calls to support children or grandchildren.

> Due to child losing their job this year ... looking after [my] grandchild for the first three and a half years of their life, supporting family members financially when in crisis and health concerns for husband and self in earlier few years of retirement.

> Term deposits rates have gone down. Share market volatility. Had to close [my] consultancy to assist daughter through postnatal issues, then became carer of elderly mother.

In the UK, almost three-fifths (57 per cent) of women feared that they were not preparing adequately for retirement, compared with two-fifths (41 per cent) of men, according to research conducted by Scottish Widows (2016). Many of those interviewed were consequently relying on their partners to support them in retirement – and a significant proportion admitted that they turned to them for advice about pension saving too, suggesting that this imbalance goes beyond a lack of funds and extends into a lack of confidence.

Similarly, women interviewed for a US study (MetLife Mature Market Institute and Scripps Gerontology Center, 2011) showed greater concern than men about their retirement security. Sixty-one per cent of those who were not confident about their ability to live comfortably in retirement believed that their savings were insufficient to last their lifetime.

One of our respondents encapsulated this uncertainty about the financial future thus:

> I'm probably quite OK between my super and a small government pension. *But* I feel very insecure as house rates rise, utilities rates rise, insurance rates rise – and I'm on a fairly fixed income. If I wasted $50 when I was working, my attitude was 'I'll make it up in next month's pay'. I now look at every $50 and make sure it is wisely spent. ... My perception of where I am and who I am has changed.

Finances are usually cited as a principal concern of retirees. About half of the women in our study expressed concern about post-retirement finances prior to leaving work, a figure consistent with that reported some years previously in survey six of the Australian Longitudinal Study on Women's Health (Women's Health Australia, 2015). Yet when we asked how financially secure they were, almost all of the women responded they felt 'very' (33 per cent) or 'moderately' (59 per cent) secure. Only a small number reported that they felt 'insecure' (6 per cent) or 'very insecure' (2 per cent). Financial resources primarily came from superannuation

38 Financial security in retirement

(73 per cent), state pension (35 per cent), partner's income (23 per cent) and/or their own private resources (35 per cent). (Some had more than one source, hence percentages add to greater than 100). A number of expected factors were associated with a feeling of security/insecurity, including source of income; partner; work breaks; age and length of retirement. Women with superannuation and those with partners felt more financially secure than those on a state pension and those without partners; women who had taken more than one long break in their employment were less financially secure than those who had taken one or no breaks. Not surprisingly, previous work position and level of education were both associated with a greater feeling of financial security: professional women and those who were better educated were more secure than non-professionals and those who were less well educated.

In another study, a substantial minority of women and men reported they were working longer to counteract insecurity (Janda, 2013). This report showed that 39 per cent of men and 36 per cent of women listed financial security as the main factor influencing their decision about when to retire. But retirement timing has never been entirely predictable or controllable. Of the women in our sample, 10 per cent retired because they had been sacked, made redundant or because there was no more work for them in their current position. The US study by MetLife found similar outcomes with 7 per cent of the women retiring earlier than they expected.

Retirement financial planning

> [I am] happy with my retirement plan. I worked in finance since I was 17 and always had my eye on the end result. Built a share portfolio, superannuation and rental income. Took advantage of work-related courses to improve my knowledge of financial and retirement opportunities.

Most of the women in our survey had made plans for retirement, primarily to ensure they maximised their financial circumstances on retirement. Only 18.5 per cent had made no plans. Yet many studies find that women's retirement plans do not adequately take account of their concerns about financial security. For the most part, men take the responsibility for financial and retirement planning; for example, double the number of men (61 per cent) compared with women (34 per cent) in the US study conducted by MetLife said that they were mostly responsible for financial and retirement planning in their households. Seven per cent of women said that they were not at all responsible for these decisions.

In the UK, the 2016 Scottish Widows study found that about one-third of women working full-time said that they were solely responsible for managing long-term financial planning in their homes (compared to almost half – 44 per cent – of men); of the remainder, almost half said that they and their partner shared the role.

A worrying aspect of planning is the situation for divorced women. The Scottish Widows study revealed that 84 per cent of divorced women reported that pensions were not discussed as part of their settlement (or they could not remember if this had occurred) at the time of their separation. As the report pointed out, 'It's important that divorced women are in the know when it comes to pension provisions or be left seriously out of pocket in retirement' (2016, p. 19).

One study of older US women and men commented that the 'do it yourself' approach to retirement planning is now common, with people managing a large portion of their retirement finances (Cahill *et al.*, 2015). Nevertheless, most (79 per cent of women and 67 per cent of men) said that they wanted professional help in managing their investments (Golladay, 2016).

Financial literacy

There has long been awareness of the importance of financial planning for women in the American Association of Retired Persons' (1991) comprehensive planning guide which advises women to save at least 10 per cent of their salaries and make this money work for them in different ways such as shares, government bonds and other investments. This well-meaning advice fails to take account of the difficulties faced by women in trying to save, as well as their relative lack of financial literacy. If women fail to grasp the essential aspects of financial literacy, their capacity to invest wisely is limited.

The OECD International Network on Financial Education defines financial literacy as 'A combination of awareness, knowledge, skill, attitude and behaviour necessary to make sound financial decisions and ultimately achieve individual financial wellbeing' (Hung *et al.*, 2012, p. 8). The most common measure of financial understanding or literacy was devised by Lusardi and Mitchell (2011a, 2011b) and consists of three questions about interest, inflation and risk diversification. These questions capture understanding of risk but not risk behaviour, although there is a correlation between understanding and behaviour. While this comprises a rather narrow measure of financial literacy, it does cover concepts that are particularly relevant to savings and investment decisions. The wording of the questions is as follows (with country-specific variations in currency):[1]

- Interest Rate Question: Suppose you had $100 in a savings account and the interest rate was 2% per year. After 5 years, how much do you think you would have in the account if you left the money to grow?
  More than $102; Exactly $102; Less than $102; Do not know; Refuse to answer.
- Inflation Question: Imagine that the interest rate on your savings account was 1% per year and inflation was 2% per year. After 1 year, how much would you be able to buy with the money in this account?
  More than today; Exactly the same; Less than today; Do not know; Refuse to answer.
- Risk Diversification Question: Please tell me whether this statement is true or false. 'Buying a single company's stock usually provides a safer return than a

40 Financial security in retirement

stock mutual fund.'
True; False; Do not know; Refuse to answer.

A report by the Global Financial Literacy Excellence Center (2017) found that only one-third of adults were financially literate in the sense of being able to answer these questions correctly. In many countries, the percentage of those considered financially literate was considerably lower. Women's financial literacy levels were consistently lower than men's. Risk diversification was the least understood concept. In a Global Financial Literacy Excellence Center Working Paper, three countries were examined in detail: the US, Germany and the Netherlands (Bucher-Koenen et al., 2016). Similarly, large gender differences in financial literacy were found in all three countries. The gender gap in financial literacy remained after taking into account marital status, education, income, and other socio-economic characteristics. Interestingly, women were unlikely to consult financial advisors to compensate for their lack of knowledge.

Reviewing nationally selected household surveys in eight countries between 2006 and 2011, Hung et al. (2012) found considerable variations in the number of women and men answering the 'interest' question correctly. For example, in New Zealand, 87 per cent of men and 85 per cent of women answered correctly, while in the Russian Federation only 37 per cent of men and 36 per cent of women knew the correct answer. Nevertheless, in all eight countries, fewer women than men answered correctly, with the greatest disparity appearing in Italy and the US. These findings about women's literacy levels are supported by studies conducted in many countries (see, for example, Almenberg and Save-Soderbergh (2011) in Sweden, Arrondel et al. (2013) in France, and Brown and Graf (2013) in Switzerland).

Bucher-Koenen et al. (2016) combined a comprehensive review of financial literacy research with their study of US, German and Dutch women and men. They confirmed 'severe' levels of low financial literacy among women, especially among single women and widows. Given that literacy is important in making financial decisions, women are particularly disadvantaged when it comes to planning for retirement and both accumulating and maintaining retirement wealth.

In Australia, the Australian Securities and Investments Commission (2015) in its longitudinal tracking of a wide range of financial issues reported that women and men differed on some but not all measures associated with financial literacy. For example, women were more likely than men to agree with the statement 'dealing with money is stressful and overwhelming'. Men were more likely than women to report they had heard of and understood risk/return trade-off. And men were more likely to accurately identify an example of 'diversification'.

There is considerable agreement that financial literacy has a positive impact on financial behaviour and financial status. Financially literate individuals do better at budgeting, saving money and controlling spending (Hung et al., 2012); handling mortgages and other debt (Lusardi and Tufano, 2009); participating in financial markets (Christelis et al., 2010; Van Rooij et al., 2011); and planning for retirement (Lusardi and Mitchell, 2007, 2008, 2011b). Arrondel et al., (2013) and Almenberg and Save-Soderbergh (2011) confirm that those with greater financial knowledge are more likely to have a clearly defined financial plan. Bucher-Koenen *et al.* (2016) also show that financial literacy is linked to key financial behaviours, all of which have consequences for retirement security. These include planning for retirement, investing in the stock market, paying attention to fees, and borrowing at low cost.

Financial risk-taking

A second key driver in increasing retirement wealth is the extent to which people are willing to make financial decisions that involve some risk. Low-risk, conservative decisions are those that entail taking few chances with savings and investments, for example putting money into low interest but safe bank accounts or only buying blue chip stocks and shares. Such cautious behaviour is likely to be relatively safe, but often means that the growth of a retirement nest egg will not keep up with inflation. If your retirement savings increase by 2 per cent per year but the cost of food and housing goes up by 5 per cent over the same period, you will be worse off financially. On the other hand, high-risk investment strategies are ones that can make or break you. These are strategies to be used sparingly unless you have deep pockets and/or have done your research thoroughly. Moderate risk investments, or a balance of high-, medium- and low-risk strategies, allow for the possibility of both safety and growth potential.

In general, women are not risk-takers. An early meta-analysis of 150 studies in which the risk-taking tendencies of male and female participants were compared (Byrnes *et al.*, 1999) showed that women were more risk averse than men in 14 of the 16 domains examined. However, certain topics (e.g. intellectual risk-taking and physical skills) produced larger gender differences than others (e.g. smoking).

There is now considerable evidence that women are more averse to financial risk than men (e.g. Bannier and Neubert, 2006; Charness and Gneezy, 2012; Collard, 2009; Grable, 2000). For example, in a study of over 1,000 women and men ranging in age from 20 to 75 years, Grable (2000) found that men were more risk tolerant than women. Risk tolerance was also associated with a combination of personality characteristics and socio-economic background and in particular, with financial knowledge.

Low levels of financial literacy together with risk-averse attitudes to financial investment mean that many women often cannot or are unwilling to make the best possible financial decisions before or during retirement. They may be over-cautious, ill-advised or lack reliable knowledge with respect to their financial decisions. This is likely to result in lower levels of retirement savings and investments in comparison with those prepared to become more informed about financial management, and to spread their investments across a range of risk options in order to maximise returns.

Collard (2009), reviewing research into investment behaviour, observed that most British consumers had limited understanding of financial risk and that they focus more

42 Financial security in retirement

on minimising financial losses than maximising financial gains. Studies also show consistently that women are more risk averse than men in their attitudes and behaviours towards investment decisions and that willingness to take financial risk tends to decrease significantly among people at or near retirement. In considering the results of 15 different studies on risk-taking in investment, Charness and Gneezy (2012) confirmed the extremely robust result that women are more risk averse than men.

Gender differences in riskiness may arise from a combination of factors, including aspects of finance such as gender inequalities in wealth and the different roles that impact on these inequalities, including gender discrimination in labour and credit markets, investment advice and information on investment decision-making, education, skills and training, and responsibility for the care of dependents (Bajtelsmit and Bernasek, 1996). Harris *et al.*, (2006) were interested in examining why women take fewer risks than men in a number of domains. Although financial risk, other than gambling, was not assessed it seems reasonable that their conclusions may be applied to financial risk. They argued that women's greater perceived likelihood of negative outcomes and lesser expectation of enjoyment partially mediated their lower propensity towards making risky choices in gambling, recreation and health domains.

Not all differences may be the result of structural and personality characteristics. Sapienza *et al.* (2009) have proposed a biological cause for women's lower levels of financial risk-taking. In humans, testosterone has been shown to enhance the motivation for competition and dominance, reduce fear, and alter the balance between sensitivity to punishment and reward. Testosterone has also been associated with extremely risky behaviour such as excessive gambling and alcohol use. However, the evidence that testosterone can affect financial risk-taking or other aspects of economic decision-making is currently mixed. Using MBA students at a US university, Sapienza *et al.* found that higher levels of circulating testosterone were associated with lower risk aversion among women, but not among men. Moreover, higher prenatal exposure to testosterone and higher circulating levels of this hormone were associated with lower risk aversion.

Although women's unwillingness to engage in financially risky behaviour may sometimes be to their advantage, in some respects being risk averse means that women tend not to maximise their financial opportunities.

Sexually transmitted debt

Court records and research show that it is usually women who acquire 'sexually transmitted debt', often agreeing to sign contracts or guarantee loans on behalf of their partner without understanding that if the partner defaults on payments, the legal liability for the debt falls on the guarantor or signatory to the contract (Australian Feminist Judgments Project, 2012). Financial debt incurred in this way is an issue for older women, including retirees, because of its potential impact on their financial security. For example, often the liability results in the loss of a family home that has been provided as security.

The main concern is that women take on debt due to the nature of their relationship, rather than an awareness of the liability or because there is some personal benefit. The cases typically arise where there is company insolvency, husband bankruptcy or a relationship breakdown. Divorce is only one of the key factors leading to sexually transmitted debt; however, it is a significant one. In the US, 40–50 per cent of marriages end in divorce (American Psychological Association, 2017); in Australia, the figure is lower, with about one in three marriages ending in divorce (ABS, 2017a). However, in both countries the median age at which divorce takes place has continued to rise, to the mid-40s for both women and men. So, increasingly, older women and men undergo relationship breakdowns that may result in the accrument of substantial financial debt.

Sexually transmitted debt can also arise in situations that tend to impact upon women in particular. Debts may be incurred because the woman wants to maintain the relationship or because the spouse is violent or exerts control over family finances. Poor financial education or experience can be a contributing factor as are the inequalities in the treatment of women by financial institutions where they are sometimes assumed to be financially incompetent or are simply discriminated against. There is not yet any consensus in Australian law as to how to address these issues. The best way to prevent sexually transmitted debt is for women to become better educated in financial matters and to be aware that such debt can pose a very real threat to their financial wellbeing.

The effects of financial inequity on women

Older single women are one of the fastest growing cohorts of people living in poverty. According to the HILDA Survey, in 2012, 38.7 per cent of older single females were living in poverty (Economics References Committee, 2016). In a study on life after retirement, 43.5 per cent of single women reported that their standard of living was worse or much worse after retirement. Of these single women, divorced women were even more likely to experience a decline in standard of living, with over half of divorced or separated women reporting that their standard of living had worsened. This was a higher proportion compared to women and men who were widows and women and men who had never married (Australian Human Rights Commission, 2009).

Reports from the US and Canada reflect similar findings. An 'Analysis of the Economic Circumstances of Canadian Seniors' (Shillington, 2012) found that poverty rates for single seniors in Canada were high, especially among women, who had a poverty rate of nearly 30 per cent. The percentage of older women in America who are in financial distress is 50 per cent higher than that of men, according to a new analysis of US Census Department data:

> For many, the consequences are serious. We are seeing evidence that older women are making choices that are untenable … They're very quietly, at home, deciding to choose between having heat in the wintertime or putting

nutritious food on the table, or they're choosing between food and the medications they need. They make choices that get them by, but they're very dangerous choices to be making. We're not talking about eating out, or buying birthday presents for grandchildren, or any of those extras. We're talking about shelter, food, clothing, and transportation – the basics we need to survive in this country, let alone thrive.

(Bennetts, 2012, p. 1)

The report analysed the living circumstances of older Americans in comparison with the Elder Economic Security Index. The Elder Index defines economic security as income sufficient to meet the necessary daily expenses without borrowing or assistance from public support programmes. According to the Wider Opportunities for Women (WOW) study reported by Bennetts, 42 per cent of all women, 63 per cent of African-American women, and 66 per cent of Hispanic women lacked economic security, a much higher percentage than for older men. As other studies have shown, marriage offers some protection. Sixty-one per cent of single seniors living alone reported household incomes below the Elder Index, compared to just 36 per cent of couples.

Other data from the US found that although economic insecurity is steadily increasing among all seniors, single women are especially vulnerable, with half of all single females financially insecure, according to the Senior Financial Security Index (Meschede *et al.*, 2011).

A qualitative study conducted by two women's health organisations in Australia (Women's Health in the North, and Women's Health Goulburn North East; Parkinson *et al.*, 2013) on women in poorer communities found a number of negative consequences of women's financial circumstances. A central concern was that the old age pension would not be sustainable into the future due to the rapidly ageing population. Some saw this period 'as one of transition away from a secure aged pension for all who need it … women spoke of uncertainty about the social security system' (ibid., p. 8–9).

> Not having any super[annuation] and the aged pension not being available until 67 years makes me very anxious.
>
> (Michelle, age 59 years; ibid., p. 9)

For some women their current financial situation was untenable. Many spoke of struggling just to survive; others developed strategies to cope such as using free showers at recreational centres, using candles to save on electricity, doing without heating in the house. There was some resentment at the relatively low state pension and one woman suggested that if more men had to live on it, it would not be so low.

Other women spoke of wanting to retire but feeling compelled to carry on working owing to financial insecurity. Indeed, some spoke of never being able to retire. Two other major areas of concern were health and a fear of losing their home and becoming homeless. The cost of health care was a significant issue and some women found that they had to choose between paying for medicine or for living expenses. Becoming homeless is now a reality for many older Australian women, with the private rental market providing few opportunities for these women to rent.

> My rent here is $950 a month [and] I only get the normal pension ... it's a real desperate worry for me. I keep thinking I'm going to end up living in my car like I've seen some people.
> *(Brenda, age 59 years; Parkinson* et al.*, 2013, p. 14)*

Many respondents in our study expressed post-retirement financial concerns and frustrations:

> I have discovered that I am not good at all at managing with much less money. It deepens my respect for my late mother and grandmother who managed so well on their pensions. I have developed a great love of travel ... However, now I cannot afford to do this, which is frustrating. I see married couples in my retirement village heading off for overseas holidays. I guess they had much more super[annuation] than I did. Most of mine went on paying off my mortgage and car, and dental work.

> [M]y husband is always with me, my son is never at home and the house is in the need of many repairs and we are unable to pay [for these] to be done. Food quantities have changed, due to money and health problems ... No, no fun when you have to beg for anything you wanted to achieve daily. [Or] do a form any time you ask for food or money at Centerlink and feel you have no right to ask, when you have been working all your life and never stopped to ask for a hand-out.

Financial traps: succumbing to a financial swindle

The number and complexity of reports involving financial abuse of older adults has grown significantly over the past decade. The available research on financial scams does not provide data on gender differences or specifically on retirees although it appears that many retirees are susceptible to exploitation.

Recent research in the US found that the rate of financial exploitation is extremely high, with one in 20 older adults indicating some form of perceived financial abuse occurring in the recent past, but underreporting is common. A recent review of seniors living on their own (Burnes *et al.*, 2017) found that one in 18 older Americans falls victim to financial fraud or scams annually, and that figure excludes seniors who have been financially abused by friends and relatives. This is likely to be an underestimate, the authors report, as victims tend to underreport the scams due to shame and embarrassment.

Financial exploitation takes many forms. While the majority of reports involve perpetrators who are related to, or in a trusting relationship with, the victim, scams and frauds by strangers are also common. These include fake telemarketing calls, sometimes using the Internet. While using the Internet is a great skill at any age, many older people find it particularly confusing, making them easier targets for automated Internet scams that are ubiquitous on the web and email programs. Door-to-door and home maintenance scams are other examples of financial exploitation. These scams generally involve promoting goods and services that are of poor quality, or not delivered at all. Unscrupulous contractors convince victims that they are in dire need of various home repairs and they overcharge them or get paid before the projects are completed and disappear.

Of even greater financial concern are investment schemes that largely target seniors looking to safeguard their cash for their later years. From pyramid schemes to complex financial products, investment schemes have long been a successful way to take advantage of older people and can leave them financially destitute.

What is commonly called 'elder financial abuse' is an example of a different type of financial exploitation. This form of abuse is not carried out by strangers but by someone known and trusted by the older person, usually a family member. Although only one aspect of elder abuse, financial abuse is by far the most common and is an increasing phenomenon in western nations, as both lifespan and the cost of housing increase. Various studies, including a review of evidence from 52 studies in 28 countries from diverse regions, including 12 low- and middle-income countries (Yon et al., 2017) find that around one in 20 older people report elder financial abuse by family members. Victims are usually seniors who live alone, are socially isolated, have cognitive deficits and/or who rely on a family member for care. In worst-case scenarios, the elderly person can be inveigled or tricked into selling their family home, changing their will or limiting their quality of life in ways that are unnecessary, given their resources. There is a profound psychological impact as a result of this form of abuse. Understandably, the victims are likely to feel devastated when members of their family, who they thought they could trust, disappoint them. They are likely to experience feelings of shame, guilt, anger and self-doubt, and may suffer financial poverty as a result. A significant outcome of this last effect is increasing reliance on government-funded programmes for financial support.

While it is difficult to protect seniors from family and outsider financial abuse, widening access to financial education and advice may prevent some older people from this type of exploitation. Focusing on financial abuse by family and trusted others, Darzins et al. (2009) consider potential strategies which may be effective, including education and community awareness campaigns, management of older people's financial affairs by independent workers, and mandatory reporting of financial abuse. However, they caution against implementation of such policies and practices without careful evaluation of their effectiveness.

Conclusion

The causes of financial gender inequality in retirement are complex and there is no simple solution. We have seen that many women are concerned about their economic circumstances. What can be done to enable women to plan for and achieve financial security in retirement? As a basic tool, there is a strong need for help with retirement planning (Golladay, 2016). In a nationwide survey of US 'millennials' most respondents (79 per cent of women and 67 per cent of men) said that they wanted professional help in managing their investments. Women were more likely than men to want help with budgeting and saving (45 per cent compared with 25 per cent). There was strong support for this advice to be provided at work to help with their overall financial health. Bucher-Koenen and her colleagues confirm the need for professional help and for increasing financial literacy. They remarked, 'The evidence suggests that it is particularly difficult for women to obtain independent, high-quality advice. Therefore, enhancing the financial knowledge of women and equipping them with the tools to make sound financial decisions should be a top priority for policymakers' (2016, p. 18).

A recent inquiry into achieving economic security for women in retirement by the Australian Senate (Economics References Committee, 2016) made 17 broad policy recommendations aimed at strengthening policy initiatives that would reduce gender inequities on retirement. These include mechanisms for developing benchmarks for the adequacy of retirement incomes to inform policy decisions, and evaluation of any reforms that ensue. The committee also recommended that all policy analysis in relation to retirement income specifically consider the impact of any proposal on men and women separately. Other recommendations were specifically related to rental accommodation in retirement, bearing in mind the greater likelihood of retired women living in poverty than men.

Grace *et al.* (2005) also proposed a range of policy responses to this inequity in addition to affirmative action policies. Most centre on aspects of childcare, such as the provision of high-quality affordable childcare, free accessible after school care, and retraining opportunities for parents who have spent time out of the paid workforce. Another focused on recognising the economic importance of carers, recommending adequate pay for those who are employed in these roles. As they noted, these policies, while expensive, serve to recompense the free labour afforded by these individuals – usually women.

Vu and Doughey (2009) made the point that there needs to be some sort of compensation, perhaps in terms of pensions, to make up for the financial discrimination women encounter before retirement in order that further discrimination does not occur after they retire.

Most writers make a strong point about women's need to have greater access to financial planning before and after they retire. This may include discussions about the diversification of investments, and about calculating the probable value of investments on retirement so that forward planning can be informed, also how to set up a budget, how to protect assets, how to develop a retirement savings plan,

48 Financial security in retirement

and understanding what their partner's benefits and assets are. Those offering financial advice need to provide women with information specifically tailored to their needs, including directing them to resources specifically for women, providing information geared at life events such as childrearing, emphasising the importance of saving early and as much as possible.

While women-centred policy changes are important goals, the reality is that these will not be enacted quickly or uniformly. If retired women are to manage on limited funds they need to develop their financial management skills. Although many women have been responsible for household budgets and for making their money 'stretch', they have often not accepted the importance of learning how to make their money grow. Financial literacy education is a key step in this process. If women do not understand important financial concepts, their post-retirement financial security is likely to be compromised.

Because of the considerable evidence that women, especially single and divorced women, leave the paid workforce with insufficient funds for a comfortable retirement, persuading them to save as much as possible for this stage of their lives is an important strategy. In an experimental setting exploring saving behaviour, Hershfield *et al.* (2011) shifted their attention from interventions that focus on present and future rewards to a complementary route that focuses on the distinction between the current and future self. Hershfield and his colleagues were able to depict vivid representations of women's future selves that led participants to 'lower discounting of future rewards and higher contributions to saving accounts' (ibid., S33).

The implication here is that if women plan for their social, intellectual and emotional lives post-retirement, they are more likely to plan financially as well. The next step, of course, is to determine whether this finding is replicated in real life.

Vu and Doughney (2009) suggest that a woman's financial disadvantage in retirement derives from two main sources: her disadvantaged position in the paid workforce and the disadvantage of performing most of society's unpaid work. As Hung *et al.* (2012) noted, women may be in greater need of long-term wealth management skills for a combination of reasons related to labour and demography. As we noted earlier, women tend to be in paid work for shorter periods, are more likely to work part-time and in lower-paid jobs than men. Jefferson (2009) reported it is widely recognised that women's patterns of care provision have adverse implications for their access to economic resources in later life. Women's capacity to provide adequately for retirement with accumulated savings and employer-funded contributions is constrained by factors such as these. The financial problem for women is exacerbated by their longer life expectancy compared to that of men. In addition, women who are lone parents and/or divorced or single suffer real economic disadvantage compared to other women and to men (Hung *et al.*, 2012).

Asked in our survey what would they do differently, many women wrote in negative terms about financial issues. One said regretfully:

> I would try not to have breaks from paid employment, so that I would have been able to contribute more to superannuation. I would have been able to

contribute longer to super (super did not exist when I first started working). I would have found out more about financial investment prior to retirement. I would have tried to have funds available to start investing in the property market sooner (for most of my early working life I lived pay to pay as I was a single mother with one wage).

Note

1 The correct answers to the three questions are (1) More than $102; (2) Less than today; (3) False

4

PLANNING AND DECISION-MAKING

Why did I retire? I started work at age 15 and felt I had worked long enough.

I resigned – internal gender politics made the job unbearable.

I retired to look after grandchildren so my daughters did not have to interrupt their careers in the way I had had to when they were born.

I retired when my husband retired so we could spend time together.

I felt I was ready.

Decisions, decisions...

What leads to the decision to retire? The five women quoted above had five different reasons, and we could doubtless find 500 more, although as we see later in the chapter these reasons do tend to cluster into categories. Sometimes there is no decision to be made – illness, circumstances, sacking or redundancy force the move to a new stage of life. A standardised retirement age would also make choice unnecessary, but in most countries and for most jobs such standardisation no longer exists. A few occupations still have a statutory retirement age, but these tend to involve work that is considered dangerous or that requires a high degree of mental or physical acuity, for example, pilot, judge, or military personnel (Australian Law Reform Commission, 2012; Vermeer *et al.*, 2015). For most occupations, however, and in many nations, mandatory retirement based solely on age falls into the category of age discrimination and is no longer legal (Agediscrimination.info, 2016, 2017; US Equal Employment Opportunity Commission, 2008). If there is no set retirement age, people have to make their own decisions about retirement timing, that is, whether they should retire 'early', 'on time', or 'late'. According to the European-based Organisation for Economic Co-operation and Development (OECD, 2016), 'on time' means around one's mid-60s; the average effective age of retirement for women is 63.6 years and 65.1 years for men.

One major barrier to early retirement is that access to state pensions is usually not possible until a specific age has been reached. This has formerly tended to fall between 60 and 65 years, but the entitlement age is gradually rising as the world population ages, because funding so many retirees for so long is a massive drain on government coffers. Similarly, although employer-funded and self-funded pensions may often be accessible as income streams at a younger age, associated taxation incentives are less likely until a designated age, usually in the mid-60s. In the UK, Australia and the US, the age of eligibility for government-funded old age pensions is currently around the mid-60s but will rise to 67 years by 2028 (UK) or 2023 (Australia, the US) (Australian Government Department of Human Services, 2017; GOV.UK, 2017; Social Security, n.d.). Pension eligibility age has traditionally been a few years lower for women, but many countries have already phased out this difference or are doing so gradually (AgeUK, 2017).

Within the limitations, exceptions and constraints described above, most working women, as they move into their senior years, will need to make a choice as to when and under what conditions they will retire from the paid workforce. As we saw in Chapter 3, financial considerations are likely to play a large part in this decision, but there are other factors as well, such as attachment to the workforce and the personal meaning and centrality of one's occupational role. In this chapter we will review research on variables affecting decision-making about retirement and the extent to which women plan for this event. We will compare retirement outcomes of women who planned their retirements with those who made fewer (or no) plans or who were constrained to retire. We will consider what happens when plans are upset by life events, and finally we will include a brief section on those women who never retire.

The decision-making process

Decision-making for this life change involves evaluating and balancing the pushes and pulls towards staying in or leaving the workforce when one reaches an age deemed suitable or normative for retirement. The process can be viewed within an approach–avoidance framework. Each option has positives and negatives associated with it, some known (e.g. how much stress you are feeling at work) and some unknown (e.g. what your social life will be like when you retire). Evaluating the various pushes and pulls will involve a mix of information-gathering, managing and predicting feelings, and making both rational and non-rational judgements. Furthermore, there are compromise positions to consider, such as working part-time or retiring 'on trial' through extended leave-taking.

Feldman and Beehr (2011) suggest that there are three phases, potentially over-lapping, in retirement decision-making: imagining the future; assessing when it is time to go; and then making the transition effectively.

Phase 1, 'Imagining the future', involves the consideration and anticipation of the general possibilities of retirement. For some women, conceiving a later-life future without paid employment might begin at a young age; for others it may not occur until very close to the moment when the decision is finally taken. Individual differences such as health status, enjoyment of the work environment, and the extent of other interests are likely to shape the imagining. For every older woman who says 'I can't imagine myself ever retiring', there will be another who spends her days thinking about a different kind of existence, away from her current workplace.

Cultural expectations will be relevant to how women imagine their lives post-work. Knoll (2011) argues that the 'spikes' in retirements of US workers at the age of 62 and 65 years are influenced not only by Social Security arrangements in that country but by norms which turn these arbitrary ages into cultural reference points, designating 'normal' times to retire. Women who retire earlier or later than their own reference group may feel out of step and be concerned about the possibility of social isolation. Illustrating this, some women in our study discussed their own reasons for retirement in terms of subjective norms, for example:

> I was an old events co-ordinator whose peers were much younger!

> I was the oldest staff member in my department.

> I felt I should retire at 68 years of age because people expected it of me. I regret leaving when I did.

It is well known that younger age groups have vastly different notions of what constitutes 'old age' compared to those who are a few more decades advanced. Many studies have demonstrated these differing perceptions. For example, one report indicated that those in the 18–20 age group judge 57 years as 'old', whereas baby boomers consider that old age begins at around 84 or 85 years (Starts at 60, 2017). A youthful group of co-workers with negative stereotypes of ageing and beliefs about its early onset may well discourage older workers from continuing to work despite feeling adequate to the task and enjoying their work or needing the money.

One's own attitudes are also relevant, not only to ageing but to retirement as a life stage. Desmette and Gaillard (2008) showed that individuals with positive atti-tudes towards retirees as a group were more motivated about taking retirement than those who viewed this stage of life negatively, associating it perhaps with 'old people' and being 'past the use by date'. Women's acceptance of their own ageing and their stereotyping of retirees will help to shape whether they approach this life stage with pleasure, dread or mixed feelings.

Many women will begin thinking about retirement possibilities as their family circumstances change. Warren (2015a, 2015b) analysed extensive data from the first eight waves of the nationally representative Household Income and Labour Dynamics in Australia Survey, which provided longitudinal information on work and retirement among older singles and couples. Using complex statistical modelling techniques, Warren concluded that there is strong evidence that working Australian couples co-ordinate their retirements in order to share leisure time. Specifically, women tend to delay their retirement if their husband has a financial incentive to continue in the labour force, or retire early to care for a partner who is in ill health. As one woman said to us:

> I might as well keep working until my husband retires or until I have some grandchildren to look after, otherwise I'll just be at home twiddling my thumbs.

In short, a complex mix of cognitions and feelings are likely to precede specific planning towards a retirement date, and these factors will differ for women and men.

Imagining is, in a sense, a first step in planning, which might involve talking to others, seeking information, developing exit strategies, and preparing for a new lifestyle. We discuss planning and its implications in more detail later in the chapter.

Phase 2 of Feldman and Beehr's process model is 'assessing when it is time to go', a stage that has been studied from several different career transition and lifespan development perspectives. These models conceptualise retirement as the final stage of career development and examine issues such as disengagement from work (e.g. Super, 1990) or commencement of new roles and activities as a way to establish a post-work persona (e.g. Barnes and Parry, 2004). At this stage, planning becomes more concrete and a retirement date may be tentatively set or firmed up. Most people at this stage find themselves investigating their likely post-retirement financial position, sometimes making plans for ways to strengthen it before they cease work entirely.

Speculations on length of life are influential in decisions both about when to move to a more leisurely existence and also about how much money is needed in savings or pension funds before retirement can be envisaged (Wang and Shi, 2014). One woman told us:

> I was 69. I didn't want to look back and regret that I had worked to 70 or 75 with no time left for leisure.

Griffin *et al.* (2012) found that for mature-aged workers, subjective life expectancy (SLE – one's estimated age of death) predicted intended retirement age and extent of pre-retirement planning. Shorter SLEs at first testing in a longitudinal study were associated with a higher likelihood of having actually retired a year later.

Fisher *et al.*, whose extensive analysis of retirement timing we consider in the next section, categorised workers as retiring 'early', 'on time', or 'late', albeit with the recognition that the ages associated with these categories are 'a bit vague' (2016, p. 251). They note that there are benefits and trade-offs for early or later retirement (the push–pull factors) so that there is no 'one size fits all' formula for making this decision. For example, while some people may retire early due to ill health, believing they can no longer comfortably handle work commitments, others may choose early retirement because their health is still good enough to travel or fulfil long-held goals (von Bonsdorff and Ilmarinen, 2013).

Other researchers like Knoll (2011) emphasise financial matters such as the advantages of putting off retirement for longer than the normative retirement age, in order to accumulate more capital to support post-work lifestyles. Knoll argues that individuals are often influenced to retire early, against their own interests, due to *cognitive biases and heuristics*. For example, she notes that in the US, 62 years is the earliest eligible age for receiving some Social Security retirement benefits, but postponing retirement until 64 years results in a significant monthly monetary increase in these payments. Individuals need to weigh up this gain against disadvantages such as the loss of freedom and leisure time associated with retiring later. She argues that many people choose to retire at the earlier age owing to non-rational factors. First, individuals tend to be *loss averse* (Tversky and Kahneman, 1974), that is, they tend to weigh losses more heavily than gains when making decisions. Loss-averse individuals may prefer to give up the potential financial gains of staying in work longer because they do not want to experience the losses associated with continuing to work – for example 'freedom', stress reduction, or more leisure time. Second, because 62 years is such a popular age at which to retire, it serves as a reference point for normal, rather than early, retirement – the *anchoring* effect, which has also been described by Kahneman and Tversky (1979). Finally, Knoll refers to a review of research on *affective forecasting* (Wilson and Gilbert, 2003) which concludes that people are not good at predicting their future happiness, and tend to 'overestimate the intensity and duration of their emotions in reaction to positive and negative future events' (Knoll, 2011, p. 20). This is another way of saying that the trade-off between retiring sooner or later can become biased towards the 'sooner' end of the equation, because we assume that the grass will be greener on the other side of the fence. Knoll's analysis seems to apply more to those who are dissatisfied with their jobs. Those who enjoy their work and whose sense of identity revolves around their occupational roles may find that cognitive biases shape their decisions in the opposite direction. They may put off retirement as a potentially negative unknown, a decision that is likely to be beneficial financially but its effects on health and wellbeing are less clear and will depend on many individual and workplace variables.

Phase 3 in Feldman and Beehr's (2011) model, 'making the transition', entails leaving the workforce and moving on to the next life stage. To do this effectively involves making satisfactory financial and social arrangements for post-work life. In the next section, we discuss further the range of variables that people take into account in deciding when to retire, with emphasis on research that focuses on women.

Timing retirement: when to go?

Fisher *et al.* (2016) take a multilevel approach in considering the antecedents of retirement timing, examining evidence for a wide spectrum of individual and demographic factors, family factors, work-related and person-job fit factors and, at the macro system level, the state of national economies.

Individual and demographic factors

Fisher *et al.* (2016) note that the most frequently cited reason for early or unplanned retirement is poor health, particularly that which results in a diminished capacity to work (e.g. van Rijn *et al.*, 2014). McGarry (2004) shows that changes in retirement expectations are more strongly affected by health status than by income or wealth changes. Fifteen per cent of our retired women research participants said that ill health was a factor in leaving the workforce, some describing specific symptoms but others stating that they were 'just tired', 'exhausted', or had 'had enough'. In a number of studies, poor mental health (usually depression) has been associated with early retirement among women (e.g. Paradise *et al.*, 2012; Rice *et al.*, 2011). Age-related cognitive decline may also be implicated in retirement, especially if the workplace is intellectually demanding or involves new learning such as mastery of constantly changing technologies (e.g. Belbase *et al.*, 2015). Among our sample of retired women, 8 per cent indicated that being unable to deal with changes in the workplace influenced their retirement decisions, while 19 per cent mentioned workplace stress as a contributing factor.

Financial status, as we have mentioned on several occasions, is a key factor in determining retirement timing. In Chapter 3, we considered women's generally reduced status with respect to the 'three pillars' of retirement finances: social security (government) pensions; employer/employee funded pensions; and savings. Interestingly, some studies have shown that women with higher incomes tend to retire earlier (e.g. De Preter *et al.*, 2013 in a study of men and women living in ten European countries; Raymo *et al.*, 2011 in a longitudinal US study). A smaller number of studies demonstrate the opposite effect, with higher wealth associated with delaying retirement (e.g. Larsen and Pedersen, 2008). No doubt other factors interact with economic variables, such as the extent to which a job is enjoyed and is central to one's definition of self. Thus, for women who have their own businesses or who are experts in their field, enjoyment of the practical, intellectual and social challenges may override financial issues and keep these women working beyond any economic 'need'.

Data on gender and retirement timing is ambiguous and subject to multiple factors. Traditionally, women have retired at earlier ages than men and in fact were sometimes legally required to do so. Some studies still show that women generally tend to retire earlier (e.g. Rice *et al.*, 2011), while others indicate a more recent tendency for women to work longer than men, possibly to make up (financially) for the likely breaks in their working lives, the 'pay gap' and their need to support themselves across longer lifespans than men. Finch (2014) in the UK, recent

56 Planning and decision-making

Australian Bureau of Statistics data (ABS, 2017b) and an Australian study by Shacklock *et al.* (2009) all found that women were less likely to take early retirement than men, and in each case this was attributed to women having been in employment less extensively in the earlier part of their careers and having consequently built up a weaker financial position.

Education is one of the moderating factors that keep individuals in the workforce longer, a consistent finding in many countries (Fisher *et al.*, 2016). Those with higher levels of education may stay in the workplace longer owing to better working conditions, more interesting jobs or perhaps because they started work at an older age due to the time taken for schooling. Relevant psychological factors that keep people working include some of the 'functions of work' variables we discussed in Chapter 2. Personal satisfaction and a sense of purpose obtained from working, identity and status, social contact and goal directedness are all implicated here. Those wondering how to fulfil these needs in retirement are less likely to retire early. For example, in the US a survey conducted by the Metlife Mature Market Institute, David DeLong and Associates, and Zogby International (2006) found that older workers in the 66–70 year age group indicated that they had continued in the workforce owing to a desire to remain active and engaged, to have the opportunity to do meaningful work, and to maintain social contacts. Zaniboni *et al.*, (2010) found that older Italian workers whose sense of identity was strongly tied to their work role were less likely to plan full retirement, intending instead to maintain part-time or casual links with their workplace even if semi-retired. In our study, women who checked 'using my talents and skills' as one of their important reasons for working were more likely to retire at an older age, as were those who showed a stronger attachment to their previous occupations through continuing to attend social events at their former workplace, retaining friendships made at work, and going to talks or meetings related to their former field of work.

An individual's leisure interests will also be influential in retirement timing. Various studies have indicated that preferences for leisure activities, club membership and involvement in volunteer work predict earlier retirement (e.g. De Preter *et al.*, 2013; Schmidt and Lee, 2008; Shacklock *et al.*, 2009). One of our study participants put it this way:

> Full-time work became too demanding with all my other commitments and hobbies!

Personality factors may affect retirement decisions (for example, low conscientiousness has been associated with earlier retirement in a US study by Lockenhoff *et al.*, 2009), but the evidence here is not particularly strong (Fisher *et al.*, 2016).

Family factors

As mentioned previously, studies indicate that married women tend to co-ordinate their retirement date with their partner's intentions regarding retirement, often so that they can retire together (e.g. Kim and Feldman, 1998; Warren, 2015). Gustman and Steinmeier (2005) showed that enjoyment of each other's company was a strong predictor of whether spouses timed their retirements to coincide with one another.

Eleven per cent of our research participants indicated that 'family reasons' affected their retirement decisions, with qualitative data suggesting that spending time with retired husbands, and sharing activities such as travel, were particularly influential. As one participant stated:

> I am lucky to share retirement with a happy, healthy, easy-going husband. How hard it would be with a grouch, or to be a grieving sad widow. I appreciate that I am very fortunate.

Plans for sharing retirement activities did not always come to fruition, as these women noted:

> I expected to spend time with my spouse, to spend time travelling together, but he is very busy with his own retirement activities.

> I expected to get on better with my spouse.

Caring for grandchildren, an elderly parent or a sick spouse can also predict earlier retirement timing for women (e.g. Dentinger and Clarkberg, 2002; Matthews and Fisher, 2013). Interestingly, the latter found that men with disabled spouses who needed care were more likely to *delay*, rather than to bring forward, their retirement date, which may of course relate to their priorities in providing the financial resources for care.

Lumsdaine and Vermeer (2015) examined the relationship between caring for grandchildren and women's retirement timing, using longitudinal data on more than 12,000 women from the US Health and Retirement Study. They found that the arrival of a new grandchild increased the probability of a woman retiring by more than 8 per cent.

A 64-year-old grandmother from our Australian study of grandparenting (Rosenthal and Moore, 2012a) typifies this trend, explaining how she originally switched to part-time work when her first grandchild (of five) was born, then took full retirement in order better to enjoy her grandparenting experience:

> Well, I was working full-time when my first grandchild was born, then I worked a nine-day fortnight so I could have a day with her. Then I took full retirement, so the grandkids had a big influence on that. They sort of showed me there was more to life than working.

For some women, their caring role and subsequent retirement was born of tragic necessity:

58 Planning and decision-making

> My daughter-in-law died giving birth to twins and I [retired to] look after them for my son.

And

> My daughter's husband died and she had a baby under one and a three-year-old to care for. I was her key supporter, so I took a 'package' [and retired] even though I had planned to work until my late 60s to build up my retirement pension.

Work factors

Barnes-Farrell (2003) argued that job satisfaction, job conditions, organisational climate and social pressures (such as retirement age norms) all affect retirement timing. Asked why they retired, some women in our study simply said things like 'I hated my job and couldn't wait to leave'; others felt that they could no longer keep up with physical or cognitive demands, as discussed earlier. A significant number retired because they perceived an organisational atmosphere of bullying, saying for example, 'I was bullied to leave after 36 years of loyal service,' and 'A bullying new CEO made work satisfaction unlikely'. Overall, as we have discussed previously, those who enjoy their jobs are likely to retire later than those who do not (e.g. Fisher *et al.*, 2016), but this is only one of the many push-pull factors influencing the retirement decision.

Some workplaces offer financial incentives to retire. A Spanish study (Potočnik *et al.*, 2010) demonstrated that these were effective in encouraging early retirement among university workers, as were organisational pressures such as the kind of bullying described above. A number of women in our study said they retired because they were 'offered a package' or were 'offered a good deal for early retirement'. On the other hand, the availability of flexible working arrangements such as additional leave or part-time opportunities, as well as supervisor support for staying longer all predicted later retirement ages across a range of European studies (e.g. Bal *et al.*, 2012; Hermansen, 2014; van Dalen *et al.*, 2010; van Solinge and Henkens, 2014).

Economic conditions

The general state of the economy has a marked effect on retirement plans. If the share market is doing well, retirement savings and pension schemes are likely to be more robust. When there is plenty of employment available, older workers have more options to delay retirement, and retirees are more able to secure part-time or casual work if they wish to boost their finances.

The global financial crisis of 2008 adversely affected the retirement savings of many workers, an effect that had more impact on those closer to exiting the workforce because these individuals have fewer years left to re-establish satisfactory pension savings. Illustrating this, a study by O'Loughlin *et al.*, (2010) examined the impact of the financial crisis on employed Australian baby boomers, aged between 50 and 64 years, surveyed in mid-2009. Nearly 40 per cent reported being financially worse off following the crisis, with women more strongly affected than men (42.4 per cent compared with 35.6 per cent). Many people decided to delay retirement in order to boost their savings, an effect that was stronger for women than men (41.4 per cent compared with 31.9 per cent).

One of our research participants explained how she had been affected by the economic downturn:

> I was confident that I would achieve my aims by putting extra money into super and going without to achieve this. Sadly, the global financial crisis changed that as I lost money just on retirement. I have never recovered and was unable to get any part-time work when I tried in the first couple of years.

Sass *et al.*, (2010) conducted a telephone survey of 1,327 American individuals aged 45–59 years to find out how the 2008 stock market crash had affected their retirement planning. These were workers whose employer-sponsored retirement pension schemes (called 401(k) plans) had lost on average about one-third of their value. As with the Australian study, about 40 per cent intended to delay their retirements to an older age than previously envisaged. The trend did not differ across gender, but was stronger for those closer to retirement and who had suffered greater asset losses. Similarly, a survey by the US-based Pew Research Center (2009) found that 52 per cent of older workers (aged 50–64 years) reported the intention to delay their retirements subsequent to the global financial crisis.

Choice or constraint?

As we have seen, many factors – personal, familial, work-related and even global – can combine and interact to shape when a person retires. Sometimes these factors are weighed up in a logical fashion before the decision is made. More often than not it seems that emotions, cognitive biases and even the desire to avoid planning are influential in retirement timing. And, of course, sometimes people have no choice in the matter and are made redundant or leave the workforce before they are ready to do so owing to factors such as illness or work stress. Whether retirement is perceived as voluntary or not has implications for future welfare, as we discuss below.

Reasons for retiring were strongly related to various aspects of life satisfaction among our sample of retired women. Those who were made redundant were significantly less satisfied, post-retirement, with their finances, their social lives, their levels of physical activity, their standards of living, life in general and with being retired, in comparison with those who were not constrained by their workplace to leave. They were also significantly more likely than the rest of the sample to self-assess as financially insecure or very insecure. Redundancy clearly limits

60 Planning and decision-making

opportunities to plan for retirement, both in terms of building up pension funds and savings adequately and in organising post-work social activities.

Other types of pressure to retire include job stress and problems dealing with change in the workplace. In our study, citing job stress as a reason for retirement was associated with lower levels of satisfaction with close family relationships, closeness of friendships, number of friends, and perceived opportunities for forming new friendships. This is a very different pattern of dissatisfactions from those expressed by the women who were made redundant. It could indicate lack of peer and family support for job-stressed women, or that stressed-out women become more difficult to relate to in general. There may be other explanations or a combination of factors may be implicated. Interestingly, those who had difficulty coping with workplace change also expressed lower levels of post-retirement satisfaction with their close family relationships, but not with their friendships. Instead, they showed a pattern of generally lowered satisfaction levels with their standard of living, being retired and life in general. Among these Australian women, retiring because of workplace problems was associated with continuing dissatisfaction in post-work life.

At least those who retire for work-related reasons can by and large leave those reasons behind. That is not the case for health problems. Of those women who nominated heath issues as one of the factors influencing their retirement, satisfaction levels were lower than for any other group. In fact, these women were significantly less satisfied than the rest of the sample on every one of the 14 measures of satisfaction we assessed, including wellbeing indicators of their financial, social, familial, physical, and life in general status.

A completely different picture emerged among those women who retired because 'they were ready'. These women, who comprised almost half of the sample, scored significantly higher than the rest on all our measures of satisfaction with retirement and aspects of life in general.

Perhaps it is stating the obvious, but women in a position to choose the time and circumstances of their retirement fare better in terms of retirement outcomes. This finding is reflected in many studies worldwide. For example, Floyd *et al.* (1992) in a US study, showed that men and women who retired voluntarily in order to follow their own interests were more satisfied with their marriages and home lives, the services available to them, their health and indeed their lives in general than those who retired because of constraints and pressures such as job stress. Hershey and Henkins (2014), studying 1,388 older Dutch workers over a six-year period, demonstrated those who retired voluntarily during the study period reported higher levels of life satisfaction than those who either remained employed or whose departure was involuntary, due to health or work organisational reasons. This latter group reported by far the lowest levels of satisfaction with life, with these results not differing across gender.

In the UK, research by Robinson *et al.*, (2010) examined personality variables, life satisfaction, quality of retirement experiences and reasons for retirement among a sample of almost 300 retirees. Consistent with other research, life satisfaction was predicted by circumstances of retirement. Interestingly, however, the personality variable of neuroticism was associated with more negative views of these circumstances, and predicted retirement life satisfaction independently of reasons for retirement. Those who scored higher on the trait of neuroticism were less satisfied in their retirement, regardless of why they left the workforce. The authors state that 'Neuroticism is the trait that is most robustly linked to reasons for retirement, life satisfaction and retirement experiences' (ibid., p. 795), but admit that the meaning of these findings is as yet 'unexplored territory' (ibid., p. 796). One possible conclusion is that while choice about when to retire is strongly related to retirement wellbeing, so is perception of whether one does indeed have that choice. These perceptions will vary not only because of 'objective' elements such as workplace policies or health conditions, but also because of subjective judgements, some of which may be grounded in personality differences.

Whether being able to exercise one's choice is an objective or subjective reality, it is clearly an important factor in achieving retirement satisfaction. One reason for this is probably because it enables people to make plans.

Retirement planning

Having had the experience I think there is not enough mental preparation- I think it is like having a baby, you can read all about it, but until you experience it nothing you read makes sense.

However well one has prepared for, or anticipated retirement, it takes time to adjust to a 'new persona' that one becomes.

You need a plan to keep busy and not allow yourself to become socially isolated *and* you need to do your sums re retirement income so that it is adequate for your lifestyle. You can't always rely on working after retirement.

Plan it. Plan activities for your days. Do not just drift. Retirement requires a plan.

As I tend to live in the present and don't worry about the future too much, I did not carefully plan my retirement but let it happen. These retirement years are proving pleasant and I am grateful for all I have.

Different women with different views on whether and how to plan! Several of these women stress the importance of making preparations, mentally as well as in terms of finances and activities. Others comment that however well one prepares, adjustments will still need to be made. The final comment is from a woman who says she didn't plan much at all, but her retirement is working out just fine.

To what extent is retirement planning common among women, and how effective is it in contributing to satisfaction post-work? Of the women in our study, 15.5 per cent said they had 'very clear plans' for what they would do post-retirement, most (66 per cent) had some plans and the rest, 18.5 per cent,

62 Planning and decision-making

had no plans. Planning was significantly associated with higher educational and occupational status.

Not surprisingly, those who had made plans were more financially secure in retirement. This is a two-way street. Longer-term planning such as saving and investing for retirement is likely to improve finances, but also, those with more money will have greater flexibility to make more adventurous post-retirement plans such as travel, study, home renovations and the like. Planners were also in better health. This latter association could be because healthier women had more opportunity and scope to plan before they retired. And indeed, those who retired due to ill health or stress were significantly more likely to have made no plans than those who did not retire for this reason.

Planning was highly dependent on retirement reasons. Those who were made redundant or who retired for family reasons were, like those who retired due to stress or illness, much less likely to have made plans for their post-work life than those who retired 'because they felt it was time'. The lack of pressure to leave the workforce gives individuals the space and time to consider how and when they intend to leave, and to develop strategies and projects for the next life stage. Again, not surprisingly, we see that the planners retained more post-retirement links to their former workplace, some continuing to do casual work, some maintaining links through professional associations, unions or conference attendance, and some meeting regularly for social events with former colleagues. Overall, satisfaction with retirement was strongly linked to pre-retirement planning. The importance of this finding is as much of relevance to workplaces as it is to individuals. It underscores the value of employers providing opportunities for older workers to be given assistance to plan both financial and lifestyle aspects of their retirement and to develop creative strategies in which former employees can maintain links with their workplaces in ways that are mutually beneficial.

What sort of plans do women make? In Chapter 3, we discussed financial planning in a general way, some of the problems women face in accumulating adequate retirement funds and their purported difficulties with financial literacy. Many people 'switch off' at the thought of financial planning, it seems. Kiso and Hershey (2017) found that nearly half of their large sample of US study participants expressed cognitive difficulties in thinking about and planning retirement finances. They noted that very few working American adults carry out 'even the most basic retirement tasks, such as calculating how much will be needed for the post retirement period of life' (ibid., p. 85). Women were more likely than men to have negative metacognitions about retirement financial planning, including that they found it hard to think about such planning, postponed thinking about it, became overwhelmed and confused by it and actually hated doing it. Women also rated their financial knowledge and the extent they engaged in financial planning activities lower than men, and they were more worried about their post-retirement finances than men. Kiso and Hershey suggest that the low levels of retirement financial planning for both sexes are reflective of the 'perceived intellectual challenges brought about by the task' (ibid., p. 86).

These data suggest there is plenty of work out there for financial planners, but pre-retiree women will only be convinced to visit these professionals for advice if they (a) perceive the need (which involves some planning, at least to the extent of thinking about the issue); and (b) trust the service provided. As a result of the global financial crisis, trust is not high partly because few saw it coming and partly because of evidence of unethical behaviour among a few professionals (Mercado, 2017; Patten, 2016).

For a few women in our study, the financial advice they received did not work out. Asked if she would do anything differently if she could re-plan her retirement, one said:

> I would trust my own instincts with financial planning and not engage a financial planner. My financial planner failed me. I had to work it out for myself.

Much more commonly however, women who met with financial advisers were happy they had done so, as these examples show:

> I was unexpectedly retrenched 15 months before I turn[ed] 65, so I had not really done any retirement planning. Fortunately, we have an excellent financial adviser so the money side of things worked well.

> [If I had the time over, I] would have contacted our financial planner about 10 years earlier.

> A voluntary redundancy was something I did not think I would ever be offered. When it was my financial adviser said it was an opportunity too good to be missed and she was right.

Listening to advice, collecting information and understanding options are important aspects of financial planning. Professional advisers can facilitate these processes, but ultimately financial management is a personal responsibility. Caveat emptor!

Lifestyle planning – thinking about and arranging retirement activities, roles and interests – is another important aspect of preparation for exit from the workforce. Retirement is a new life stage that involves transition from the worker role to … something else. Perhaps it will be to work of a different kind, or to becoming a more active and involved grandparent, or to checking off a 'bucket list' of travel destinations. Perhaps it will involve a change of housing, an opportunity to focus on gardening, cooking, genealogy, learning French, or nurturing a hitherto neglected creative talent. Daily life will need to be structured differently, something that can only be planned in advance to a certain extent. Price and Nesteruk (2015) quote from interviews with recently retired women, noting that one major theme was their realisation that a new routine was needed. Resolutions to 'organise the cupboards' or 'sort out the family photos' proved just as uninteresting in

64 Planning and decision-making

retirement as they were when the women were working. One 68-year-old woman from Price and Nesteruk's study said this:

> Once retired, I had thought I would clean out the drawers, the cupboards and the cabinets ... so far I've got two drawers cleaned out. I would watch 'Good Morning America' and then I'd lay there and go back to sleep. I thought I just can't keep doing this ... what am I going to do?
>
> *(Ibid., p. 424)*

One factor that has been implicated in whether people tend to be planners or non-planners is time perspective, described by Lewin as 'the totality of the individual's views of his psychological future and psychological past existing at a given time' (1951, p. 75). Zimbardo and Boyd (2008) developed the idea further, proposing five different types of time perspective: past positive, past negative, present fatalistic, present hedonistic, and future oriented. Those who are future oriented are more likely to plan, and are highly attuned to considering the future consequences of current behaviours. More 'present oriented' individuals are more inclined to live in the moment, either focusing on its pleasures (hedonistic) or how external forces are the cause of their current condition (fatalistic). Earl *et al.*, (2015) used these concepts to explore the role of time perspective in retirement planning using a three-wave longitudinal study of 367 Australian retirees, of whom 46 per cent were female. Three aspects of retirement planning were assessed: public protection (accessing government benefits and services available for retirees); self-protection (lifestyle planning, specifically in terms of health and wellbeing); and self-insurance (managing own finances and financial planning). Women scored significantly lower than men on each aspect of planning. Future time perspective was positively associated with each type of planning, as expected. Interestingly, a 'present hedonistic' time perspective also related to planning; perhaps those who enjoy life 'in the moment' are more motivated and skilled at looking after themselves. As in our own study described above, greater planning was linked with better retirement outcomes, including retirement adjustment, health and life satisfaction.

Plans do not always work out

> The best laid schemes o' mice an' men / Gang aft agley
>
> *Robert Burns, 1785, 'To a Mouse'*

Of course, there is only a certain amount of planning possible for the future. The best-laid plans of women, too, can go astray. Circumstances change in financial investments, social and family relationships, and health. Expectations about what one will enjoy in retirement are not always fulfilled; new opportunities and challenges may appear out of the blue. As with any stage of life, flexibility is important, being ready to tweak plans or totally change them if need be.

Flexibility in changing plans is not always easy, especially as we age. Opportunities for older women to improve their financial position through going back to work or taking on casual jobs are limited through systemic factors like age discrimination and (in some places) high unemployment. They can also be limited by health and sensory deteriorations that so often accompany ageing, for example eyesight and hearing difficulties, lack of energy or cognitive decline. Some women feel socially isolated and find new friendships difficult to develop; for some, there is great disappointment because family relationships do not evolve as expected.

While the majority of women in our study were satisfied that their retirement plans were working out as expected, a significant number mentioned situations in which their expectations had not been fulfilled or their plans had come adrift, as illustrated in these varied responses to the question 'Is your retirement working out as you expected?':

> Definitely not, so far. I expected joy and relaxation and good company. Instead I have been bullied and harassed by other residents in other units [in my retirement complex].

> No – we had planned to become grey nomads – but realised we didn't really enjoy caravanning!

> No – it is more financially challenging and a lot lonelier. I have joined some organisations in the hope of making new friends and participating in new activities but these have, on the whole, not turned out as well as I expected, leading to much disappointment.

To end this section on a positive note, it is important to say that at least 10 per cent of women thought that their retirements were working out *even better* than they had planned or imagined.

> So much better. I actually have a *life now*.

> It is far better than I expected. I love learning new things and there are so many opportunities to do that in retirement. … Life is great in retirement. Previously, the things I do now were just a dream, now I'm making that dream reality.

Women who never retire

Stories of women who are 'still working' in their 80s, 90s and even at 100 years of age are loved by social media, and can certainly be quite inspirational if these women are experiencing enjoyment and fulfilment in what they do. Certain jobs lend themselves more readily to participation by older workers, most usually ones

66 Planning and decision-making

in which the worker can choose their hours and pace of working. Examples include small business management, or creative careers pursued by artists or writers.

Among a number of Australian women recently profiled in the media were Jean, aged 92 years, who works up to 38 hours per week in the family's motorcycle spare parts business (and dislikes holidays), and 84-year-old Annabelle who manages a trendy clothing store in central Melbourne and nominates these years as some of the best of her life (Carbone, 2016). While the participation rate in employment of those over 70 years of age is currently relatively low, it is increasing sharply, especially among women (ABS, 2010; *The Guardian*, 2017).

Perhaps the most famous of these 'women who never retire' is someone who has hardly changed her working pace and commitment for the last 70 years, namely Her Majesty Queen Elizabeth II. The vow she made publicly on her 21st birthday in 1947, 'I declare before you all that my whole life whether it be long or short shall be devoted to your service and the service of our great imperial family to which we all belong' has not been broken. Her motive is one of duty, but we hope she also experiences pleasure in her role.

5

THE PSYCHOSOCIAL JOURNEY

From worker to retiree

How dull it is to pause, to make an end,
To rust unburnish'd, not to shine in use!

Tennyson, 1833, Ulysses

In the previous chapter we considered imagining retirement, planning for it and deciding when to leave the workforce (or having this decided for us). In this chapter, we discuss the leap from theory into practice as the transition to a new life stage begins. For the king in Tennyson's poem, *Ulysses*, the thought of leaving his active life for a sedentary retirement was a noxious one but by the end of the poem, he had redefined his goals and purposes, realising that ''Tis not too late to seek a newer world', and that even in our senior years, 'Some work of noble note may yet be done'. How are today's women managing this psychological journey?

Retirement as a life transition

First, let us consider what the literature has to say about life transitions in general. These are developmental and social changes that involve discontinuities with previous life events. In any transition, including retirement, it becomes necessary for us to learn new ways of being and to adjust to a different set of expectations and roles. Even the most benign and desired life changes such as winning the lottery or getting married involve ups and downs, adjustments, and psychological work as we shape new goals, relationships and ways of being. Emotions, both positive and negative, can surface at unexpected times. The sense of freedom from routine and stress on one day can be replaced by boredom and disorientation on another, until new patterns of behaviour become established.

Retirees will follow a range of different pathways through the transition process. It is possible that those who retire gradually over a number of years will experience

68 From worker to retiree

their transition more gently. On the other hand, sociologists have often discussed the power of 'rites of passage' in which the movement from one state or life stage to another is made quickly, publicly and in high definition by the employment of a ceremony marking the change. These ceremonies acknowledge the transition, make it feel 'real' and often invoke emotional support from friends and family. Marriage, baptisms and birthday parties are common examples; retirement farewell parties or events are less common. Nevertheless, there is at least one study suggesting that such functions may be implicated in facilitating retirement adjustment (van den Bogaard, 2017).

Schlossberg (2004) argues that retirement involves not just one but multiple transitions, first over the time span from new to established retiree, but also across different life domains, such as health, finances and relationships. For example, in early retirement, friendship networks may remain similar to those of one's working years, but later in retirement, distance and diverging interests may lead to significant changes in these networks.

To complicate matters, ageing is a transition that occurs simultaneously with adapting to retirement, so it is not always easy to differentiate the effects of one from the other. Browning *et al.*'s (2017) 16-year longitudinal study of 1,000 older Australians examined the predictors of ageing well in people aged over 65 years at the start of their study. Three distinct groups emerged. The first group included those who remained independent as well as physically and mentally healthy across the 16 years. The second group initially aged well but then deteriorated, and the third group started in relatively poor health and remained that way throughout the study. Interestingly, men who began the study in poor health had a one in five chance of improving their health in a subsequent testing period, but the probability of this happening for the women in the sample was negligible. Does this imply that retirement provides fewer health benefits (such as stress reduction) for women than it does for men? This issue is ripe for further research.

Best predictors of good health for both sexes were lower age and fewer medical conditions at first testing. Restful sleep was an independent predictor for women only. For men there were many more predictors, including good nutrition, decreased strain, being a non-smoker and strong social support. The authors suggest that these different health trajectories in how we age remind us that older people are not a homogeneous group, and that a 'one size fits all' approach to public policies relating to ageing is bound to be inadequate. The same reminder could well be applied to consideration of how individuals deal with retirement. Men and women will differ in their patterns and pathways to adaptation and, as we will see in Chapter 6, health is likely to be one of the key influencing factors in this adaptation.

Some theoretical perspectives on transitions

Meleis *et al.* (2000) developed a theory of transitions based on their work with hospital patients and it was extended to other transitions such as migration. Key variables in their model relevant to retirement include the retiree's level of engagement with the process of adjustment, the extent of the changes to be dealt with, the time span of the transition and whether critical points or events occur as the journey proceeds. Retirees will vary in their level of engagement, for example in their degree of planning, information seeking, search for role models of successful retirement, and the attention they give to understanding and actively addressing their own social, emotional, physical and financial needs. They will also vary in the degree of change they experience, for example a part-time worker who retires but continues some work on a voluntary basis will experience far less disruption to her way of life and have fewer adjustments to make than one who retires from a high-pressure, full-time job to a quiet life in the country.

The time span of adapting to retirement will also vary from person to person, with some moving seamlessly and quickly to a new identity and lifestyle while others take a more gradual route. Some, but not all, will experience periods of disequilibrium, instability, confusion and distress. Finally, transitions are often marked by critical incidents that can either assist or hinder the rate of psychological change. Retiring because one has been made redundant, or having retirement plans thwarted through death or illness of a partner, are negative examples of such critical incidents, whereas events such as the birth of a grandchild or finding a new hobby that one is passionate about are positive examples.

A related theoretical perspective is that of Bamber *et al.* (2017) who discuss the concept of liminality, referring to a state of being 'betwixt and between'. Particularly in the early stages of retirement, retirees can feel this way, having lost their identity as workers but having not yet found satisfactory new ways of being. As one woman in our study so neatly put it, 'Who am I without a business card?' Liminality is another way of referring to the transitional state, characterised as a period of ambiguity and uncertainty, but also potentially as a period of productivity and creativeness as the constraints of work are thrown off and new possibilities can be sought and explored.

Stages of the retirement transition

One woman from our study described her retirement experience as a series of stages thus:

> In my case, the experience of retirement can be divided into a number of stages. The first stage lasted for about four years: the novelty of being a free agent; the novelty of volunteering; the novelty of experiencing the arrival of four grandchildren in four years and the novelty of contributing to their infancy; the satisfaction that came from mentoring young women.
>
> The second stage, also about four years, was confronting the appearance of the frailties of ill health and 'getting older'.
>
> The third stage, which I am well into now, is redefining aims and expectations to accept physical limitations and to maintain interests and rebuild self-esteem.

70 From worker to retiree

Cussen (2018) describes four stages occurring post-retirement that many women experience as part of the transition period. These are the 'honeymoon phase, 'disenchantment', 're-orientation' and 're-establishing a routine'. It is important to point out that not all retirees will traverse each of these stages, nor necessarily experience them in the same order. And, as pointed out previously, retirement can involve more than one transition, so the stages may be experienced more than once over time. Despite these caveats, many women will recognise their own process of adjustment to retirement as occurring in stages, perhaps similarly to those described either by Cussen or by the woman who supplied the quotation above. Acknowledgement of the typicality of different stages of retirement may assist self-understanding and provide guidance for those considering post-work life in the future.

Honeymoon phase

The honeymoon phase refers to the feeling that a burden has been lifted, that life is about to become less stressful and complicated. The everyday slog of working life need no longer tie one down. Even among those who love their jobs, there will be some features they are glad to slough off, and some new opportunities they can now visualise, be it travel or just sleeping in. 'Freedom' was one of the most popular responses from women when we asked them to name the best aspects of this new life stage. It was freedom 'to do what I want when I want', or 'to have control over my day-to-day activities'. It was freedom from conflicts with employees or colleagues, bullying bosses, rigid schedules, boring meetings, paperwork, the long commute every morning and evening – the list goes on.

Along with freedom goes more time. Time to see all those movies you missed, catch up on old friends and the latest novels, cook healthy meals, organise the garden and plan interesting excursions. Time to spend with grandchildren, give back through volunteering, keep fit, engage in hobbies and take up new challenges.

Many of the women in our study expressed a great sense of satisfaction – and often surprise – at how well this new life stage was turning out for them.

> It is far better than I expected. I love learning new things and there are so many opportunities to do that in retirement. ... I'm in my seventh heaven!
>
> Wish I'd done it sooner. [I've got] freedom and peace and no power-hungry and self-interested people around me. There is far more to life than a paid job.

But for some women the increase in time, freedom and self-directedness brought problems of their own. The honeymoon period – if it occurred at all – did not last long. They felt bored, lonely or at a loss as to what to do with their days.

> I'm still working out where I'm going. My house is super clean (not something that I'm interested in). Meals are cooked – just to keep busy. There's a lack of volunteer positions available that interest me.

I'm alone too much. I haven't yet found something I want to do, paid or for free.

For some women, especially those who have pre-planned interesting post-retirement activities and projects, the honeymoon period can last for years. With immediate goals to fulfil, any feeling of having too much time or freedom is delayed. Perhaps that feeling never arrives for some. However, there is no doubt that many retirees experience a period during which they question how to give their lives more meaning and purpose once paid work is finished. This questioning may be preceded by the next stage.

Disenchantment

> After longing for 'freedom' I got jack of it within four months. Is this all there is?

Some people call this the 'retirement blues'. It's that experience of wondering, like the woman quoted above, 'is this all there is?' It's the realisation that, unless one does something about it, ageing is the only certainty that the future holds. One of the participants in Price and Nesteruk's study of 230 retired American women expressed it thus:

> At first it felt like a vacation for about three weeks and then it didn't feel so good anymore. I was just floundering around like a fish out of water.
>
> *(2015, p. 424)*

Disenchantment can occur when retirees realise that all that time on their hands can be boring, directionless and lonely. Some experience apathy, lack of motivation or even depression as the realisation dawns on them that future goals and activities probably need to be self-initiated and self-directed. These feelings are not abnormal or even unusual; they are part of the process of adapting to transition and change. A disenchantment phase may occur more than once during retirement as one project or life stage ends (for example, the grandchildren go to school and no longer need to be minded) and the need to reassess how to meaningfully fill one's days arises yet again. Disillusionment and disenchantment may also occur when expectations about retirement are not met, for example because illness intervenes, funds are not available for the planned activities, or the new hobby turns out to be unfulfilling.

What to do? Talk it over with the family, perhaps? It seems that this is not a common practice. Researchers Damman and van Duijn (2017) posed the question as to whether older workers drew support from their families during the retirement process, and found that this was relatively unusual. Only about 20 per cent of the 697 fully retired Dutch participants in their study agreed that their children offered support during this life transition. Those without a partner and with poorer finances were more likely to receive support, reflecting their greater needs. Also,

recipients of family support were retirees who offered something in return, specifically those who regularly looked after their grandchildren. There were no differences between male and female retirees in terms of the extent of family support
they received.

The retirement blues might best respond to a proactive approach. It's a time to
try moving out of one's comfort zone, experimenting with new activities, plans
and social groups, developing new purposes and life goals that are both realistic and
fulfilling. As one woman said, 'Work motivated me, now I have to motivate
myself'. Another told us:

> You need to replace things that were part of your work life, such as socialising,
> keeping your brain active, keeping physically active in order to have a happy
> retirement. I worked hard to make this happen.

Relevant here is consideration of the work of developmental psychologist Erik
Erikson (1963). As discussed in Chapter 1, Erikson wrote about how psychosocial
maturity is something that grows and develops through different stages of life. Each
life stage has its emotional upheavals as we travel the pathway to becoming a fully
functioning adult. For those at mid-life and beyond, Erikson postulated that
development of a sense of generativity was one of the keys to life satisfaction and
maturity. A generative person is one who contributes to society and future generations rather than focusing only on self-related concerns. Failure to find ways to
contribute can lead to becoming self-obsessed (for example with one's ageing or
ailments), as well as to feelings of disconnection from one's community and social
groups. The 'disenchantment' phase of retirement could be interpreted as part of
this struggle to move from a self-absorbed state to more mature fulfilment, which
can often be achieved through 'giving back' actions, such as volunteering, helping
out in one's family, mentoring the young, or engaging in creative pursuits and
activities that link the generations, such as genealogical interests. Instead of thinking
'I'm bored', the generative person is able to think, 'How can I help?' or 'What
good uses can I put my talents to?'

Reorientation

Many, perhaps most, retirees overcome the disenchantment phase, moving on to
re-establish themselves in different roles, building a new, non-work-based identity,
like this woman:

> The first three years of my retirement were marked with grief and loss. I hated
> not working. My partner left me, as I was too hard to be with. I was caring for
> an elderly loved one who eventually died. My daughter was struggling [with
> many life issues]. I attended regular classes at U3A [University of the Third Age]
> which stimulated my brain and I began to have grief counselling which helped
> enormously. Then I fell into my current voluntary work and I'm happy now.

Reorientation involves reshaping one's sense of self through establishing new, often non-work-based, activities and purposes. It usually also involves significant changes to one's social network. Social activity is likely to become based less around workplace contacts and more on family and leisure-based pursuits. We consider these changes in turn.

Reorienting of identity

> I sometimes ponder the change of job from 'Geospatial Information Systems Analyst and Programmer' to 'Retired'. I have realised that I was really the only person who cared about my position title and it makes no difference to the people I give it to, except that I no longer have to spell it out. This has been a good wake up to the important things in life.

Reshaping one's identity as someone who has worth and purpose beyond the role of a paid worker requires effort and 'psychological work'. It does not necessarily involve leaving aside all links with work, or even giving up all paid work, but it does mean a change in balance and focus. Cussen (2017) says that this is the stage at which retirees ask questions like 'Who am I, now?' 'What is my purpose at this point?' and 'Am I still useful in some capacity?'

Retirement is an identity disruptor. A person with a strong sense of identity is someone who knows who she is and where she is going, a person who has some clarity about her values, goals and purposes. Paid work is important to identity not only because of the number of hours we spend in this role. Jobs also provide status and sense of purpose; they mark us as responsible adults who contribute to family and community, as people to be taken seriously. Family and domestic roles may be part of one's identity, but for those who have spent a significant portion of their lives in paid work, occupational roles are often front and centre of how we present ourselves to the world. We are teachers, engineers, salespeople, managers, nurses and technicians. The role of 'domestic goddess' (or 'domestic slave') is not one aspired to by most modern women for a range of reasons, including, for example, its low social status, boredom and (potentially) social isolation.

Many women in our study felt their loss of identity and sense of purpose keenly, making comments such as:

> [I miss] feeling worthwhile. I think I'm of the generation who sees my value in terms of the job I do. I feel I have lost my identity.

> I miss the satisfaction of doing a job well, and the acknowledgement of and respect for my talents and expertise in my field of work. I loved my work; it was an expression of my 'natural' abilities. I have found the loss of my sense of 'identity' hard at times.

> [I miss] the sense of purpose. While it was hugely stressful, I felt useful. Now I keep feeling at a bit of a loss, as if I should be doing something. Doing housework is absolutely unsatisfying and does not absorb my mind.

The women acknowledged that work had 'made a contribution to my sense of who I am', 'contributed to my self-esteem', 'provided intellectual stimulation' and 'gave me a sense of making a contribution'. We found that those who had retired from higher-status occupations (professional and managerial) were more likely to experience these identity-enhancing features of their job, a finding consistent with previous research on identity and occupational status among both men and women (e.g. Schieman and Taylor, 2001).

Not all were troubled by a loss of identity or purpose on retirement, particularly those in lower-status or less satisfying occupations. One woman put it this way:

> What do I miss? Not much. My work life was never very rewarding and was simply a means to an end – namely paying the bills and keeping a roof over my head and that of my daughter. I was not a 'career' person [but was] largely a non-working wife in my 23 years of marriage.

Workplace attachment and identity disruption

We tested how the strength of women's attachment to their pre-retirement occupational roles was associated with their adjustment to retirement. Women who expressed stronger ties to work were less satisfied with retirement than women with weaker ties. It is not surprising that those who are committed to their jobs and who spend long hours at work or thinking about it have less time to develop and nurture non-work activities and social connections; therefore, they may feel more at a loss when they retire. Post-work, they need time to process their change of status, experiment with new roles and channel their passions in new directions. As this chapter indicates, retirement is a psychosocial journey, not simply a change of state. Nevertheless, the association between workplace attachment and retirement satisfaction was less evident among women who had been retired for a longer time, were more active in their retirement and more socially connected. The feeling of missing work was apparently one that dissipated as women found other meaningful ways to fill their days.

Findings from previous research about the association between strength of attachment to work and retirement satisfaction are equivocal. Some show positive relationships – the committed worker becomes the well-adjusted retiree – although this effect may not always be manifest in the early stages of the transition (Wetzel et al., 2016). Others, like the women in our study, show negative relationships, with retirees missing the cut and thrust of the working day (Reitzes and Mutran 2004, 2006; Reitzes et al., 1996; Wang and Shi, 2014). Variations between studies on participants' time since retirement and in measures of both workplace attachment and retirement outcomes are likely to account for these differences. As mentioned above, we found that negative associations decreased over time, as did Reitzes and Mutran (2006). We also found that while greater worker attachment was linked to lower levels of retirement satisfaction, this effect did not generalise to satisfaction with life in general, which showed no such association.

Two small qualitative studies have examined identity issues among retired women who had had professional careers. Price (2003) conducted two in-depth interviews with each of the 14 retired professional women, focusing on how they had renegotiated life roles and identity. The women were aged between 64 and 82 years, and they had all been retired for at least seven years. Several reflected on their initial struggle to find a new purpose in life, and their experience of 'role-lessness'. For most, however, any disruption to their sense of self was relatively short-lived. One comment that encapsulated this way of thinking was from the woman who said that she 'always thought of myself as a person, as not just an occupation' (Price, 2003, p. 348).

Three identity-maintaining strategies were noted. First, women reported that their self-concepts had always been multifaceted, never totally tied to their work but including roles in the community and among family and friends. Second, all but one of the women continued to practise their professional skills after retirement, a strategy that helped them to maintain a sense of competence. They could do this as casual or part-time workers or in a voluntary capacity. Third, all practised 'role expansion', seeking new interests or discovering new skills and outlets once retirement allowed them the time to do so. They substituted these new opportunities and activities for their loss of full-time professional roles.

Professional women in a small qualitative study by Borrero and Kruger (2015) similarly renegotiated their sense of self in retirement by developing new roles such as volunteering, learning new skills, and focusing on the nurture of their social networks. Most recognised that this 'psychological work' involved moving beyond one's comfort zone, for example, seeking out others to socialise with, maintaining professional contacts where possible and finding ways to contribute to the community.

Gender and the identity transition

Do men and women differ in their capacities to adjust to retirement, to manage the reorientation from worker to retiree? Early studies concluded that men had more problems than women in adjusting to retirement (e.g. Tibbitts, 1954). The reasons postulated were first that men were more committed to their workplaces and had stronger identities as workers, and second that women had stronger non-work social networks and their identities were more likely to be shaped (at least in part) by family and domestic activity (Barnes and Parry, 2004).

Strong growth in women's employment over the last 50 years and women's greater representation in higher-status occupations calls for a re-examination of gender differences in adjustment to retirement. Barnes and Parry's research (2004), is one of the few relatively recent studies available. They conducted interviews with 22 men and 26 women, aged 50–65 years, who were approaching retirement or were already retired. According to the study authors, 'traditional gender roles predominated', in participants' responses to their transition out of the paid work-force. Men reported more negative emotions than women about their retirements and were more likely to have viewed work as central to their identity. For example, one man who had been a coalminer typified the responses to retirement of the men in the study. He grieved over the loss of camaraderie and the sense of purpose that his job had provided. Six years after retiring, he was suffering boredom and insomnia, unable to find activities that interested him. His wife, on the other hand, had experienced few problems adjusting to retirement from paid work, as she continued with domestic and family-related tasks that had been – and still remained – at the core of her sense of self.

A few women in the Barnes and Parry study did express post-retirement adjustment problems. A teacher, who had to retire before she felt ready to do so, reported feelings of grief, as if she were mourning her loss of self. But, overall, the study authors concluded that the men they interviewed found the transition to retirement more difficult, because they interpreted it as stripping away part of their masculine identity. Home-based domestic roles and leisure pursuits did not adequately compensate for this loss.

Identity continuity

Of course, retirement does not necessarily mean total relinquishment of one's worker identity. In answering the question, 'What do you do?' many retirees will answer, 'I'm a retired teacher/doctor/manager/electrician…' Retirement researchers Reitzes and Mutran point out that '[r]etirees still think of themselves in terms of their former careers. Even when they no longer occupy the role, their identity lingers' (2006, p. 354). One's sense of self in retirement comprises a mix of new and former roles.

The extent to which the worker role remains salient to identity is likely to relate first to how important it was during working life, second to time since retirement, and third to the availability and attractiveness of new retirement activities and purposes. The speed and success of the reorientation stage will depend in part on this renegotiation of identity, but it will also be influenced by one's integration into a social network. This too will change, as we discuss in the next section.

Renegotiating social relationships

Retirement is likely to herald significant changes in one's social networks. Women can find themselves more alone than they are used to, or in the case of some part-nered women, spending more time with their husbands than ever before. These changes may be perceived as desirable or undesirable, depending on the person and the context. There will be more time to spend with family members, but expecta-tions of retirees and their families do not always converge. Furthermore, workplace social interactions – connections with customers and colleagues – no longer fill the day. For many retirees, this means making the effort to stay socially integrated through proactively seeking alternative friendship and community outlets.

Marital status and social connection

Being married can be a protective factor against the uncertainties associated with retirement, including changes in financial status and the risk of loneliness and isolation. Research is clear that married retirees usually enjoy better psychological and physical wellbeing than single or widowed retirees (e.g. Price and Joo, 2005; Tamborini, 2007). This participant in our study was not unusual in commenting on her retirement satisfaction in a way that reflected her marital satisfaction:

> I have settled in the country with my husband, and we enjoy a very pleasant, if quite simple, lifestyle. We engage with our community in many ways, and retirement enables us to have a freedom of choice about what we do, as we hoped it would. We are fortunate!

However, even among happily married couples, retirement can lead to unanticipated relationship stresses. Szinovacz and Davey used data from a large sample longitudinal study of health and retirement to show that 'retirement transitions undermine married retirees' satisfaction if they enhance the other partner's influence in the relationship' (2005, p. 387). They based this conclusion on the finding that when one partner kept working after the other retired, and this was associated with an increase in the working partner's power in household decision-making, then the retired partner was more likely to show lower levels of retirement satisfaction than other married retirees in their sample. This was true whether the retired member of the couple was the husband or the wife.

In our study, although being partnered was linked with greater retirement satisfaction in general, qualitative data indicated that there could be tensions. When both partners retire, greater time together can result in discovering that they have few common interests. Expectations about shared activities, domestic responsibilities and extent of 'togetherness' may not be mutually held. One woman put it this way:

> It isn't [working out as expected] because my husband and I are not on the same page. I desperately want to travel while we are physically able. He is not particularly interested. I feel resentment that I may never get to do it. I would be prepared to go it alone but ... I don't know how that will be received.

Another complained about her husband's dependency:

> I miss time to myself, my husband is home quite a lot and does not have as many interests as me and seems to want to rely on being with me. I thought he would find more activities for himself.

Despite these stresses of marital life, those living alone are more vulnerable to distress in retirement. Single women are more likely to experience financial stress and poorer health when they retire (e.g. Kendig *et al.*, 2017; Patulny, 2009; Social Security Administration, 2016; Tamborini, 2007). Living with a partner (or other independent adults) is more economical because of shared resources, and it tends to promote healthier lifestyles, for example through regular meals and joint activities.

Perhaps more importantly, co-habitation is a buffer against loneliness, which in itself is a factor strongly implicated in poorer health and premature mortality, as will be discussed in Chapter 6 (e.g. Holt-Lunstad *et al.*, 2010; Steptoe *et al.*, 2013; Steffens *et al.*, 2016).

Many of the retired women in our study lived alone (37 per cent), either because they had never married, were divorced or had been widowed. Social isolation was, not surprisingly, one of the most common issues mentioned as a negative aspect of retirement. Women said things like:

> Being alone and single [in retirement] is stressful, lonely and embarrassing and socially limiting.

> I don't fit what seems to be the common expectations. Single women don't participate the same as couples. I have found it harder to socialise after retirement partly because the 'market' is dominated by couple images and expectations.

Eleven per cent of our sample were widowed, a reflection of the lifespan gap between men and women. Sadly, many reported the following experience:

> [Retirement is] nothing like what I had planned. I never thought I'd be spending my retirement as a widow.

In our study, social isolation was experienced by a noteworthy number of retired women with some, as in the examples above, mentioning it in relation to their single status or widowhood. Interestingly, however, there was no statistical association between retirement satisfaction and either living alone or marital status. Overall, as length of retirement increased beyond the first two years, women in all living arrangements expressed increasing satisfaction with their retirement and with life in general, suggesting a learned adaptation to the retirement transition.

Post-retirement changes in family relationships

Retirement for women can herald not only changes in intimate partner relationships, but with the extended family as well. Expectations about spending more time with one's adult children or with grandchildren may or may not be fulfilled. Some women find that when they relinquish paid work in retirement, their days are soon filled by unpaid work as carer, family support person or babysitter. Indeed, some retire so they can contribute more to their family support network, such as these women, who found their caring responsibilities rewarding for the most part:

> I retired for not only me but for my family. I decided that [my stressful career] wasn't fair to anyone. I love my family enough to put their needs on an equal footing to my own. However, I find that during retirement the hardest thing

to do is keep sight of 'me' and not have my entire personality disappear down a funnel of other's needs.

I took retirement early. The grandkids had a big influence on that. They sort of showed me there was more to life than working. Now if I have the kids I can devote myself to them, I don't have to do a hundred other things at the same time.

(Rosenthal and Moore, 2012b, pp. 79–80).

But this pattern of post-retirement family caring, or expectations about caring, can be stressful, and does not always sit well with dreams of a more relaxed and leisurely older age. This is particularly an issue for women, because gendered expectations surrounding nurturance mean that women are more likely to regard caring for a partner or family member as an obligation. They spend more time doing so than men, a state of affairs that has been linked to increased stress (Colombo *et al.*, 2011).

One daughter expects me to come whenever she calls for babysitting even though it disrupts my own plans. It is expected of me as I am the non-working grandmother.

(Rosenthal and Moore, 2012b, p. 117)

As we discuss in more depth in Chapter 7, sometimes the amount of childcare expected of retired grandmothers can be a cause of conflict (as reflected in the quotation above), and the demands of caring for elderly relatives can result in exhaustion, depression and other negative health outcomes. Negotiating and adjusting family expectations about time spent together and extent of caring and support required from the older generation is part of the retirement transition for women who no longer have the 'excuse' that they are working!

Finding replacements for workplace socialising

For most occupations, the workplace provides extensive social connections, ranging from informal chats in the lift or around the coffee machine, to in-depth discussions of work-related and personal issues. Many casual acquaintanceships and, often, close personal friendships are formed. After retirement, these social connections may not be so readily maintained, especially if many friends and colleagues are still working. Extra efforts may be required to develop new friendship networks and/or keep work-based ones alive.

I realise now I thought it would be much easier to establish new friendship networks, and it's not. If that's the goal then you have to be very strategic in the group you join, the level of involvement you agree to and the personal contacts you actively pursue.

When we asked women retirees what they missed most about work, many mentioned friends and colleagues:

> [I miss] the daily banter and camaraderie.

> [I miss] the social interaction with all different types of people at all levels, especially the younger ones.

> [I miss] being with work colleagues who are friends willing to listen and also to be listened to in supportive ways.

Retired women appear to be less vulnerable to loneliness and social isolation than retired men, due it seems to their greater efforts at maintaining non-work friendship networks both pre- and post-retirement (e.g. Patulny, 2009). For example, Patulny showed that Australian women, both workers and retirees, perceived that they had more friends to confide in, greater social support, more contact with their friends and family, and lower levels of loneliness than men. Overall, independent risk factors for loneliness include being male, poor physical health, chronic work and/ or social stress, small social network, lack of a spousal confidante, and poor-quality social relationships (Hawkley and Cacioppo, 2007; Hawkley *et al.*, 2008).

Regaining 'social connectedness' can be a key challenge for retirees. Social connectedness involves a sense of belongingness to a social group in which there is trust, shared purpose and mutual obligation. A review of nearly 150 studies found that those who reported lower levels of social connection had a greater risk of early death than those who smoked, drank or were obese (Holt-Lunstad *et al.*, 2010).

Recently, Steffens *et al.* (2016) studied a group of UK seniors across the first six years of their retirement, monitoring their mortality, quality of life and social group membership. Retirees who were members of more social groups following their transition to retirement – and who retained these memberships post-retirement – had better quality of life and greater longevity than those with fewer or less long-lasting group memberships. These patterns were not evident among the matched group who were still working, suggesting to the authors that group membership had 'a distinct role to play in the process of adapting to new circumstances following retirement' (ibid., p. 6). Underscoring the importance of social connectedness, it was noted that its effects on both quality of life and longevity were comparable in size to those of physical activity, a well-established factor in maintenance of health during the senior years.

There are various strategies that retirees can use to overcome social isolation and increase connectedness. Several women from our study described the changes they made to their lives to avoid loneliness:

> After the first 12 months [of retirement], I made an effort to maintain professional networks and now see former (retired) colleagues at regular lunches, attend work reunions and have an extensive Facebook network of

colleagues. I am also active in a couple of volunteer community organisations. … The other benefit is that I now walk every day, which is good for me and the dog.

I joined U3A when I retired. I have been involved for the past 12 years both as a participant, committee member and volunteer. When you retire you must get out there and get involved. No use sitting at home. Social interaction and giving to your community is so valuable for your wellbeing. The new friendships have enriched my life.

It is very important to keep busy, to stay connected with family and to make time for leisure activities as well. I joined the local Probus club when we moved to a new area and the club has allowed me to meet new friends and keep active with the walking club.

These women mentioned a range of approaches they used to develop and maintain social connections. They made active efforts to do things like keep in touch with former work colleagues, nurture family ties, join classes in order to learn new things and to keep fit, volunteer their time for worthy causes, and utilise social media. One summed up this proactive approach thus: 'Retirement is what you make it … it is important to keep occupied'.

In summary, the reorientation stage of the retirement transition involves psychological work and social adaptation. As retirees, we need to rethink and replan our daily activities and goals to enable maintenance of social contacts and also of a sense of purpose. During this time, our sense of identity – of who we are – is also likely to undergo significant changes. Successful adaptation to retirement requires that we develop ways to find meaning and direction that is not tied to life in the paid workforce.

Moving on

In time, new routines develop as retirees work through the challenges and emotions associated with leaving the workplace. As with most transitions, a period of upheaval is likely to be followed by relative stability as retirees adapt to their new realities.

For some women this occurs readily:

It's better [than I expected]. I liked being a busy young thing and now I'm enjoying being a slow old thing.

I had been a workaholic and was surprised that I did not miss work much at all. Retirement is better than I expected.

For others, it can take longer and there will be fits and starts:

> I thought that I was ready to retire mentally but I found that it actually took me three years to adjust. I grieved for my job and the process took that long.

> I have retired four times so far.

> It took me a long time (at least two years) to admit that I was retired and not 'semi-retired'.

Over time, most retirees readjust their sense of self to encompass new identities that are less concerned with drawing life meaning from paid work and which are more attuned to purposes and meanings that relate to family, community and hobby or leisure interests. New routines, different social worlds and reimagined goals are established. Many women describe these years as the best of their lives, to be enjoyed with gratitude before the next set of life challenges present themselves.

In summary, the retirement transition takes women on a psychological journey that may engender a range of emotions including confusion, boredom and sadness, relief, pleasure and contentment. Honeymoon and disenchantment phases are common (although not universal) as the retiree readjusts cognitively and emotionally to new or modified activities, purposes, relationships and ways of making social connections. Good health is an important facilitator of adaptation to the different routines and roles of retirement. Relationships between ageing, health and retirement adjustment are discussed in the next chapter.

6

RETIREMENT AND HEALTH

> I did not expect retirement to be this good. I thought that I would be bored and would have too much time on my hands. I feel that I am fortunate to be in good health, and able to enjoy life as it is.

> I expected my health to be better, and to be more mobile than I am. This is restricting me in many ways. ... I can no longer join some friends for brisk walks, hikes with backpacks etc. ... I thought I would have heaps of time to do heaps of things, but I didn't factor in the fact I have less strength and get tired quicker.

Predicting how retirement affects health is difficult because retirement is usually synonymous with ageing, and retirees are typically older than those still working. Teasing apart the separate effects of retirement and ageing is a complex task. But we also know that research in this area is difficult because, just as retirement can influence health, health can influence retirement decisions. Moreover, research has not generally examined the relationship between health and the number of years spent in retirement. It is possible that health will initially improve when somebody retires and then, after a while, start to deteriorate due to reduced physical activity and social interaction. In a comprehensive review, Sahlgren (2013) concluded that being retired is associated with decreases in physical, mental and self-assessed health. The adverse effects increase as the number of years in retirement increase.

In this chapter we take up these issues and examine how retirement affects women's health and wellbeing. The contrasting quotations above suggest that there is no single answer to this question.

Ageing and health

As a result of increases in life expectancy, the number of older people in the population will continue to increase. The number of those aged 65 years or above is projected to grow from an estimated 524 million in 2010 to nearly 1.5 billion in 2050, with most of the increase occurring in developing countries (World Health Organization (WHO), 2011).

Advances in medical science, particularly the control of communicable diseases, are major factors responsible for increased life expectancy (WHO, 2011). Even in low-income countries, the majority of older people die from chronic diseases such as cardiac disease, cancer and diabetes, rather than infections. One major health consequence of a longer lifespan, placing considerable demands on the health care system and on long-term care, is the increase in prevalence of dementia. The risk of dementia rises sharply with age, with an estimated 25–30 per cent of people aged 85 years or above showing some evidence of this condition. In addition to illness and disease, social attitudes to the aged can have negative impacts on their wellbeing. One form of social 'abuse' is the ageism and consequent marginalisation that exists in many, but not all, societies. Stereotyping of older people can be reflected in structural aspects of society such as compulsory retirement age, or in the lack of appreciation of older people's competencies.

As both the proportion of older people in communities and the length of life increase throughout the world, key questions arise. Will an ageing population be accompanied by a longer period of good health, a sustained sense of wellbeing, and extended periods of social engagement and productivity? Or will this be associated with more illness, disability and dependency?

Factors that influence retirement health

Older people today spend many more years in retirement than was once the case. For example, in Organisation for Economic Co-operation and Development (OECD) countries in 2014, men lived in retirement for an average of 17.6 years, and women for 22.3 years. In 1970, the figures were 11 and 17 years, respectively (OECD, 2015).

As mentioned in the introduction to this chapter, a key issue for researchers in estimating the effects of retirement on health and wellbeing is that these are confounded with age. Thus, what might seem to be a consequence of retirement may merely be part of the ageing process. Teasing out the effects of retirement on health and wellbeing can be difficult as these effects could be grounded in pre-retirement factors and the nature of the transition to retirement rather than simply retirement itself. Moreover, our interest is in retired women's health and wellbeing and few studies focus on this population either specifically or incidentally as part of sampling. We reveal gender differences in those studies where comparisons have been made.

Behncke (2009) reports outcomes from the English Longitudinal Study on Ageing, which showed that the percentage of retired individuals with chronic conditions such as diabetes, stroke and cancer was almost twice that of those still employed. There were some gender differences reported. Compared to the overall sample women had a higher risk of being diagnosed with cancer and a lower risk of developing cardiovascular diseases. For male retirees, estimated effects were higher than the overall sample for heart attack, stroke and psychiatric problems, but smaller for arthritis and cancer. Behncke notes that poorer health outcomes among retirees cannot be regarded as causal because of the many differences between individuals in both employed and retired groups even after adjusting for age. She concludes, as do others, that when estimating the impact of retirement, these confounding factors must be controlled.

A number of studies have used careful methodologies, such as adjusting for selection bias (e.g. pre-retirement work and health history, timing of retirement) to overcome these difficulties. The importance of this is revealed in analysis of data from the US Health and Retirement Study. Dave *et al.* (2008) found that these confounding biases accounted for most (80–90 per cent) of the observed differences in health between retirees and non-retirees over time. Dave *et al.* examined the effects of retirement on health status using indicators of physical and functional limitations, illness conditions, and depression. They found that:

> [C]omplete retirement leads to a 5–16 per cent increase in difficulties associated with mobility and daily activities, a 5–6 per cent increase in illness conditions, and a 6–9 per cent decline in mental health. ... The adverse health effects are mitigated if the individual is married and has social support, continues to engage in physical activity post-retirement, or continues to work part-time upon retirement. There is also some evidence that the adverse health effects are larger in the event of involuntary retirement.
>
> *(Ibid., pp. 28–29)*

Dave and colleagues go on to suggest that retiring at a later age may lessen or postpone poor health outcomes, improve wellbeing, and reduce the utilisation of health care services, particularly acute care, a conclusion supported by Sahlgren (2013).

Others have reported consistent findings. Calvo *et al.* (2013) found that retiring at an earlier age than usual can be more problematic, culturally and institutionally, for both physical and emotional health than retiring later. In a US study, Wu *et al.* (2016) found that retiring one year older was associated with an 11 per cent lower risk of mortality, notwithstanding a wide range of sociodemographic, lifestyle and health factors. The negative impact of early retirement extends to cognitive functioning. Analysing data from large-scale studies, Rohwedder and Willis (2010) found that early retirement has a significant negative impact on general cognitive functioning, measured by instruments such as the Mini-Mental State Examination, a widely used tool for assessing cognitive status. There is also evidence that work requiring greater mental demands protects against cognitive decline in retirement, notwithstanding education level and socio-economic status (Fisher *et al.*, 2016).

A number of researchers have taken advantage of the ongoing longitudinal US Health and Retirement Study to examine health-related issues. Moon *et al.* (2012) investigated the association between the transition to retirement and the risk of stroke and heart attack by following US Health and Retirement Study participants aged 50 years or more in the paid workforce and free of major cardiovascular disease for up to ten years. They noted whether or when participants who self- or proxy-reported either stroke or myocardial infarction transitioned to full retirement. After adjusting for age, sex, childhood and adult socio-economic status, and co-morbidities, Moon and his colleagues found that those who were retired were 40 per cent more likely to have had a heart attack or stroke than those who were still working at the same age. Interestingly, this difference was more pronounced during the first year of retirement, but then levelled off. There were no significant interactions by sex, indicating that there were no differences between men and women in these outcomes.

A longitudinal study of British civil servants by Jokela *et al.* (2010) yielded results that conflicted with those reported above; both on-time retirement and voluntary early retirement were related to higher levels of physical functioning and mental health compared to those who remained in the workforce. In addition, their results indicated that mental health and physical functioning could prospectively predict taking earlier retirement. Jokela and colleagues suggested that these results support a causal relationship between statutory and early voluntary retirement and positive health outcomes. They do note, however, a caution in this interpretation, recognising the likely selection bias of their sample, which although large, comprised mainly middle-class, white-collar participants working in the relatively sheltered environment of the British public sector.

Clearly, studies proposing that retirement leads to either better or worse health outcomes need to be examined carefully in terms of their methodology and sampling. There are likely to be a multitude of factors influencing both health and retirement, and considerable individual differences in how people factor in their health status when making retirement decisions. For example, women who choose to retire early may do so because of poor health or because, although healthy, they want to enjoy retirement activities while still fit enough to do so.

Lifestyle activities and retirement health

There is abundant evidence showing the importance of physical activity in maintaining and enhancing good health. A balanced diet and sustaining a healthy weight are among the pillars of health promotion, as is moderation in alcohol intake and avoidance of smoking. These factors, especially in relation to physical activity and diet, have been the subject of research into the health outcomes of retirement. It is clear that retirement provides the opportunity to engage in physical activity that may have been limited by the demands of full-time work. As one woman in our study told us, her increased physical activity after retirement was a consequence of health problems rather than the converse:

> Health and fitness issues were unexpected. I have become more physically active (cycling and walking) than at any other period of my life, which wasn't planned but evolved through circumstances.

Retirees may also have more time to focus on preparing a nutritious diet and maintaining healthy weight levels than they did when working. It is evident that not all are doing so. In western nations, levels of obesity are worryingly high and the so-called obesity epidemic has profound public health effects because of the likelihood of conditions such as heart disease, diabetes and some kinds of cancer. In 2013, one-third of adults in the US and one-quarter of those in the UK and Australia were classified as obese. Even in France, which has the least number of obese adults among western nations, 15.6 per cent of adults were classified as obese (Food and Agricultural Organization of the United Nations, 2013).

Does retirement lead to health-promoting lifestyle improvements? The evidence is mixed. Duberley *et al.* (2014) analysed data from a large-scale UK data set to provide information on health outcomes post-retirement by age and gender. The annual British Household Panel Survey consists of a nationally representative sample that initially comprised about 5,500 households recruited in 1991. For all age groups except the oldest (80 years and over), women's subjective wellbeing was significantly lower than men's. Women were more likely to report that their daily activities were limited by ill health. In contrast, for most age groups, men were more likely than women to participate in physical activity (walking, swimming or playing sport) on a weekly basis. The exception was 50–64-year-old women who were more likely to participate in these activities than men of the same age. Part of the explanation for women's reported lower subjective wellbeing may be attributable to their lower employment participation rates and lower incomes since both were related positively to subjective wellbeing. Women's greater propensity to undertake informal care may also be implicated, as informal carers report lower subjective wellbeing in some studies, particularly if their care obligations require a considerable time commitment. Ill health was also, unsurprisingly, negatively associated with maintenance of a wellbeing-oriented lifestyle, and women were more likely to report that ill health limited their daily activities. In contrast, participation in regular physical activity was related positively to wellbeing, but within most cohorts women were less likely than men to participate in regular physical activity. In short, women aged between 65 and 80 years – likely to be retirees – reported less physical activity and lower subjective wellbeing than men in the same age group.

In contrast, women's physical activity was positively associated with retirement in an Australian study reported by Zhu (2016). She estimated the causal effect of retirement on health outcomes of women in Australia using data from a large ongoing national survey, the Household, Income and Labour Dynamics in Australia (HILDA). Zhu showed that not only did retirement have positive effects on women's self-reported physical and mental health but also that these positive effects coincided with increased physical activity and reduced smoking. Moreover, there were additional health benefits from spending a longer time in retirement. In our survey of retired women, most told us that in retirement their health was the same or better than when they retired, but a substantial minority (15.4 per cent) reported that their health was worse. Unlike Zhu, we found that those who had retired more recently were more likely to say that their health had improved or stayed the

88 Retirement and health

same than those who had retired some time ago. This may be because the mean age of our sample was six years older than Zhu's (67 years and 61 years, respectively) and our age range was significantly wider (55–94 years in our sample; 50–75 years in Zhu's). Again, in our study, those who retired at the (currently) normative age (60–63 years) reported significantly better health, and greater satisfaction with their health, than those who retired 'early' or 'late'.

Sjosten *et al.* (2012) examined the relationship between retirement and physical activity in the French GAZEL Cohort Study. Participants were employees of Electricité de France-Gaz de France (EDF-GDF), the French national gas and electricity company, who had retired at the statutory age and for whom there was at least one pre- and one post-retirement measurement of physical activity and, in a separate study, change in weight. In one analysis, the annual prevalence of higher physical activity (walking ≥ 5 km/pw) four years before and after retirement was analysed. Prevalence estimates showed that physical activity increased by 36 per cent among men and by 61 per cent among women during the transition to retirement. This increase was also observed among people who had a higher risk of physical inactivity, such as smokers and those with elevated depressive symptoms. A second analysis examined change in weight as a function of pre- and post-retirement physical activity. Not surprisingly, weight gain was greater among physically inactive persons compared with those physically active. While the authors note limitations in their results (e.g. lack of a measure of alcohol intake, use of self-reported data), the study did have several strengths. This prospective study of a large and stable cohort included yearly and long-term measurements that enabled them to obtain accurate estimates of physical activity during the actual retirement transition.

The observed increase in physical activity after retirement confirms findings in other studies (Forman-Hoffman *et al.*, 2008; Henkens *et al.*, 2008; Lahti *et al.*, 2011; Touvier *et al.*, 2010). Touvier *et al.* found that women retirees who increased their walking duration by two hours or more per week spent less time watching TV, whereas in the case of men, the increase in time spent watching TV was more than twice as high in retirees as in workers. The positive change in physical activity following retirement was mainly related to an increase in activities of moderate intensity, such as walking.

Forman-Hoffman and her colleagues found no significant weight change among men but women who had retired were more likely to gain weight than those who continued to work part-time, who were of normal weight upon retiring and those who retired from blue-collar occupations.

Of course, weight gain may not only be caused by less physical activity but by changes in eating habits. It is feasible to expect changes in weight to be associated with retirement. As we age, the role of nutrition becomes even more important. There is little research examining the specific links between good nutrition and retirement. In one study, Helldan *et al.*, (2012) examined a sample of current and former Finnish employees from Helsinki. They found that healthy eating habits increased more among retired women than among those continuously employed, whereas among men healthy food habits were not associated with retirement.

Given the many benefits associated with a healthy diet and proper nutrition apart from weight loss, including resistance to illness and disease, higher energy levels, and increased mental alertness, it could be hypothesised that, post-retirement, the health of these women would be better than that of their male peers.

Finally, the experience of loneliness and social isolation may be linked to poor health. While not specifically a problem among retirees, retirement may trigger increased loneliness and decreased social connections among some individuals, particularly those who are single. There is strong evidence that social isolation and loneliness heighten the risk for premature mortality, and that this risk exceeds that of many key ill-health indicators. Researchers have shown that loneliness can be a bigger killer than obesity and should be considered a major public health issue. A review of 218 studies into the health effects of social isolation and loneliness (Holt-Lunstad *et al.*, 2010) found that lonely people have a 50 per cent greater chance of premature death, while obesity increases the chance of early death by 30 per cent. The team found that the risk of early death associated with loneliness, social isolation and living alone was equal to or greater than the premature death risk associated not only with obesity but also with other major health conditions.

Retirement: opportunity or pitfall?

A review of the literature on the link between retirement and a healthy lifestyle could help us to clarify the often-conflicting findings reported above. Zantinge *et al.* (2014) asked whether retirement was an 'opportunity or pitfall' for a healthy lifestyle. Thus, their focus was not on medical illness or disease. Systematic searches of relevant databases resulted in 20 papers published between 2001 and 2013 being selected for the review. All studies allowed for a comparison between retirees and those still in employment. Search terms included, in addition to 'retirement', '(change/increase/decrease) in alcohol, smoking, dietary habits, physical activity.' Zantinge and her colleagues concluded from their examination of these studies that while retirement may be associated with lifestyle changes, the impact is 'hetero-geneous' and related to both positive and negative changes. Thus, an increase in alcohol consumption in retirement seems to be associated with involuntary retire-ment. Leisure time physical activity, especially moderately physically intense activ-ity, increases slightly. Finally, Zantinge and colleagues found that studies of smoking and dietary habits were too limited to draw any conclusions.

We might expect that better-educated retirees or those with greater wealth might be more aware of the benefits of a healthy diet and adopt (or retain) heal-thier food habits. Although they did not test this proposition, it is interesting that Geyer *et al.* (2014) found, using a wide variety of wealth measures and contrary to expectations, that associations of wealth and health were inconsistent among German retirees although there was a moderate association between health and home ownership. So, a carefully conducted review of research over a 13-year period makes it clear that there are no generalisable relationships between health/ lifestyle and retirement.

90 Retirement and health

Various factors such as the reason for leaving the workforce are likely to moderate relationships between health and retirement. Van der Heide *et al.* (2013) systematically summarised the literature on the health effects of retirement, with the aim of describing differences in terms of voluntary, involuntary and regulatory retirement and between blue-collar and white-collar workers. Twenty-two longitudinal studies were included. Strong evidence was found for retirement having a beneficial effect on mental health, which, they speculated, may be linked to a reduction in work-related stress. Conflicting evidence was found for retirement having an effect on perceived general and physical health, with some studies showing positive effects and others negative effects. Only one study indicated that involuntary retirees were more likely to report declines in general health after retirement than voluntary retirees, but most of the research examined did not analyse this issue. Regarding occupational characteristics, van der Heide *et al.* found no clear differences between blue-collar and white-collar workers in retirement health outcomes.

Fisher *et al.*'s comment is a reminder of the difficulty or perhaps the futility of seeking such relationships:

> There are many inherent challenges associated with estimating the impact of retirement on health, including methodological limitations, limited and cross-sectional data, differences in cultural norms, labor markets, and economic incentives, and failure to differentiate between voluntary and involuntary retirement. Furthermore, there are important gender, class, and national differences to consider. For example … higher levels of education and greater wealth are related to health status and longevity and nations differ in healthcare services and policies.
>
> *(2016, pp. 244–245)*

The difficulty in establishing clear links between physical and mental health and retirement suggests that it may prove more productive to examine psychological 'health', in this case how women adjust to retirement and how satisfied they are with this life transition.

Adjustment to retirement: difficult or easy?

> [Retirement] has become a development of my life growth and interests. I have continued to learn new things and ways of looking and understanding. I have spent some time on becoming less stressed. I have seen relationships differently and needed to offload some. I have become less of a garbage bin for other people's problems. Maybe I have fewer contacts with others in some ways but they are better contacts and relationships. I have lost good friends from illness and death and can see this will continue. It is part of life's journey. I am more reflective. I could not have anticipated these things clearly from when I stepped away from full-time work at around 50, having started work at 14. The second half of my life has been a different kind of work, not full-time paid work but full-time learning about life in many areas I had not explored so thoroughly before.

> I thought that I was ready to retire mentally – but found that it actually took me three years to adjust – I grieved for my job and that process took that long. There was no help or recognition about the grieving process. I had to work through that myself and it was only after I came out the other end that I realised what had happened to me. I now am very unstressed and enjoying my retirement.

These two women from our study were among many who commented at length about their adjustment to retirement. Some, like the first woman, found retirement to be a gradual process of opening up opportunities for personal growth; others, like the second woman, found the adjustment to retirement to be a stressful and difficult progression. Others made the transition smoothly without any sense of disruption to their lives.

Although the term 'adjustment' is commonly used in these studies, few have actually measured pre- and post-retirement psychological adjustment specifically and most rely on life satisfaction or satisfaction with retirement as a surrogate for this. Although our study contained no specific measure of psychological adjustment, it is clear that on two adjustment-like measures, self-esteem and stress levels, the women in our sample had different experiences post-retirement. When asked if their self-esteem was better, the same or worse than before they retired, two-thirds reported 'same', one-quarter reported higher self-esteem post-retirement and only 14 per cent had worse self-esteem. Those whose self-esteem was better or the same reported significantly better health post-retirement, as well as greater satisfaction with their health than those whose self-esteem was worse. When asked about stress, three-quarters reported being less stressed, one-fifth was equally stressed and only 7.4 per cent were more stressed. Most of our participants reported being more or equally satisfied with life post-retirement (46.3 per cent and 38.5 per cent, respectively), with the remainder being less satisfied.

Early studies of life satisfaction in retirement found that the majority of people were satisfied with their lives (Monette 1996; Reitzes *et al.*, 1996). In a large-scale study of later life families, the majority of all retired men (70 per cent) and women (76 per cent) said that retirement was easy for them (Wolcott, 1998). However, in an excellent and extensive review of the literature on life satisfaction and retirement, Heybroek *et al.* (2015) note that findings about the association between life satisfaction and retirement are inconsistent. These are largely due to methodological and/or disciplinary differences and are a particular function of other factors including economic and social correlates (see below for a discussion about this).

In order to enable a closer examination of wellbeing in retirement, several researchers have identified different patterns of adjustment to retirement (Pinquart and Schindler, 2007; Wang, 2007). Wang's longitudinal study yielded three different patterns: maintaining a stable level over time; improvement in adjustment; and a group whose adjustment was worse after retirement but improved over time. Heybroek *et al.* analysed data from the first 11 waves of the HILDA survey and extended Wang' classification. Using measures of life satisfaction before and after retirement, the authors report that 40 per cent of their retired participants maintained high life satisfaction during the transition to retirement; 28 per cent experienced declining life satisfaction from a high level after retirement; 14 per cent experienced increasing life satisfaction from a low level pre-retirement; and 18 per cent reported a declining low level of satisfaction. Heybroek and his colleagues conclude that this diversity in life satisfaction in retirement is concealed when overall averages are the focus of analyses. Moreover, taking into account differences such as those reported will result in a more accurate examination of the factors that predict life satisfaction in retirement.

What of depression in retirement? Depression is a significant health issue. It reduces productivity at work and increasingly is becoming the main reason for early retirement. There is convincing evidence that depressed individuals retire at a significantly younger age than those without depression. Post-retirement depression has also been documented but less convincingly. Although Sahlgren (2013) showed that being retired increases the risk of clinical depression by 40 per cent, not all studies have demonstrated such a strong effect and some not at all. More research is clearly needed in this area to tease out the effects of pre-retirement psychological health, retirement, social isolation, ageing and lifestyle factors on depression.

What predicts life satisfaction after retirement?

There has been extensive research on predictors of adjustment to retirement. And while many retirees are able to negotiate retirement without serious adjustment problems, some do not appear to have the resources to refashion their lives. For example, in our study, some women complained about the 'emptiness' of their retirement lives:

> It can be tedious, boring and even though I am a loner, more solitary than I would sometimes like. I don't fit much of the community programs and even some of the other activities that are around.

Slevin and Wingrove (1995) reviewed early studies of women's adjustment to retirement and nominated a large number of predictors, most of which are noted below. Where studies contrasting men and women had been conducted, findings were often contradictory. Although there were differences in the relative importance of the determinants of satisfaction, many of the same factors apparently accounted for retirement satisfactions for both genders. These included self-perceived health, financial adequacy, retirement planning, activities and marital status. While these issues affect some but by no means all retirees, the loss of financial resources is a major concern for many, especially women, as we have seen in Chapter 3. Inadequate finances can affect many aspects of life satisfaction, for example through limiting access to secure housing and adequate health care, and reducing opportunities to engage in new roles and activities because of their cost.

Since 2010, a number of reviews conducted by groups of researchers that address the determinants of adjustment to life during retirement have been published, reflecting the growing interest in this field (Wang *et al.*, 2011; Wang and Hesketh, 2012; Wang and Shultz, 2010). As Barbosa *et al.* (2016) report in their systematic review of predictors of adjustment to retirement, these meta-analyses present not only convergent results but also three methodological issues: (a) grouping different outcomes without describing grouping criteria; (b) not showing how much evidence supports each predictor; and (c) not describing their article search strategies. Regarding the first issue, Barbosa *et al.* labelled variables such as quality of life, depression and attitude towards retirement as retirement adjustment (using the categorisation system adopted by Wang *et al.*, 2011). Marriage quality and positive and negative influences during retirement were labelled as wellbeing (following Wang and Hesketh, 2012) and wellbeing, retirement planning, and emotions and feelings towards retirement were labelled as retirement adaptation.

In planning their review, Barbosa and colleagues investigated retirement adjustment as a latent construct measured through five variables: retirement adjustment; life satisfaction and wellbeing (as cognitive and affective subjective evaluations); quality of life (referring to personal domains, including control, autonomy, pleasure and self-realisation); and retirement satisfaction (defined as contentment with life during retirement). In their evaluation of 115 articles, they found of 26 classes of adjustment predictors. Barbosa *et al.* identified four groups of predictors:

(1) Those assessed in many studies (more than 30) and with a high proportion of positive results for adjustment (more than 60) included physical health, finances, psychological health and personality-related attributes, leisure, voluntary retirement, and social integration.
(2) Predictors with a moderate proportion of positive results for adjustment (more than ten studies and positive results for adjustment between 40 and 60 per cent) included preparation for retirement, marital relationships, spirituality, characteristics of pre-retirement jobs, post-retirement jobs, duration of retirement, parenthood, and education.
(3) A third group of predictors was assessed in a small number of studies (ten or fewer) with a high proportion of positive results for adjustment ($\geq$50 per cent). These included community resources, volunteer work, family, professional identity, goals, and physical activity.
(4) Finally, a fourth group that failed to predict adjustment included age, sex, household composition, timing of retirement, and ethnicity.

This careful systematic review of predictors of retirement adjustment is of considerable benefit in providing an overview of this complex set of factors. But it may leave the reader confused about contributions of specific individual factors. Most of the relationships found by Barbosa *et al.* confirm those shown by other researchers but some are at odds with these findings. For example, they claim that duration of retirement appeared for the first time as a relevant predictor of adjustment to retirement. In seven of the 15 studies that assessed duration of retirement, participants who had been retired longer reported better quality of life, wellbeing, and

94 Retirement and health

satisfaction with retirement and with life. Time since retirement had no effect in six studies and only two studies indicated that time was a risk factor for retirement.

Silver (2010) examined the relationship between duration of retirement and three subjective measures of wellbeing (depressive symptoms, financial worries, and health) among three groups: recent retirees (retired two years or fewer), long-term retirees (retired up to eight years) and self-identified homemakers. She found that recent retirees were younger, reported the fewest health conditions and the highest levels of activity compared to long-term retirees and homemakers. All three measures of wellbeing were significantly better for long-term retirees relative to homemakers. Silver concluded that participating in the paid labour force may have been a protective factor with regard to self-assessed wellbeing.

Among retirement transition-related factors, voluntary retirement (Reitzes and Mutran, 2004; van Solinge and Henkens 2007, 2008) and retirement planning (Petkoska and Earl 2009; Reitzes and Mutran, 2004; Wang, 2007) are positively related to retirees' psychological wellbeing. From a life course perspective, the timing of retirement can have a significant influence on psychological wellbeing. As discussed earlier in this chapter, people who retire earlier than expected or planned are more likely to experience decreased psychological wellbeing on entering retirement (Isaksson and Johansson, 2000; Wang 2007). Calvo (2006) found that continuing to work in older adulthood is related to higher levels of life satisfaction. However, the type of work did affect the results. Not surprisingly, working in undesirable jobs was not associated with the positive effects of paid work on mood indicators and mortality. A related issue is the extent to which work role identity is related to psychological wellbeing in retirement. Retirees who strongly identify themselves with their work are likely to experience a decrease in life satisfaction on retirement (Reitzes and Mutran, 2004). In our study, we found that women who had retired from higher-level occupations were significantly more likely to retain links, post-retirement, with work. Retaining links with work was in turn related to satisfaction with retirement and life in general.

One interesting additional study reminds us that small events can play a role in the retirement transition. We tend to pay little attention to retirement rituals yet, in a Dutch study, van den Bogaard (2017) examined the relationship between the experience of retirement rites of passage and post-retirement satisfaction with life. Retirement rituals were measured in two ways: the perceived effort put into the ritual and the presentation of a retirement gift. The author found that the experienced retirement ritual was positively associated with post-retirement satisfaction with life, and particularly so for those who perceive themselves as highly competent in their work. Van den Bogaard concludes that we need to pay attention to farewell ceremonies and the rules and customs that surround them and their effect on retirement outcomes. However, Osborne (2012) warns that retirement farewells from employers and colleagues need to avoid giving the impression that the time has come to dispose of entities that are no longer required. Instead, such ceremonies could be considered as genuine rites of passage.

What about the women?

Barbosa *et al.* (2016) found that sex (gender) was included as a potential predictor in 103 of the 115 studies they reviewed, but its effect on adjustment was assessed in only 35 of the final statistical models. In 22 of the cases (62.9 per cent), sex presented no effect on retirement adjustment. In the remaining 13 studies, the results were contradictory: both sexes were predictors of better adjustment in some of the studies and predictors of worse adjustment in others. In a study reported to the Gerontological Society of America, Coan *et al.* (2016) examined changes in life satisfaction from full-time employment to retirement for men and women and found that life satisfaction increased in retirement for both men and women. However, when controlling for occupational factors, women experienced significantly less improvement in life satisfaction on retirement relative to men. The authors suggest that while men and women both experience a sense of freedom in retirement, the fact that women continue to carry out household labour means that they are not entering the same period of leisure as are men (van Solinge and Henkens, 2005).

Kubicek *et al.* (2011) found interesting gender differences in their study of pre-retirement resources and retiree wellbeing. They established that their sample of US retirees reported moderate to high levels of positive psychological functioning and low levels of depressive symptoms. There were significant, but small, gender differences, with women scoring higher on psychological functioning yet reporting more frequent symptoms of depression than did men. Women scored higher than men on environmental mastery, personal growth, positive relations with others, and purpose in life, while the converse was true for autonomy. Kubicek and her colleagues hypothesised that possessing key resources prior to retirement as well as losing or gaining resources in the transition to retirement influence retirees' wellbeing and that these effects are partially conditioned by gender. They found that some resources (pre-retirement physical health, tenacity in the pursuit of goals, and flexibility in goal adjustment) benefited men and women's wellbeing equally. But financial assets and job dissatisfaction were more strongly related to men's psychological wellbeing in retirement while pre-retirement social contacts were more strongly related to the wellbeing of women, particularly their level of depression. A related issue raised was the gendered pattern of financial, social and work resources. Men and women differed in their employment experiences and financial resources as well as in their friendships and social contacts. Their gendered experiences throughout the life course seemed to translate into different patterns of resource needs for men and women's psychological wellbeing during retirement.

While many reported findings on retirement adjustment derive from comparisons between men and women, thus providing valuable information about gender differences, Price (2003) notes the importance of also conducting detailed, thorough studies of women's experiences. These allow for greater depth of analysis of the impact of retirement on women's health and wellbeing. She reports that researchers who have examined women's retirement independently of men have

96 Retirement and health

found that low self-esteem and negative retirement attitudes, early or late retirement, and obligatory family-centred responsibilities in retirement predict adjustment problems for women. What remains unclear is the extent to which women's employment history influences the retirement adjustment process. Significant differences in attitudes to retirement, timing of retirement and work attachment between professional and non-professional retirees have been shown in a number of studies. Participation in leisure activities and positive morale predicted successful retirement adjustment for professional women while women who retire from lower-status occupations experience greater adjustment difficulties. In a qualitative study designed to extend understanding of professional women's retirement experiences, Price (1998) interviewed 14 women who had been retired for between seven and 15 years. The women repeatedly described their adjustment to retirement as part of a 'linear process and appeared to draw comfort from the sequential nature of their lives' (ibid., p. 346). Price goes on to interpret these women's retirement adjustment in terms of her process model and concludes:

> [R]etirement is not a monolithic process that all individuals experience similarly. Rather, retirement is a process based on experiential variables specific to one's life circumstances, and for this sample of women, retirement adjustment was indeed an ongoing process – one that was largely influenced by former professional roles and responsibilities. In spite of existing limitations (e.g., variation in time since retirement, health status, and financial security of sample participants), these women's narratives provide valuable insight into the retirement behaviors of a neglected segment of women.
>
> *(Ibid., p. 353)*

The current literature implicates some consistent health and wellbeing consequences of retirement but there are many factors whose impact is uncertain or contradictory. A key challenge is to establish methodologically sound studies that take into account the many contextual factors associated with the transition to retirement and the health-related experiences of this life stage.

7

WHAT NEXT?

I am so happy in retirement, far more than I expected. I feared boredom and loss of meaning, but it's been easy to find so many worthwhile activities that I've never been busier ... all sorts of interesting casual odd jobs have come my way and enriched my life and my networks. I've been able to study for sheer pleasure and interest, and I've been able to travel from Antarctic to Europe, Asia to America, Africa to Arnhem Land, within three years. As someone said to me recently: 'You live the life we all aspire to'. What's not to love?

I hoped to be able to spend time with friends, instead I needed to actively create opportunities to find and make new friends (not easy for me). It's a work in progress. Learning to travel alone. Go to events alone. Somewhere I had a dream to go off around Australia, then realised I could no longer change a tyre? Work motivated me, now I have to motivate myself.

The contrast between these two experiences of retirement for women in our study is sharp. The first has engaged in activities that make retirement a happy and fulfilling stage of her life. For the second woman, constructing an active and rewarding retirement life has not been easy. Yet considerable research has shown that those who are active in retirement are happier and healthier – physically and mentally. For example, a study of 1,583 retirees conducted by the Teachers Insurance and Annuity Association (TIAA) in 2016 found that three-quarters of those (men and women) who participated in ten or more activities said that they were 'very satisfied' with life compared with half who engaged in between one and four activities. Indeed, a meta-analysis of the impact of social isolation (e.g. lack of friends, living alone) found that this was a risk factor for mortality comparable with other established risk factors for ill health such as smoking, poor diet and obesity (Holt-Lunsted *et al.*, 2015).

Many who are retired see this time as an opportunity for freedom from the structure and routine of work. As we noted in Chapter 5, when we asked our research participants 'What is the best thing about retiring?' by far the most common response from these women was freedom, either explicitly or implicitly ('freedom to please myself'; 'no alarm clocks ever!'; 'being able to choose what I do and when'). On the other hand, some women reported that they were bored, with little interest in their life.

In today's hyperactive world, expectations for retirees have changed. No longer regarded as the end of life, retirement can be considered as a next stage in which activities delayed by full-time work can be pursued and new life choices made. One researcher captured this approach to retirement, coining the term 'proto-retirement', a term that defines the desire to retire with the positive idea of pursuing meaningful and fulfilling activities (Hudson, 1999). It is an opportunity to engage at last in those pursuits that matter most to each individual.

A large and growing literature base examines the uptake and maintenance of leisure activities after retirement and we review some of these studies in this chapter. We then focus on several more general issues of relevance to how retired women spend their time, which is not always in the pursuit of leisure.

Leisure activities

The substantial self-help literature available to retirees and seniors is replete with suggestions for staying active in retirement. While most offer general advice (have a routine; keep active; stay in touch) with examples of how this might translate into action, others are less realistic about the options available. For example, an American journalist suggests 'fun' alternatives to retiring at home. These include travelling long-term, cruising, taking care of a property for absent owners, 'hitting the road' in a motor home, and spending half the year in a different climate (Stich, n.d.). While many retirees might dream of taking up one of these suggestions, most cannot afford, financially or otherwise, to do so; they engage in other, less ambitious leisure pursuits. The most common retirement activities people plan to pursue when they retire include travel, hobbies of various sorts, gardening, sport, getting fit through exercise, reading and relaxing, home renovations and volunteering (e.g. Eisenberg, 2016). How does the reality match these aspirations?

We asked women about their participation in different leisure activities, and their profile of participation was similar to those recorded in other studies. Of note is the fact that they were least likely to be engaged in organised sport or monitoring financial investments, activities that are typically associated with men. Most women (81 per cent) spent their time reading, watching TV and listening to music. Over half reported engaging frequently in home-related activities just as they might well have done before they retired – cooking, domestic chores, and spending time with family. Nearly half often spent time on the Internet, worked in their gardens, pursued hobbies, or volunteered. In our sample, participating in casual paid work was uncommon, as was church attendance. Playing sport was not high on these women's agendas, but undertaking various forms of exercise was. Exercise appears to serve other purposes for women, as well as keeping fit. Mobily *et al.* (2017)

found a number of factors associated with continued exercise among retired women. Social support and socialising helped women to complete a session and to remain committed to the programme; women felt better when they completed a class and worse if they missed one; and several described exercise classes as being an 'organising' element in their day, structured and scheduled, much like work had been.

There is considerable evidence that leisure activities make a positive contribution to retirement adjustment, life satisfaction and wellbeing (see, for example, Earl *et al.*, 2015; Nimrod, 2007; Park and Park, 2016; Zaninotto *et al.*, 2013). Our research also showed that the more women engaged in activities, the more satisfied they were with retirement and with life in general. Life and retirement satisfaction were predicted by many activities, especially travel, spending time with friends, 'keep fit' activities, attendance at clubs, and engaging in hobbies. Interestingly, satisfaction was not predicted by volunteer work, caring for grandchildren or time spent on social media.

Relatively few studies directly compare women and men's preferred leisure activities. The 2016 TIAA study mentioned above found that retired women and men had different activity patterns. Women were more likely than men to be caregivers (46 per cent compared with 26 per cent), to socialise with friends (75 per cent compared with 52 per cent) and family (80 per cent compared with 60 per cent) and to give time to volunteering (58 per cent compared with 42 per cent); retired men were more likely than women to play sport (38 per cent compared with 18 per cent), do casual work (28 per cent compared with 19 per cent) or engage in aspects of their previous job or career such as attending talks or meeting former colleagues (26 per cent compared with 14 per cent). Women were also slightly more likely to engage in exercise or creative pursuits than men.

Avital (2017) used two large European data sources (Survey of Health, Ageing and Retirement in Europe and the Organisation for Economic Co-operation and Development) to assess gender differences in three types of leisure patterns: going to sports or social clubs, participating in a course or educational class, and volunteering. She found, in general, that men were more active physically than women and that retirement increased the likelihood of participating in sports club activities that are exclusive to men. Avital concluded that a country's expenditure on culture and recreation contributed significantly to women's participation in leisure activities and substantially reduced the gender leisure gap.

Volunteering

Several studies have demonstrated gender differences in volunteering. Rotolo and Wilson (2007) found that the amount of time devoted to volunteering did not differ substantially but that the type of volunteering activities did. Men tended to take on leadership positions (teaching, maintenance work) while women were more likely to 'help out', preparing and serving food or assisting at events. Similarly, Manning (2010) found that women's volunteering was characterised by

100 What next?

caring tasks, while men were more likely to be engaged in leadership positions. Jaumont-Pascual *et al.* surmise that because of the relational nature of women's upbringing they 'tend to choose activities where social interaction is either the main activity or a requirement for activities such as volunteerism and community service to take place' (2016, p. 85). They invoke the belief that an ethic of care, namely behaviour that responds to the needs of others, constrains women's choices of leisure activities. The dominance of an ethic of care is implicated in the choice of activities described above.

While our own research did not demonstrate this, many studies have shown that volunteering has positive physical and mental health benefits for older adults, for example increased self-esteem, self-efficacy and life satisfaction, and even decreasing mortality (Greenfield and Marks, 2003; Morrow-Howell *et al.*, 2009; Zaninotto *et al.*, 2013). There is evidence that volunteering or 'civic engagement' partially offsets role losses encountered in later life, including those that come about through retirement. This is particularly so among those for whom work or career comprise a central aspect of their self-concept (Greenfield and Marks, 2003).

Nesteruk and Price (2011) interviewed 40 retired women to examine attitudes and practices towards volunteering. They described three categories of women based on their engagement with volunteering: traditional formal volunteers, represented by over half the women in their study, who donate their time to community agencies and organisations; non-volunteers who reject the idea of volunteer work for personal reasons related to time commitments, dissatisfaction with earlier experiences, or a lifetime of doing things for other people; and unrecognised volunteers, especially informal or family carers. Nesteruk and Price contend that women in this last category 'represent a legion of informal volunteers that go unnoticed and unvalued. In response to cultural expectations for community engagement, the women in this study expressed a sense of guilt for not contributing in more formal ways' (ibid., p. 104). Women in the traditional category 'expressed a need to give back and they described how volunteering gives back to them in terms of social integration, structured time, and finding meaning in their lives' (ibid.), as well as being a way to implement personal agency. In their analysis, Nesteruk and Price discussed societal expectations about 'giving back' and advocated against assigning social value only to those retirees who meet the criteria for productivity in the type of volunteering (formal or informal) that they undertake.

Wired women or the impact of the internet

One of the most profound changes to occur in the past few decades has been the proliferation of Internet use as a source of communication. Although access to and use of the Internet is significantly more common among young people than old, the percentage of older people who are regular users is increasing. One recent study revealed that in 2016, 85 per cent of European Union members had access to the Internet from their own homes and 71 per cent used it daily (Eurostat, 2017). More than half (57 per cent) of those aged 55–74 years were regular Internet users.

While these data are not disaggregated by gender, they tell us that a substantial number of older people use the Internet on a regular basis. Thus, in addition to the more familiar pastimes described above, the Internet occupies the time of many retirees as they email (the most common activity) and seek information about goods and services. Interestingly, over one-third of older people in the Eurostat study reported that they also engaged in social networking through various platforms such as Facebook, Instagram, LinkedIn, Skype and Twitter. A recent Australian study (Australian Communications and Media Authority, 2016) found that proportionally more Australians aged 65 years and above (79 per cent) had used the Internet at some point in their lives than their British or American counterparts and that this number had increased over the previous five years. Nearly all users (98 per cent) had accessed the Internet from their own homes, indicating ready availability and privacy.

Given concerns about the negative effects of social isolation and the importance of maintaining social relationships, clearly the Internet is a valuable tool. Popular apps such as Skype, FaceTime and Viber facilitate easy (and free) communication across locations and generations. Indeed, some women in our earlier study of grandmothers (Rosenthal and Moore, 2012b) reported that they used Skype to talk to their grandchildren who lived a great distance away from them; others employed this platform to play games with their small grandchildren as a means of establishing or maintaining a relationship in the absence of physical contact. In addition to other activities (banking, paying bills, access to news and commentary), the Internet plays a significant role in providing information about health and services although less so than might be hoped. In 2015, about one-third of older UK Internet users had accessed the Internet for information about health and services, more than those in Australia (15 per cent) and less than US seniors (74 per cent). Perhaps not surprisingly, a recent study of Australian women found a strong preference among older women for sourcing health information offline rather than online, but the converse held for their young counterparts (Jean Hailes, 2017)

So, older people are embracing the digital life with the opportunities this brings for continuing engagement with others, for information and for ongoing learning. A new and increasingly common phenomenon is the use of online dating services by older women whose partners have died, who are divorced or who have never partnered. One of the largest computer dating companies reports older people as its fastest growing group, while a service that analyses Internet audiences found that in one month more than 1.6 million women and men aged over 65 years visited online personal sites (King, 2005). As this report was carried out more than a decade ago, there is a strong likelihood that these numbers have substantially increased.

But there is a darker side to the Internet. Newspapers and other media abound with horror stories of older women and retirees seeking love or companionship and who have been victims of fraud or scammed in some way (see, for example, Olson, 2015; Quinn and Cribb, 2013; Reinitz, 2012). Victims report financial exploitation, pervasive lying and unwanted sexual aggression, among other negative outcomes of their experiences (Vanderweerd et al., 2016). So why do older

102 What next?

women (and men) use these sites? There are clearly some good reasons, as well as risks. Expanding their social networks, for friendship and romance, the perceived ability to control risks and knowing more about one's partner were reported benefits of online dating according to 45 women over the age of 50 years interviewed by Vanderweerd and colleagues.

Kang and Hoffman (2011) used data from a large-scale project to examine factors that lead to online dating. Although not targeting older people, they found that neither age nor gender influenced the probability of online dating, but there were two significant predictors: those who used the Internet for more tasks were more likely to use online dating sites; and individuals who were more trusting of others were less likely to use these sites. Although the authors note limitations to their study, including the measure of trust, this latter finding is intriguing and counter-intuitive and needs to be replicated.

As a source of companionship, online dating may offer some of today's retirees rewarding social relationships, but the weight of evidence suggests that, at the very least, women should be wary of the possible distressing downsides of this action.

Being a carer

> Being freed up from working in a reasonably demanding job, means I'm now available for the other demands of life – looking after aged parents, supporting my husband (now I get to do all the housework) and getting caught up in his transition to retirement business – means not a great deal of freedom to pursue my own interests. I don't feel very relevant any more.

> I am trapped – caring for a demanding and often aggressive elderly mother. I see no end in sight and it is very difficult. I care a lot also for little grandchildren … and also have to pick up the child going to school. I provide back-up when the girls are too sick for childcare. It is so hard to plan your day.

> Because my friend has become increasingly dependent on me and less able to do things for herself, I am unable to get away for a holiday as she is not yet ready for respite [care] and I am unwilling to leave her alone. We have no family in this country.

These three quotes from women in our study show a variety of caring responsibilities, whether for partner, parent(s), grandchildren, or friends. Some are onerous and exhausting; others – especially when grandchildren are involved – can add a joyous new dimension to life (Rosenthal and Moore, 2012b). The grandmothers we surveyed who were the primary carers of their grandchildren recognised rewards as well as challenges. They were more likely than other grandmothers to feel valued and that they had status in the family. They acknowledged the downside of this role, but many spoke of the pleasure it brought:

> It's been wonderful for us to have this light-filled house again with this little boy – it's so lovely.

> I think as we go through middle age we close ourselves up a bit ... and a child just opens your arms back up. You sort of embrace thing again with a new energy.
>
> *(Ibid., p. 31)*

Not all of the women in our survey took on carer roles in retirement, but neither was caring for others an uncommon activity. Asked whether they looked after or babysat grandchildren, around half did this sometimes (29 per cent) or often (24 per cent). Fewer were carers for other relatives, although 11 per cent did this often and another 25 per cent sometimes. Qualitative data suggested that these women were mostly looking after either their husbands or elderly parents.

With an increasingly ageing population, many retirees are likely to have parents who are frail and need assistance. A recent survey by the (ABS, 2015) found that women accounted for 68.1 per cent of primary parental carers and that there was a division of caregiving duties. Women were more likely than men to help with personal and daily domestic tasks while men more often undertook occasional tasks such as doing repairs or installing equipment in the home.

It seems that caring for elderly relatives is not a matter of who has the time or resources – it is largely a matter of gender. Research drawing on a longitudinal panel study that surveys a nationally representative sample of more than 26,000 Americans over the age of 50 every two years (Grigoryeva, 2014) found that daughters provide an average of 12.3 hours of care to elderly parents each month compared to sons' 5.6 hours, a ratio that has remained static since 1995. Sons reduce their relative caregiving efforts when they have a sister, while daughters increase theirs when they have a brother. This gender inequality in elderly parent care is particularly significant due to the consequences of elder care for caregivers. Numerous empirical studies report negative mental and physical health consequences, including a higher mortality rate, for people who provide care for elderly family members. While a great deal of caring is done by women in the pre-retirement phase of their lives, for retirees there is often considerable stress associated with having to give up or delay substantially their retirement plans. As Dow and Meyer (2010) note, the need to care for a partner or older relative can be an unanticipated outcome or a precipitator of retirement. Retirement may coincide with illness or disability of a parent or partner, or may be forced by the demands of caring. The financial impact of having been a carer during one's working life may also be felt most keenly on retirement, through the lack of opportunities for savings and retirement fund co-contributions.

There is some evidence to suggest that informal caregivers are more likely to be forced into retirement and retire earlier when compared with non-caregivers (Dentinger and Clarkberg, 2002; Szinovacz and Davey, 2005). A study of the association between caregiving intensity (hours of weekly care) and retirement status among 55–69-year-old Canadians showed that higher intensity caregiving was associated with being fully retired (relative to working full-time) for women and men. For women, but not men, higher intensity caregiving was also associated

104 What next?

with working part-time and being a labour force non-participant (Jacobs *et al.*, 2014). It seems for women, unlike men, the amount of time devoted to caregiving is associated with multiple paths to retirement.

Studies such as these emphasise the negative aspects of caring. While caring for another can be difficult and demanding, there are positive aspects too. We noted above how full-time carer grandparents enjoyed and appreciated their role. It can also be fulfilling to care for an elderly spouse or parent. Consequences of these roles can include becoming closer, 'giving back', increasing one's understanding of the person being cared for, or even the healing of old wounds.

> I have been retired [for] 13 years and it is in some ways the most enjoyable period of life – far less stress and worry. ... Another benefit is that it allowed me to care for my mother until she died, and to help my daughter with her child as she is a single parent.

> [Retirement] allowed me to spend the last few years of my mother's life (she was 98) as a special time.

In an interesting shift in focus, Gonzales *et al.* (2017), using longitudinal population-based data, examined whether informal caregivers *un*retire, that is, return to work after retirement when their caregiving duties are no longer required or become less intense. 'Unretirement' is an emerging phenomenon that is likely to continue as the population ages, with retirement policies encouraging people to work longer, and many seniors recognising that they have accumulated inadequate retirement savings. People's desire to remain socially engaged may well be a further incentive to return to work after such an absence. Participants in the US Health and Retirement Study were aged 62 years or above in 1998 and claimed retirement status at that time. 'Unretired' participants reported being partly retired and working part- or full-time in paid work in subsequent waves during the period 2000–2008. They were asked about the informal care of a spouse and/or parent(s). Informal care comprised two types: activities of daily living (e.g. bathing, dressing, eating, or going to the toilet), or instrumental activities of daily living (preparing meals, shopping, help with taking medication). Approximately 6 per cent of retirees returned to work in subsequent waves, of whom three-quarters returned in the first two waves. Post-retirement jobs were mostly part-time (an average of 18–21 hours worked per week during the observation period). When compared with non-caregivers, helping a spouse with either type of informal care reduced the odds of returning to work in the subsequent wave. There was no statistical difference in returning to work between non-caregivers and helping parents with either type of care. Gonzales *et al.* suggest that the reason for the latter finding is that parents may have others available to assist them (e.g. other children, their own spouse/partners, friends or formal help). The absence of gender differences in the return to work of those who provide parental care is surprising, especially in light of previous research that suggests that parental caregiving was negatively associated with labour force

What next? **105**

participation for women, but the relationship was not significant for men (Lee *et al.*, 2015).

Relocation as an option

Finding a new home might appear to be an unusual topic for this chapter; however, for some women, choices about housing in retirement are a critical aspect of their post-work life. In fact, in one study, researchers refer to 'the consumption context of housing after retirement' (Kopanidis *et al.*, 2014). Although at least one study has shown that late mid-life workers and retirees expect to age in their family home (Robison and Moen, 2000), their physical and social contexts have an impact on these expectations. Older, rural and less well-educated people had the strongest expectations that they would remain in the family home and not relocate. Interestingly, the health of study participants or their spouses did not predict their future housing expectations, although Robison and Moen reported that prior expectations did predict actual moves within two years.

The need to change housing arrangements may arise for a number of reasons: inadequate finances (discussed earlier); the desire to capitalise on the family home; poor health and/or increasing dependency; or serious chronic illness or death of a partner. Furthermore, the motivation to change residence may simply relate to a wish to make life easier through 'downsizing', a move that brings with it fewer household and garden maintenance tasks, less housework, and (ideally) reduced expenditure on items such as energy bills and rates.

The research literature mainly focuses on retirement communities or villages as the housing destination for retirees and seniors who are obliged to give up independent living. However, 2011 Australian census data (ABS, 2013) showed that most older people live in private dwellings (94 per cent of Australians aged 65 years and above). Some live with a spouse/partner, some with children, and some live alone. In every age group of older people, women were less likely than men to be living with a spouse or partner, and more likely to have other living arrangements such as living alone, living with a child or other relatives, or in supported living accommodation.

Of those who lived in non-private dwellings, the great majority were in some type of cared accommodation. The most common were nursing homes (67 per cent) and accommodation for the retired or aged (not self-contained) (25 per cent). The proportion of older people living in non-private dwellings increased with age from 2 per cent of people aged 65–74 years to 6 per cent of people aged 75–84 years. Interestingly, women accounted for just over half of older people in the census, but for 69 per cent of older people in non-private dwellings.

Moving to a retirement village is a housing option sometimes used by older adults. Women comprise the majority of the residents of these communities due, in part, to living longer. While living in a retirement village can be a positive experience (one of our participants told us that 'Moving to a retirement village was one of the best things I did, I love living here'), for others difficulties surface over time. The positive benefits of physical activity and social participation for retirees and older people have been discussed in earlier sections of the book. Thus, an important issue is the extent to which living in a retirement village facilitates these health-enhancing activities. Several studies have reported on levels of activity (Bjornsdottir *et al.*, 2012; Holt *et al.*, 2016). Holt *et al.* audited physical activity facilities in 50 retirement villages and interviewed 200 residents to identify neighbourhood barriers to walking, and to obtain information on use of facilities at the retirement villages. Although larger retirement villages provided significantly more facilities and programmes for physical activity, this had no impact on use. Overall, only half the residents used the facilities and programmes available, suggesting the importance of understanding the enablers and barriers to physical activity in these settings.

A contemporary issue for retirement communities is a probable need for support for non-heterosexual people as the global increase in older people will also mean an increase in the number of women identifying as lesbian. Neville and Henrickson (2010) surveyed lesbian, gay and bisexual (LGBT) people's accommodation plans for old age and found that they were least likely to choose living in a retirement community/facility, possibly for fear of discrimination or because these services were not geared to their specific needs. However, if unable to live independently the majority of respondents indicated that they would prefer to live in a retirement facility that specifically catered for people who did not identify as heterosexual. In a study of providers of retirement and residential care for the elderly, few had experiences with non-heterosexual residents; there was poor inclusion of LGBT issues in policy, and little understanding of same-sex law reforms (Horner *et al.*, 2012). These studies show that the residential support sector needs to be prepared to provide a service that is free from discriminatory practices and that meets the needs of consumers regardless of sexual orientation.

Are retirement villages the best option for retirees and older people? Gardner *et al.* (2005) assessed the quality of life among people in two independent living retirement villages and compared this with a group of older people who had decided to continue to live in the community. They found that those in the former group had higher overall satisfaction with life and with their social life than those in the community group. Crisp *et al.* (2013) conducted a survey of community residents aged 55 years and above to identify the characteristics associated with retirement villages that influence relocation decisions. Factors that would encourage older people to relocate to a retirement village included the provision of outdoor living areas, support in maintaining independence, assisted living facilities and accessibility to medical facilities. A fear of losing independence and loss of privacy were the most influential factors in discouraging relocation.

A low-cost alternative to moving into a retirement village in the UK is a 'park home' (commonly called a mobile home in the US).

> Park home living is a unique tenure where the resident owns their home, but pays a 'pitch fee' to the owner of the site for the right to station it on their

land. The sector offers an attractive choice for some people, often older persons downsizing from conventional family homes. Sadly, not all sites are managed well and there is still evidence that some site owners do not fully comply with their responsibilities or respect the rights of residents.

(Department of Communities and Local Government, 2017, p. 4)

Bevan (2010) interviewed 40 residents of park homes and found that most shared very positive experiences of park home living and its benefits, although there were some dissenters. Bevan interpreted the residents' experiences in terms of two conceptual frameworks: 'elective belonging', a perspective that affirms residents' sense of biographical continuity despite having moved to a new location; and 'biographical disruption', when residents' lives had not followed the expected path and allowed them to cope with circumstances that tainted their new lifestyle.

Finally, we give one example of a new trend, the development of co-living housing. In the UK, a group of women have planned and organised housing that is entirely run by residents who support each other through old age. Most of the residents, aged between 50 to 87 years, are retirees. Two-thirds own their customised apartment and the remainder pay rent; there are rosters for cooking and cleaning and there are group outings. But as the originator of the project says, 'The architecture is lovely but the important architecture is the social fabric. ... The sense of community doesn't just happen, and we have done a lot to create it and to sustain it' (Fraser, 2017, para. 9). It may be unlikely that the many 'for profit' retirement villages that house older people would make the necessary financial and social investment in this ideal form of housing. However, more communities of this kind could be developed with the assistance of not-for-profit organisations, as has this UK development.

Maladaptive behaviours

Some women in our survey reported that retirement was boring; they missed the structure, the challenges and the companionship of their working lives and found little to replace this. Some fill the void with replacement behaviours that are problematic for their physical and mental health. We include here a brief discussion of three such behaviours among older women: alcohol abuse; prescription drug misuse; and problem gambling. These addictive behaviours of older women are largely hidden and relatively little researched. Very few studies focus on women retirees; however, it is clear that findings about older women and the causes for their problem behaviour are equally relevant to those women who have retired.

Alcohol misuse. Alcohol use and misuse is partly a hidden problem among older women as much drinking is done in private and goes 'under the radar' (Dare *et al.*, 2014). Nevertheless, figures have been published that indicate that the 'prevalence of alcohol use among older adults is staggering', according to a recent review by Bamburger (2015, p. 93). In the US, Grant *et al.* (2004) reported that the overall prevalence of alcohol abuse in women had significantly increased over a ten-year period, with rates of alcohol abuse and dependence increasing almost ten-fold in women aged 65 years and above. In contrast, among men aged 65 years and above, there has been a lower (but still worrying) four-fold increase. Bamburger (2015) surveyed more recent studies and confirmed the disturbing prevalence of women's alcohol misuse in a number of countries, including the US, the UK, Japan and Brazil. The detrimental health consequences of alcohol misuse have been widely documented.

Among the small number of studies that have examined the link between alcohol misuse and retirement some argue that retirement precipitates and/or exacerbates drinking problems (Bamburger, 2015), although results are equivocal. For example, Kuerbis and Sacco (2012) concluded that retirement plays a minor direct role in older adults' problem drinking. The retirement-alcohol link is likely to be mediated by many intervening factors such as negative emotional states. There appears to be a consensus that it is not retirement per se that affects drinking behaviour, but the retirement process itself.

After reviewing existing studies in the context of current theories of the association between problem drinking and retirement, Bamburger concludes that there is a complex interaction of factors relating to the pre-retirement and disengagement process with individual attributes and personal history. He gives one example of how this might relate to problem drinking for women:

> [T]here is evidence that the effects of certain work-based stressors can linger following work disengagement. Such lingering strain can also emerge when the disengagement from work is forced rather than volitional, particularly among older adults reporting higher levels of job satisfaction.
>
> *(2015, p. 105)*

Yogev (2017) summarises factors that impact on alcohol consumption in retirement. These include reasons for retiring (voluntary or involuntary); the nature of the retiree's social networks, both within or outside of work; the stress levels within the work environment; age at retirement (youthful retirees may be more likely to misuse alcohol); financial stress that could lead retirees to alcohol use; and the state of the retiree's marriage or partnership where an unsatisfactory post-retirement relationship could be a trigger for alcohol misuse. Retirement in and of itself does not cause alcohol misuse; it is the combination of any or more of these factors, or the complex network of relationships, individual characteristics, and the social and physical environment both pre- and post-retirement that make retirees susceptible to this problem behaviour.

Substance abuse. Here we discuss briefly older women's abuse of prescription drugs, which is by far the most common category of drug abuse among this group. The drug-taking patterns of psychoactive prescription drug users can be described as a continuum that ranges from appropriate use for medical indications through misuse to persistent abuse and dependence. Abuse of prescription drugs among older adults does not typically involve the use of these substances to 'get high' and the users do not usually obtain them illegally. Instead, unsafe combinations or amounts of medications may be obtained by seeking prescriptions from multiple doctors, by obtaining medications from family members or peers, or by stockpiling medications over time (Culberson and Ziska, 2008).

Misuse and abuse of prescription drugs is a growing problem although the overall prevalence is difficult to estimate and, despite considerable data on the epidemiology of alcohol misuse and abuse among older people, few comparable data are available on prescription drug misuse and abuse. Culberson and Ziska (2008) note that the prevalence of abuse may be as high as 11 per cent, with female gender and social isolation factors that increase risk. Koenig and Crisp (2008) report studies that show that older women who use psychoactive prescription drugs become addicted faster than any other group and are much more likely than older men to self-medicate in order to alleviate a large number of environmental and personal stressors, including anxiety, poverty, social isolation and bereavement.

There are a number of barriers that make it difficult to treat women who misuse and abuse prescription drugs, according to Koenig and Crisp. Conventional stereotypes of 'drug abusers' may result in older women's prescription drug use not being recognised and acknowledged. Financial barriers may lead to older women failing to get appropriate treatment; women who seek help from their physicians may be subjected to inadequate or inappropriate treatment through lack of knowledge. Relationships can be another barrier in sustaining drug use if a woman's partner is a user or if the woman has few social contacts and thus limited opportunities to be identified as a drug user by others.

Gambling. Is excessive gambling a problem for older women? Holdsworth *et al.* (2012), in a review of women's problem gambling, assert that this activity is becoming increasingly feminised and a 'mainstream pastime' for women, largely because of the expansion of electronic gaming machines (also known as 'pokies' or slot machines) in the past two decades. Although more men than women gamble, their gambling patterns tend to be quite different (ibid.). Men tend to gamble on games where some skill is considered to be involved – betting on card games such as poker, racing and other sports, and even the stock market – and are characterised as 'action' gamblers. Women, however, are often 'escape' gamblers and prefer to wager on activities such as bingo, lotteries or slot machines, activities in which winning is based solely on luck. Shaffer and Korn (2002) found that 73 per cent of female problem gamblers preferred slot machines and gambled to reduce boredom, to escape responsibility, and to relieve loneliness rather than for financial gain, pleasure or excitement. Holdsworth and her colleagues support and extend these findings. They suggest that gambling motivations particularly associated with women 'include social isolation, the need to escape from everyday stress, and psychological co-morbidity' (2012, p. 204). In the latter case, depression and anxiety disorders are key factors that coexist with problem gambling. However, the researchers note a caveat in terms of temporal sequencing, questioning whether the depression precedes or is the result of problem gambling. To date, there are no longitudinal studies to determine causation.

110 What next?

In an effort to explain gender differences in gambling, Holdsworth *et al.* integrate a range of contemporary theories with outcomes of gambling research.

> For instance, drawing on social capital concerns and the importance of social networks, in conjunction with gender role theory, may illuminate why, for some older women especially, gambling increases as their traditional gendered caring role decreases (most commonly when children leave home). This stage in many women's lives can be a time when a sense of loss can take place leading to feelings of loneliness and social isolation. For women especially it would appear that gambling in venues provides a safe place to go and where a sense of belonging can be achieved which can in turn ease feelings of loneliness and isolation.
>
> *(2012, p. 209)*

They also implicate the gender pay gap, discussed in Chapter 3, as a potential reason for women's problem gambling and cite research that shows that women's progression to problem gambling appears to be quicker than men's, with women likely to face economic difficulties sooner as they frequently do not have the financial buffer that men have (Brown and Coventry, 1997). Holdsworth *et al.* conclude with a plea that more research be conducted that takes into account women's experience of life and insight into their specific concerns.

Continuity and change in retirement activities

Whether retirees respond to their newfound unstructured time by continuing to engage in pre-retirement leisure activities or whether they begin new activity patterns has been the focus of interest for some researchers. Continuity theory (Atchley, 1999), which predicts the maintenance of pre-retirement activities, has had considerable support. However, as Jaumont-Pascual *et al.* (2016) point out, some activities may have to be abandoned owing to loss of physical capacity or energy or life-changing circumstances. As such, retirement may cause discontinuities in behaviour and act as an opportunity to begin anew.

Lahti *et al.* (2011) examined changes over a period of five to seven years in leisure time physical activity of moderate and vigorous intensity for 40–60-year-old employees facing the transition to retirement. Retirees significantly increased their time spent in moderate-intensity physical activity, with men doing so more than women but there were no changes in physical activity among those who remained in employment. Follow-up studies showed that leisure time physical inactivity decreased among retirees but not among older employees of nearly the same age, while in the former group the prevalence of physical inactivity was relatively low following retirement.

Earl *et al.* (2015) found that enjoyment of activities and their familiarity affected maintenance and continuation of these activities post-retirement. Continuity was also evident in a study conducted by Scherger *et al.* (2011) as part of the English

Longitudinal Study of Ageing. Longitudinal analyses showed that participants continued their pre-retirement activities (hobbies, club membership, participation in cultural events), although retirement resulted in increases in having a hobby. In a cross-national study of Israeli and American retirees, country differences were revealed (Nimrod et al., 2008). In the US there was a general inclination towards continuity of leisure pursuits while in Israel there were significant increases in rates and frequency of participation in new pursuits. The authors suggest that these differences are due to the already higher pre-retirement participation in leisure activities in the US. Pushkar et al. (2010) investigated whether continuity or change in retirement activities occurred over a two-year period. Assessment of retirees' activities showed that continuity of activities dominated with only a small percentage (13 per cent) of frequency of activity scores changing over time.

Although there is evidence for both continuity and disengagement post-retirement, there has been little focus on innovation, that is, the development of new interests and skills post-retirement (see, for example, Nimrod and Kleiber, 2007). Using a very different approach from other studies, Jaumont-Pascuel et al. reported on gender differences in patterns of initiation (innovation) and continuity in 'meaningful' activities, defined by the authors as 'those that allowed the development of new skills and interests and reinforced relationships' (2016, p. 83). Employing narrative analysis with a Spanish sample of ten women and ten men who were highly engaged in leisure activities prior to retirement, they found that women were more innovative than men in their retirement leisure activities, while men tended to continue in their lifelong activities. Thus, women tended to add more leisure roles after retirement rather than eliminate them, falling into Nimrod's 'expander' category. They conclude that 'what really enables women to cultivate leisure in later life is not their status as ... retirees, but their liberation from gender role responsibilities that have heretofore defined their lives' (2007, p. 99).

Conclusion

We have seen in other chapters that being active in retirement has many benefits for women, not the least being in terms of their physical and mental health and their degree of satisfaction with retirement. While some women engage in behaviours that are detrimental to their wellbeing, the great majority take advantage of this stage of life in order to pursue a wide range of leisure activities. If anything, research suggests that women are more active than men, especially in pursuits that enhance social communication and reduce isolation. Although retirees continue with pre-retirement leisure pastimes, women are more likely than men to seek new ways of engagement when freed from work. Certainly, most women in our study seemed to regard retirement as an active, busy phase of life rather than one in which they gave in to ageing and loss of function.

8

ACCENTUATE THE POSITIVE

Like life itself, retirement is what you make it.

Remember you are in control of your life – you make the decisions – you are not a victim.

I believe it is important to have a positive attitude to this stage of life, be open to change and to keep busy.

These comments from three women in our study reveal a positive, optimistic approach to the future, reflecting agency rather than a passive acceptance of retirement as simply opting out. In fact, as we have seen in earlier chapters, attitudes to retirement have changed. No longer does retirement signal the end of a productive life; rather, it is the opening of a new chapter of experiences for many people. One writer labels retirement as 'the possibility years' – neither a perpetual vacation nor an inevitable surrender to diminished resources and declining health.

Our study participants were keen to offer advice emphasising these possibilities to other women considering retirement. They took issue with society's negative stereotypes about retirement and ageing. Retirement was described as a 'legitimate position' by one; another asked that we find 'an alternative word, as "retirement"/ "retired" does not explain how I spend the rest of my life'. A recurring theme was the need to 'fight the stereotypes and misinformation in society about ageing'. Some wrote about their perception that society places no value on older people and the contribution that they can make. An earlier research focus in which ageing was generally associated with ill health, incapacity and dependency tended to reinforce these ageist stereotypes (Australian Psychological Society, 2000). More recently, there has been a different focus, which stresses the maintenance of good health and a purposeful lifestyle.

Accentuate the positive **113**

There is now considerable evidence that attitude to retirement – and perception of the attitudes of others – makes a difference to retirees' functioning. Holding negative stereotypes is associated with poorer retirement outcomes, including worsening physical functioning and memory (e.g. Hess and Hinson, 2006; Levy *et al.*, 2012; Sargent-Cox *et al.*, 2012). Illustrating this is an interesting experiment by Levy *et al.* (2014) who attempted to overcome ageist stereotypes in older individuals and explore the effects of this on wellbeing. They found significant improvement in the physical functioning of people aged between 60 and 90 years when they were subliminally presented with positive stereotypes of ageing across four one-week intervals. Even more powerfully, a longitudinal study of retirees by Lakra *et al.* (2012) examined whether attitudes towards retirement could impact longevity. They followed 394 participants for 23 years. Participants with positive attitudes towards retirement at the start of the study lived significantly longer than those who did not share these attitudes. This survival advantage remained after controlling for age, functional health, socio-economic status, and whether employed or retired. A similar benefit was reported in a different study by Ng *et al.* (2016). Importantly, Lakra *et al.* concluded that 'psychological planning for retirement is as important as the more traditional forms of planning'. By 'psychological planning' the researchers were referring to retirees adjusting their mental attitudes towards ageing and viewing the possibilities of these senior years more positively and proactively.

The negative impact that stereotypes have on ageing and retirement is a fitting background to the introduction of a relatively new branch of psychology that has great possibilities for developing a well-lived retirement.

Positive psychology and retirement

Patricia Edgar and Don Edgar (2017) argue that late middle age can be a time during which we capitalise on all we have experienced and learnt. Living longer means that we need to rethink our responsibility for looking after ourselves and contributing to society beyond our 50s and 60s. Their book uses recent research to explore opportunities and impediments to productive ageing. Research into longevity shows clearly that those who age successfully have enjoyed fulfilling lives. They have used their later years well, continuing a 'purposeful' life and being resilient in times of hardship.

We know that wellbeing is tied to having meaning and purpose in life, to having a reason to get out of bed for every day. A positive attitude is correlated with happiness, health and better relationships, as are activities that contribute to one's sense of generativity such as volunteering, helping others, mentoring and active grandparenting. Those who view ageing as a negative process, believing, for example, that they are no longer useful, experience poorer outcomes than those who perceive their senior years more confidently, focusing more on what they can do rather than what they cannot.

The title of this chapter suggests that retirees should 'accentuate the positive', taking on board an emphasis on positive thinking, as have researchers in the past

114 Accentuate the positive

two decades. Positive psychology is a theoretical approach to research that seeks to explain how healthy people can achieve richer and fuller life experiences (Seligman and Csikszentmihalyi, 2000). Asebedo and Seay (2014) used this framework to examine retirement satisfaction among a sample of over 5,000 retirees. They drew on Seligman's wellbeing theory and operationalised wellbeing as five elements: positive emotion (being optimistic); engagement (maintaining interest in the world); relationship quality; sense of meaning/purpose in life; and perceived mastery/accomplishment (Seligman, 2012). Retirement satisfaction was associated with dispositional optimism, feelings of perceived mastery and accomplishment, maintenance of a purpose in life, and family support. The authors noted the importance of encouragement and development of these positive characteristics as part of educational programmes and counselling strategies for retirees and those making the transition to retirement.

Other examples of positive psychology approaches have been demonstrated within the literature, although not necessarily embedded in Seligman's theoretical work (Burr et al., 2011; Donaldson et al., 2010; Kim and Moen, 2002). For example, Kim and Moen (2002) assessed both wellbeing (via a morale scale) and ill being (depression) among New York retirees. Their finding that women in their sample entered retirement with more depressive symptoms and lower morale than men is worrying. However, those women who did experience higher levels of retirement wellbeing were also those with a stronger sense of personal control, better quality marital relationships, and greater awareness of good health. Donaldson et al. also found personal mastery (the degree to which one feels a general sense of control over what goes on in his or her life) positively influenced adjustment to retirement within a sample of semi-retired and retired Australian men and women aged 45 years and older. These findings once again suggest the potential for pre-retirement education and counselling that emphasises positive and proactive approaches to maintaining good morale in one's senior years.

The power of mindset to influence physical and mental health is dramatically illustrated by the research of Ellen Langer, who studies mindfulness and its beneficial effects on wellbeing. In her early book, *Mindfulness* (1989), Langer explained that we are 'mindless' when we treat information in a rigid way, as though it were true regardless of the circumstances. When we are 'mindful', we are open to surprise, present-oriented, aware of context, and able to think beyond old mindsets. Although Langer has contributed a large body of highly original experiments to the study of mindfulness, one innovative study is particularly relevant here, because the participants were elderly (and presumably retired) (Langer, 2009). Langer was interested in whether it was possible to turn back the clock physically. Drawing on landmark work in the field and her own experiments, she described her 'counter-clockwise' (or 'reverse ageing') study, in which elderly men lived for a week as though it was 1959, dressing in 50s clothes, eating 50s food, sleeping in a room decorated in 50s style, etc. They showed dramatic improvements in their hearing, memory, dexterity, appetite, and general wellbeing. Cued by stimuli reminiscent of their youth, it seems that they were able to behave more like their younger selves.

Langer stresses the need to be aware of the ways we mindlessly react to social and cultural cues (such as ageist stereotypes) and she challenges the idea that the limits we impose on ourselves are real. She argues that with only subtle shifts in our thinking, language, and expectations we can begin to change the ingrained behaviours that sap health, optimism and vitality from our lives.

The conclusion from these studies is that positive psychology has considerable relevance for retirees' wellbeing and that the elements comprising Seligman's (2012) theory are worthy of further study in determining the social and personal factors that influence the 'good' retired life. We have seen in earlier chapters the importance of some of these elements such as family support; we now need to focus on internalised factors such as dispositional optimism, perceived mastery or control, and sense of generativity. One variable that as far as we know has never been researched in relation to retirement adjustment and health is perceived appearance. Given the role appearance plays in women's life satisfaction, it would not be surprising if those women who most strongly mourned their loss of youthful appearance found retirement adjustment more difficult. Relevant here is another of Langer's interesting studies that potentially points in this direction (Hsu et al., 2010). Among a sample of 47 women aged between 27 and 83 years visiting the hairdresser for a cut or colour, those who thought their new hairdo made them look younger actually experienced reduced blood pressure. The possible implications of both 'the hair salon study' and 'the reverse ageing study' are tantalising, but clearly more rigorous research is needed to examine these phenomena further.

Temporal focus can influence retirement satisfaction

> As I tend to live in the present and don't worry about the future too much, I did not carefully plan my retirement but let it happen.

In Chapter 1, we wrote how an individual's perceived time perspective could influence their motivational priorities, and in Chapter 4, time perspective was discussed in relation to retirement planning. It is fitting that we revisit the relevance of time perspectives to retirees' wellbeing in some detail in this final chapter. Individuals' views of the past, present and future and how this affects their attitudes, morale and behaviour has, in fact, been of interest to researchers for 70 years or more (for recent examples, see Bal et al., 2010; Kerry and Embretson, 2018).

Research shows that as we age, there is a shift in time perspectives with, at retirement age, a focus on the present and the future. Strough et al., (2016) suggest that older people's emotional wellbeing stems from having a limited future time perspective that motivates them to maximise wellbeing in the here and now. Interestingly, they found that during middle age individuals focused more on opportunities in the future than on limited time, but at around the age of 60 years, the balance changed. Increasingly, people focused more on limited time and less on future opportunities, even when factors such as perceived health and retirement status were taken into account. In one of the few studies that reported gender differences, Strough *et al.* found that at all ages women concentrated more on future opportunities and men on limited time. An emphasis on future opportunities was associated with reporting less preoccupation about negative events; focusing on limited time was associated with reporting more preoccupation with such events.

Zimabardo's early conceptual model (Zimbardo and Boyd, 1999), discussed in Chapter 4, has been subsequently extended. Boniwell and Zimbardo (2004) proposed the theoretical concept of Balanced Time Perspective (BTP) as a predictor of wellbeing. BTP is defined as having the mental ability to switch flexibly between temporal orientations to meet the demands of any given situation, rather than having a bias towards a specific perspective that may influence decisions and actions in a negative manner. Zimbardo and Boyd (2008) proposed that in order to maximise wellbeing and maintain good psychological health, it is necessary for people to have a temporal balance. An individual with a balanced time perspective would have mostly positive orientations (past-positive, present-hedonistic, and future) and fewer negative orientations (past-negative and present-fatalistic)

In one of the few studies of retirees that reflects on positive thinking in the context of past, present and future time perspective, Mooney *et al.* (2017) investigated the influence of BTP on retirement planning, defined as planning behaviour during, rather than before, retirement. Mooney *et al.* found that deviation from a balanced time perspective was associated with less retirement planning, as well as with more depression, anxiety, stress and negative mood. They concluded:

> [o]ur findings reveal that older individuals who deviate less from the balanced ideal are happier, report feeling less stressed, less depressed, less anxious, and they are in a more positive mood. They also care about their future more because they actively make more plans than those who are less balanced. ... The results revealed participants with a more balanced temporal view were more likely to be proactive in making plans toward their retirement. ... Thus, we could reliably conclude that having a healthy time balance allows one the ability to alternate between different temporal views of their life, as necessary, in order to put measures in place to ensure they promote or maintain their well-being during their retirement.
>
> *(Ibid., p. 1)*

So, in another example of the power of positive thinking, this study suggests that a positive perspective on one's past, present and future improves planning during retirement and reduces negative aspects of psychological functioning that impede wellbeing.

What do we make of these studies? As a general conclusion it is clear that older people, whether retired or not, who are optimistic about their lives, whose temporal focus is on the present, and who have positive views of their future and past are those who have higher levels of satisfaction and wellbeing.

What factors might mediate these associations? In a study of young people (mean age 20 years), Felsman *et al.* (2017) examined how frequently participants focused on the present throughout the day over the course of one week. They also examined whether being present-oriented predicted improvements in two components of subjective wellbeing over time – how people feel and how satisfied they are with their lives. They found that these young participants were present-focused for two-thirds of the time and that focusing on the present predicted improvements in life satisfaction (but not happiness) over time by reducing rumination (recyclic negative thinking), a known factor in the recurrence of depressed mood (Papageorgiou and Wells, 2004).

> This is consistent with the idea that meaningfully engaging in the world, which requires present focus, promotes life satisfaction. ... [W]e also find evidence that the better we feel, the more likely we are to attend to the present – supporting the idea that when we encounter negative experiences, we are more likely to engage in mental time travel as an emotion regulation strategy (e.g., look forward to when this hard thing is done) – and that the strategies we take in this scenario are very likely to be moderated by age.
>
> *(Felsman, personal communication, 1 April 2018)*

An interesting extension of this study would be to replicate it with a wide range of ages, including retirees, to determine if the benefits of present focus are found among the elderly and those retired.

We do concede that little of the research cited here involves retirees and still less centres on women. Nevertheless, the concepts described above, the value of positive thinking, mindfulness and time perspectives have clear relevance to an older population and to retired women. In fact, this research opens up some exciting possibilities for future researchers and for the development of programmes that maximise retired women's wellbeing and satisfaction with life.

We sum up by inviting retirees to reflect more on positive than negative experiences and to set new goals while also appreciating what we have. This thoughtful response from one study participant captures, in an optimistic way, the challenges in determining the future:

> This is an exciting stage of my life, with not a day to be wasted! However, it feels like uncharted territory. I am challenged to work out what is the purpose of this stage. Some find meaning in self-pleasing activities, travel or grandparenting or voluntary work. ... Given that each individual's choice to allocate meaning to their various activities is valid, where do these choices come from? Do the various choices have different moral or ethical value?

Making the most of retirement

Research shows that many women are not confident in their ability to retire with a comfortable lifestyle. In a major US study, Collinson (2015) found that only 14 per

118 Accentuate the positive

cent were very confident and 40 per cent were not confident that they could do so. Clearly, there is room for advice – from those who have personal experience of retirement and through professionally developed programmes. In this section, we consider the kind of advice offered to female retirees from participants in our study. Many referred to the importance of planning, especially with regard to financial matters:

> Try to be in a better financial position prior to taking retirement so super-annuation could last longer.

> I would never have handed over all my wages to my husband, nor co-signed loans for his business, or become guarantor for anyone. I regret being financially disabled all my married life. Since I retired, I live from pension to pension.

Other women wrote about the need for more general planning and understanding of retirement, beyond the financial aspects:

> I would have sought a far broader understanding of the 'retirement' stage of life, beyond the limited financial planning that is available.

> I would not assume that I knew as much as I thought I did about retirement.

Some specifically addressed the transition to retirement:

> If it were possible to set up some services before retirement and spend a bit more time establishing links with social and community aspects that would survive transition from 'work' to 'retirement'.

> [I] would like better transition to retirement options, recognition of work skills and some commitment by organisations (where possible) beyond paid work to utilise talent.

The need to 'expect the unexpected' was a common theme. While planning for retirement is important, life does not always follow an anticipated path and plans must be flexible enough to accommodate this:

> Sometimes life throws curveballs. No amount of planning can prepare a person for curveballs. The ability to remain flexible, resourceful and true to yourself is key to being able to survive them. Planning my retirement would not have helped me with regard to unexpected violence and trauma … the only thing that helped has been to have faith that good people will come into your life and support you through that transition as best as possible. The danger in 'planning' is it sets up 'expectations'.

Accentuate the positive **119**

As we know, expectations are not always fulfilled. We asked women in our study 'Is your retirement turning out as expected?' Most answered, 'yes' to this question, elaborating on what they had expected. Others said retirement was better than hoped for, or that they had not had any expectations. But a significant number told us that retirement had not lived up to their expectations:

> I had not expected my husband to die. We had planned that … we would retire together.

> I was expecting to travel … but my health will not allow it, nor my financial situation.

> I didn't expect the social isolation – didn't realise how few friends I had outside work.

> No, nothing like what I had planned. Never thought I'd be spending my retirement as a widow.

Sources of advice

As we have seen above, the women in our study were clear about the need for advice about how to retire well. This advice could come from others who have experienced the highs and lows of retirement, from stories in seniors' magazines and other popular literature, and/or from professional programmes designed to ease the path into and during retirement.

Many women in our study took seriously the invitation to provide advice to those about to retire. Commonly cited was enjoy the moment, try new activities, don't delay. Learn how to manage your time, travel, join classes, or volunteer were some of the activities mentioned. Recognise that retirement is a process, not a stage, that follows the end of paid work, so that this period of your life will not be static and unchanging. Below are some examples of women's thoughtful comments, emphasising acceptance, flexibility, positivity and openness to change:

> Accept what is and stay open for new experiences. One never knows where things lead and who one might meet. Accept you will lose contact with some. Accept that it's not because they have forgotten you, they are still working and have little time as you once did. … Embrace new experiences and new folk.

> Do it [retirement] gradually if you can, rather than one day full-time, next day nothing. Be prepared to be flexible and try new things. Plan your trips early because your health might not hold up later. Let yourself get bored occasionally so you can think through what you really want to do with the time you have left.

120 Accentuate the positive

Do things that bring you joy.

However well one has prepared for, or anticipated retirement, it takes time to adjust to a 'new persona' that one becomes. This need not be a negative outcome depending on the satisfaction one experiences in other aspects of one's life.

Fortunately, there are government agencies or organisations that provide assistance for retirees, taking responsibility for various aspects of wellbeing. The US, for example, has a number of national organisations that run educational courses for retirees and seniors. For example, the National Council on Aging provides programmes on healthy ageing, 'ageing mastery', chronic disease management and other relevant topics. The American Association for Retired Persons lobbies and provides assistance for older retired persons but also organises voluntary programmes in which seniors can participate, such as providing mentorship and tutoring to school children. AgeUK offers similar services in Britain, with one of their goals being to tackle loneliness in older people. They do this through helping seniors to connect online as well as running fitness classes and befriending programmes across the country.

Another type of support available in the transition to retirement is the provision of employer-funded outplacement services. An Australian example is Outplacement Australia (www.outplacement.com.au). Their 'transition to retirement' coaching programmes and workshops are designed to offer individuals considering retirement the tools, strategies and pragmatic support they need to confidently deal with the complexities of this important step.

Support of a different kind can be available following retirement, voluntary or involuntary, from highly stressful or otherwise unsafe workplaces. For example, in Victoria, Australia, Retired Peer Support Officers (RPSOs) are former members of the Victoria police force, available to assist any former employee of this organisation who may be experiencing stress, depression, post-traumatic stress disorder or other mental health conditions likely to have arisen in the work environment. RPSOs are trained to recognise various symptoms and problems, and assist their colleagues through listening, understanding, providing appropriate options and assisting with referrals where necessary.

Some employers are taking a share of the responsibility for the mental wellbeing of their staff once they exit the workplace. SuperFriend is an Australian national mental health foundation focused on creating positive, healthy and safe working environments where every employee can be well and thrive. A SuperFriend programme called Mentally Healthy Retirement holds seminars at workplaces for those nearing retirement age (www.superfriend.com.au). The programme aims to help retirees to:

- form realistic expectations about retirement by understanding the link between expectations, satisfaction and wellbeing;

- learn which factors contribute to adjusting well or poorly to retirement;
- understand the importance of planning not just a financially healthy retirement but a mentally healthy one;
- learn strategies to foster wellbeing during retirement.

While most of us will not have had the benefit of such formal programmes, there is a good deal of sound and practical advice in the popular literature aimed at retirees and those about to retire. In addition, the Internet provides a wealth of information which, judiciously used, can be helpful in allaying concerns and indicating ways forward. In a nutshell, this advice focuses on how to manage retirement finances, continuing to use one's skills and talents purposefully, maintaining and developing relationships and social contacts, finding ways to 'give back' to the community, looking after one's health, and actively rejecting the stereotypes of ageing.

What of the future?

Nobel Peace Prize winner, Muhammad Yunus, writing about unemployment, has a warning to offer future generations:

> The problem [of unemployment] is made worse by trends such as automation, the spread of robotic technology, and advances in artificial intelligence, all of which are making it possible for companies to eliminate workers in many fields without diminishing output. In addition, people are living longer, healthier lives, which means they both want and need to work longer to support themselves, putting additional pressure on the employment rolls. It seems likely that in the years to come, politicians and governments will become more and more overwhelmed by the issues of job creation and unemployment management.
>
> *(2017, p. 69)*

What does this mean for the future of retirement? Will people who have jobs stay in them longer so that they can support themselves in this extended old age? Will there be more redundancies as jobs disappear, placing many individuals into early retirement before they are ready? Will part-time work and job sharing become the norm, enabling a greater number of people to remain in the workforce – and potentially allowing for a gentler transition to retirement than the 'cold turkey' approach we discussed in Chapter 1. Specifically, what are the implications for women and retirement?

While Yunus and other writers are no doubt correct about the demise of certain occupations though automation, it is worth remembering that such changes have been ongoing throughout history. Where are today's wheelwrights, barrel makers, rat catchers, leech collectors, spinners and weavers? New jobs are created as society changes, but there are also certain jobs that technology and robots can never

122 Accentuate the positive

replace. Many of these are stereotypically 'women's work' – roles that involve relational skills such as communicating well, empathy and emotional intelligence. Will robots ever replace carers, schoolteachers, nurses, therapists, historians, hairdressers and lifestyle bloggers?

What might happen is that as 'heavy lifting' jobs are phased out occupations may become less gendered. This is already occurring as more men move into nursing and carer positions and more women move into politics and leadership roles. Social changes to gender roles now encourage men to be more involved in childrearing and domestic duties. This (ideally) may lead to both sexes seeking more flexible workplaces and preferring occupational set-ups that allow for a better balance between work and 'life' than traditional full-time work commitments. Perhaps it is time to revisit the quotation with which we began this book – 'a woman's work is never done' – and change it to 'human work is never done'. It's a reminder that in a sense, retirement is but a different phase in the working lives of both women and men, with its own set of tasks, challenges and rewards.

REFERENCES

Agediscrimination.info (2016). *Summary of age discrimination law in Australia, 19 August 2016.* Available at www.agediscrimination.info/international-age-discrimination/australia.

Agediscrimination.info (2017). *News: The latest UK and international age discrimination news from around the web.* Available atwww.agediscrimination.info/news.

AgeUK (2017). *Changes to state pension age.* Available at www.ageuk.org.uk/money-matters/pensions/changes-to-state-pension-age/.

Almenberg, J. and Save-Soderbergh, J. (2011). Financial literacy and retirement planning in Sweden. *Journal of Pension Economics & Finance*, 10(4), 585–598.

American Association of Retired Persons (1991). *Focus your future: a woman's guide to retirement planning.* Washington, DC: American Association for Retired Persons.

American Psychological Association (2017). *Marriage and divorce.* Available at www.apa.org/topics/divorce.

Arrondel, L., Debbich, M. and and Savignac, F. (2013). Financial literacy and financial planning in France. *Numeracy*, 6(2), Article 8.

Asebedo, S. D. and Seay, M. C. (2014). Positive psychological attributes and retirement satisfaction. *Journal of Financial Counseling and Planning*, 25, 161–173.

Atchley, R. C. (1999). *Continuity and adaptation in aging: creating positive experiences.* Baltimore, MD: Johns Hopkins University Press.

Australian Bureau of Statistics (ABS) (2010). *Older people and the labour market* (No.4102.0). Available at www.abs.gov.au/AUSSTATS/abs@.nsf/Lookup/4102.0Main+Features30Sep+2010.

Australian Bureau of Statistics (ABS) (2012). *Fifty years of labour force: now and then* (No. 1301.0). Available at www.abs.gov.au/ausstats/abs@.nsf/Lookup/1301.0Main+Features452012.

Australian Bureau of Statistics (ABS) (2013). *Reflecting a nation: stories from the 2011 census* (No. 2071.0). Available at www.abs.gov.au/ausstats/abs@.nsf/Lookup/2071.0main+features902012–902013.

Australian Bureau of Statistics (ABS) (2015). *Disability, ageing and carers, Australia: Summary of findings* (No. 4430). www.abs.gov.au/ausstats/abs@.nsf/mf/4430.0.

Australian Bureau of Statistics (ABS) (2016). *Gender indicators* (No. 4125.0). Available at www.abs.gov.au/ausstats/abs@.nsf/mf/4125.0.

124 References

Australian Bureau of Statistics (ABS) (2017a). *Marriages and divorces* (No. 3310.0). Available at www.abs.gov.au/ausstats/abs@.nsf/mf/3310.0.

Australian Bureau of Statistics (ABS) (2017b). *Retirement and Retirement Intentions, Australia, July 2016 to June 2017* (No. 6238). Available at www.abs.gov.au/ausstats/abs@.nsf/Latestproducts/6238.0.

Australian Communications and Media Authority (2016). *Digital lives of older Australians.* Available at https://www.acma.gov.au/theACMA/engage-blogs/engage-blogs/Research-snapshots/Digital-lives-of-older-Australians.

Australian Feminist Judgments Project (2012). *Sexually transmitted/emotionally transmitted debt.* St Lucia: TC Beirne School of Law, University of Queensland. Available at https://law.uq.edu.au/files/5954/STD.pdf.

Australian Government Department of Human Services (2017). *Age pension.* Available at https://www.humanservices.gov.au/customer/services/centrelink/age-pension.

Australian Human Rights Commission (2009). *Accumulating poverty? Women's experiences of inequality over the lifecycle.* Sydney: Australian Human Rights Commission. Available atwww.humanrights.gov.au/our-work/sex-discrimination/publications/accumulating-poverty-women-s-experiences-inequality-over.

Australian Human Rights Commission (2014). *Face the facts: older Australians.* Sydney: Australian Human Rights Commission. Available at www.humanrights.gov.au/sites/default/files/FTFOlderAustralians.pdf.

Australian Law Reform Commission (2012). Recruitment and employment law. *In Grey areas: age barriers to work in Commonwealth Laws* (no. 78). Available at www.alrc.gov.au/publications/2-recruitment-and-employment-law/compulsory-retirement.

Australian Psychological Society (2000). *Psychology and ageing: a position paper prepared for the Australian Psychological Society (APS).* Melbourne: Directorate of Social Issues, APS.

Australian Securities and Investments Commission (2015). *Australian financial attitudes and behaviour tracker wave 3: March–August 2015.* Available at www.financialliteracy.gov.au/research-and-evaluation/financial-attitudes-and-behaviour-tracker.

Avital, D. (2017). Gender differences in leisure patterns at age 50 and above: micro and macro aspects. *Ageing & Society*, 37(1), 139–166.

Bajtelsmit, V. L. and Bernasek, A. (1996). Why do women invest differently than men? *Financial Counselling and Planning*, 7, 1–10.

Bal, P. M., De Jong, S. B., Jansen, P. G. W. and Bakker, A. B. (2012). Motivating employees to work beyond retirement: a multilevel study of the role of i-deals and unit climate: I-deals and continuing working. *Journal of Management Studies*, 49(2), 306–331.

Bal, P. M., Jansen, P. G. W., van der Velde, M. E. G., de Lange, A. H. and Rousseau, D. M. (2010). The role of future time perspective in psychological contracts: a study among older workers. *Journal of Vocational Behavior*, 76, 474–486.

Bamber, M., Allen-Collinson, J. and McCormack, J. (2017). Occupational limbo, transitional liminality and permanent liminality: new conceptual distinctions. *Human Relations*, 70(12), 1514–1537.

Bamburger, P. A. (2015). Winding down and boozing up: the complex link between retirement and alcohol misuse. *Journal of Work, Aging and Retirement*, 1(1), 92–111.

Bannier, C. E. and Neubert, M. (2006). Gender differences in financial risk taking: the role of financial literacy and risk tolerance. *Economics Letters*, 145, 130–135.

Barbosa, L. M., Monteiro, L. and Murta, S. G. (2016). Retirement adjustment predictors: a systematic review. *Work, Aging and Retirement*, 2(2), 262–280.

Barnes, H. and Parry, J. (2004). Renegotiating identity and relationships: men and women's adjustments to retirement. *Ageing & Society*, 24(2), 213–233.

References 125

Barnes-Farrell, J. L. (2003). Beyond health and wealth: attitudinal and other influences on retirement decision-making. In G. A. Adams and T. A. Beehr (eds), *Retirement: Reasons, processes, and results.* New York: Springer Publishing Co, pp. 159–187.

Baxter, J. and Chesters, J. (2011). Perceptions of work-family balance: how effective are family-friendly policies? *Australian Journal of Labour Economics*, 14(2), 139–151.

Behncke, S. (2009). *How does retirement affect health?* (Discussion Paper No. 4253). Available at http://ftp.iza.org/dp4253.pdf.

Belbase, A., Khan, M. R., Munnell, A. H. and Webb, A. (2015). *Slowed or sidelined? The effect of 'normal' cognitive decline on job performance among the elderly* (no. 2015–2012). Chestnut Hill, MA: Center for Retirement Research at Boston College.

Bennetts, L. (2012). Census data reveals elder women's poverty crisis. *The Daily Beast.* 28 March. Available at www.thedailybeast.com/census-data-reveals-elder-womens-poverty-crisis.

Bevan, M. (2010). Retirement lifestyles in a niche housing market: park-home living in England. *Ageing & Society*, 30(6), 965–985.

Bianchi, S. M., Milkie, M. A., Sayer, L. C. and Robinson, J. P. (2000). Is anyone doing the housework? Trends in the gender division of household labor. *Social Forces*, 79(1), 191–228.

Bjornsdottir, G., Amadottir, S. A. and Halldorsdottir, S. (2012). Facilitators of and barriers to physical activity in retirement communities: experiences of older women in urban areas. *Physical Therapy*, 92, 551–562.

Blair-Loy, M., Hochschild, A., Pugh, A. J., Williams, J. C. and Hartmann, H. (2015). Stability and transformation in gender, work, and family: insights from the second shift for the next quarter century. *Community, Work & Family*, 18(4), 435–454.

Boniwell, I. and Zimbardo, P. G. (2004). Balancing time perspective in pursuit of optimal functioning. In P. A. Linley and S. Joseph (eds), *Positive psychology in practice.* Hoboken: Wiley, pp. 165–178.

Borrero, L. and Kruger, T. M. (2015). The nature and meaning of identity in retired professional women. *Journal of Women & Aging*, 27(4), 309–329.

Briggs, H. (2014). Mothers' average age hits 30. Available at www.bbc.com/news/health-28329737.

Bronfenbrenner, U. (1979). *The ecology of human development: experiments by nature and design.* Cambridge, MA: Harvard University Press.

Brown, M. and Graf, N. (2013). Financial literacy and retirement planning in Switzerland. *Numeracy*, 6(2), Article 6.

Brown, S. and Coventry, L. (1997). *Queen of Hearts: the needs of women with gambling problems.* Melbourne: Financial and Consumer Right Council.

Browning, C. J., Enticott, J. C., Thomas, S. A. and Kendig, H. (2017). Trajectories of ageing well among older Australians: a 16-year longitudinal study. *Ageing & Society*, 1–22.

Bucher-Koenen, T., Lusardi, A., Alessie, R. J. M. and van Rooij, M. C. J. (2016). *How financially literate are women? An overview and new insights* (No. 2016–2011). Available at http://gflec.org/wp-content/uploads/2016/02/WP-2016-1-How-Financially-Literate-Are-Women.pdf.

Buhlmann, F., Elcheroth, G. and Tettamanti, T. (2010). The division of labour among European couples: the effects of life course and welfare policy on value–practice configurations. *European Sociology Review*, 26(1), 49–66.

Burnes, D., Henderson, C. R., Sheppard, C. and Lachs, M. S. (2017). Prevalence of financial fraud and scams among older adults in the United States: a systematic review and meta-analysis. *American Journal of Public Health*, 107(8), 1295.

Burr, A., Santo, J. B. and Pushkar, D. (2011). Affective well-being in retirement: the influence of values, money, and health across three years. *Journal of Happiness Studies*, 12, 17–40.

126 References

Byles, J., Tavener, M., Robinson, I., Parkinson, L., Smith, P. W., Stevenson, D., Leigh, L. and Curryer, C. (2013). Transforming retirement: new definitions of life after work. *Journal of Women & Aging*, 25(1), 24–44.

Byrnes, J. P., Miller, D. C. and Schafer, W. D. (1999). Gender differences in risk taking: a meta-analysis. *Psychological Bulletin*, 125(3), 367–383.

Cahill, K. E., Giandrea, M. D. and Quinn, J. F. (2015). Retirement patterns and the macro-economy, 1992–2010: the prevalence and determinants of bridge jobs, phased retirement, and reentry among three recent cohorts of older Americans. *The Gerontologist*, 55(3), 384–403.

Calvo, E. (2006). *Does working longer make people healthier and happier?* (WOB No. 2). Chestnut Hill, MA: Center for Retirement Research at Boston College. Available athttp://crr.bc.edu/briefs/does-working-longer-make-people-healthier-and-happier/.

Calvo, E., Sarkisian, N. and Tamborini, C. R. (2013). Causal effects of retirement timing on subjective physical and emotional health. *Journals of Gerontology, Series B: Psychological Sciences and Social Sciences*, 68(1), 73–84.

Carbone, S. (2016). Senior citizens working full time in their 80s and 90s are not the retiring type. *The Age*. 28 April. Available at www.theage.com.au/victoria/senior-citizens-working-full-time-in-their-80s-and-90s-are-not-the-retiring-type-20160427-gogrcm.html.

Carriero, R. (2011). Perceived fairness and satisfaction with the division of housework among dual-earner couples in Italy. *Marriage & Family Review*, 47(7), 436–458.

Carstensen L. L. (2006). The influence of a sense of time on human development. *Science*, 312(5782), 1913–1915.

Catalyst (2017). *Women CEOs of the S&P 500*. Available at www.catalyst.org/knowledge/women-ceos-sp-500.

Centers for Disease Control and Prevention (2015). *Births and natality*. Available at www.cdc.gov/nchs/fastats/births.htm.

Charles, M. (2003). Deciphering sex segregation: vertical and horizontal inequalities in ten national labor markets. *Acta Sociologica*, 46(4), 267–287.

Charness, G. and Gneezy, U. (2012). Strong evidence for gender differences in risk taking. *Journal of Economic Behavior & Organization*, 83(1), 50–58.

Christelis, D., Jappelli, T. and Padula, M. (2010). Cognitive abilities and portfolio choice. *European Economic Review*, 54(1), 18–38.

Coan, V., Calasanti, T. and Carr, D. C. (2016). Gender and life satisfaction in retirement: recent findings from the HRS. *The Gerontologist*, 56(Suppl. 3), 625–626.

Cohen, P. N. and Bianchi, S. M. (1999). Marriage, children, and women's employment: what do we know? *Monthly Labor Review*, 122, 22–31.

Collard, S. (2009). *Individual investment behaviour: a brief review of research*. Available at http://citeseerx.ist.psu.edu/viewdoc/download?doi=10.1.1.323.4768&rep=rep1&type=pdf.

Collinson, C. (2015). *Fifteen facts about women's retirement outlook: select findings from the 15th Annual Transamerica Retirement Survey of Workers*. Available at www.transamericacenter. org/docs/default-source/resources/women-and-retirement/tcrs2015_sr_womens_retirem ent_outlook.pdf.

Colombo, F., Llena-Nozal, A., Mercier, J. and Tjadens, F. (2011). The impact of caring on family carers. In *Help wanted? Providing and paying for long-term care*. Paris: OECD Publishing, pp. 85–120. Available athttp://dx.doi.org/10.1787/9789264097759-en.

Commonwealth of Australia (1998). *Equal pay handbook*. Available at www.humanrights.gov. au/sites/default/files/content/pdf/sex_discrim/equal_pay.pdf.

Commonwealth of Australia (2016). *'A husband is not a retirement plan': achieving economic security for women in retirement*. Available at www.aph.gov.au/Parliamentary_Business/Committees/Senate/Economics/Economic_security_for_women_in_retirement/Report.

References **127**

Craig, L. (2007). Is there a second shift, and if so, who does it? A time-diary investigation. *Feminist Review*, 86(1), 149–170.

Crisp, D. A., Windsor, T. D., Butterworth, P. and Anstey, K. J. (2013). What are older adults seeking? Factors encouraging or discouraging retirement village living. *Australasian Journal on Ageing*, 32, 163–170.

Culberson, J. W. and Ziska, M. (2008). Prescription drug misuse/abuse in the elderly. *Geriatrics*, 63, 22–26.

Cussen, M. P. (2018). Journey through the six stages of retirement. *Investopedia*. 20 January. Available at www.investopedia.com/articles/retirement/07/sixstages.asp.

Cutler, D. M., Meara, E. and Richards-Shubik, S. (2011). *Healthy life expectancy: estimates and implications for retirement age policy*. Available at www.nber.org/aging/rrc/papers/orrc10-11.pdf.

Damaske, S. andFrech, A. (2016). Women's work pathways across the life course. *Demography*, 53(2), 365–391.

Damman, M. and van Duijn, R. (2017). Intergenerational support in the transition from work to retirement. *Work, Aging and Retirement*, 3(1), 66–76.

Damman, M., Henkens, K. and Kalmijn, M. (2015). Women's retirement intentions and behavior: the role of childbearing and marital histories. *European Journal of Population*, 31(4), 339–363.

Dare, J., Wilkinson, C., Allsop, S., Waters, S. and McHale, S. (2014). Social engagement, setting and alcohol use among a sample of older Australians. *Health & Social Care in the Community*, 22, 524–532.

Darzins, P., Lowndes, G. and Wainer, J. (2009). *Financial abuse of elders: a review of the evidence*. Victoria: Monash University. Available atwww.eapu.com.au/uploads/research_resources/VIC-Financial_Elder_Abuse_Evidence_Review_JUN_209-Monash.pdf.

Davaki, K. (2016). *Differences in men's and women's work, care and leisure time*. Available at www.europarl.europa.eu/RegData/etudes/STUD/2016/556933/IPOL_STU(2016) 556933_EN.pdf.

Dave, D., Rashad, I. and Spasojevic, J. (2008). The effects of retirement on physical and mental health outcomes. *Southern Economic Journal*, 75(2), 497–523.

De Preter, H., Van Looy, D., Mortelmans, D. and Denaeghel, K. (2013). Retirement timing in Europe: the influence of individual work and life factors. *Social Science Journal*, 50(2), 145–151.

Dentinger, E. and Clarkberg, M. (2002). Informal caregiving and retirement timing among men and women gender and caregiving relationships in late midlife. *Journal of Family Issues*, 23(7), 857–879.

Department of Communities and Local Government (2017). *Review of park homes legislation*. Available at www.gov.uk/government/consultations/review-of-park-homes-legislation-call-for-evidence.

Desmette, D. and Gaillard, M. (2008). When a 'worker' becomes an 'older worker': the effects of age-related social identity on attitudes towards retirement and work. *Career Development International*, 13(2), 168–185.

Donaldson, T., Earl, J. K. and Muratore, A. M. (2010). Extending the integrated model of retirement adjustment: incorporating mastery and retirement planning. *Journal of Vocational Behavior*, 77, 279–289.

Dow, B. and Meyer, C. (2010). Caring and retirement: crossroads and consequences. *International Journal of Health Service*, 40, 645–665.

Duberley, J., Carmichael, F. and Szmigin, I. (2014). Exploring women's retirement: continuity, context and career transition. *Gender, Work & Organization*, 21(1), 71–90.

Earl, J. K., Bednall, T. C. and Muratore, A. M. (2015). A matter of time: why some people plan for retirement and others do not. *Work, Aging and Retirement*, 1(2), 181–189.

128 References

Earl, J. K., Gerrans, P. and Halim, V. A. (2015). Active and adjusted: investigating the contribution of leisure, health and psychosocial factors to retirement adjustment. *Leisure Sciences*, 37, 354–372.

Economics References Committee (2016). *'A husband is not a retirement plan': achieving economic security for women in retirement.* Available at www.aph.gov.au/Parliamentary_Business/Comm ittees/Senate/Economics/Economic_security_for_women_in_retirement/Report.

Edgar, P. and Edgar, D. (2017). Peak: reinventing middle age. Melbourne: Text Publishing.

Eisenberg, R. (2016). Retirement life: men and women do it very differently. Available atwww.forbes.com/sites/nextavenue/2016/04/20/retirement-life-women-and-men-do-it-very-differently/#4eb395bb3dd8.

Ekerdt, D. J. (2010). Frontiers of research on work and retirement. *Journals of Gerontology, Series B: Psychological Sciences and Social Sciences.* 65B(1), 69–80.

Ellis, K. (2017). Letter to constituents in the Australian Federal seat of Adelaide.

Erikson, E. H. (1963). *Childhood and society.* New York: Norton.

Eurofound (2013). *Women, men and working conditions in the European Union.* Luxemburg: Publications Office of the European Union.

European Institute for Gender Equality (2014). *Gender equality and economic independence: Part-time work and self employment.* Luxembourg: Publications Office of the European Union. Available athttp://eige.europa.eu/rdc/eige-publications/gender-equality-and-eco nomic-independence-part-time-work-and-self-employment-report.

European Institute for Gender Equality (2015). *Women and men in decision-making* (database). Available at http://eige.europa.eu/gender-statistics/dgs/browse/wmidm.

Eurostat (2017). *Internet access and use statistics.* Available at http://ec.europa.eu/eurostat/statistics-explained/index.php/Internet_access_and_use_statistics_-households_and_individuals.

Even, W. E. and Macpherson, D. A. (2009). Managing risk caused by pension investments in company stock. *National Tax Journal*, 62(3), 439–453.

Everingham, C., Warner-Smith, P. andByles, J. (2007). Transforming retirement: re-thinking models of retirement to accommodate the experiences of women. *Women's Studies International Forum*, 30(6), 512–522.

Ewert, H., Adams, J., Price, D., Pike, T. M., Corna, L. M., Platts, L. G. and Glaser, G. (2016). *How do gender differences in lifecourses affect income in retirement?* (Briefing Note. 92). Available at www.pensionspolicyinstitute.org.uk/briefing-notes/briefing-note-92—how-do-gender-differences-in-lifecourses-affect-income-in-retirement.

Feldman, D. C. and Beehr, T. A. (2011). A three-phase model of retirement decision making. *American Psychologist*, 66(3), 193–203.

Felsman, P., Verduyn, P., Ayduk, O. and Kross, E. (2017). Being present: focusing on the present predicts improvements in life satisfaction but not happiness. *Emotion*, 17(7), 1047–1051.

Finch, N. (2014). Why are women more likely than men to extend paid work? The impact of work-family life history. *European Journal of Ageing*, 11(1), 31–39.

Fisher, G. G., Chaffee, D. S. and Sonnega, A. (2016). Retirement timing: a review and recommendations for future research. *Work, Aging and Retirement*, 2(2), 230–261.

Floyd, F. J., Haynes, S. N., Doll, E. R., Winemiller, D., Lemsky, C., Burgy, T. M., Werle, M. and Heilman, N. (1992). Assessing retirement satisfaction and perceptions of retirement experiences. *Psychology and Aging*, 7(4), 609–621.

Fondow, M. andEmery, C. (2008). Effects of retirement on health among men and women in the health and retirement study. *Annals of Behavioral Medicine*, 35(S1), S68.

Food and Agriculture Organization of the United Nations (2013). *The state of food and agriculture.* Available at www.fao.org/publications/sofa/the-state-of-food-and-agriculture/en/.

Forette, F., Salord, J-C. and Brieu, A-M. (n.d.). *Living longer, working longer: a French challenge*. Available at www.ilc-alliance.org/images/uploads/publication-pdfs/Article_living_longer_working_longer.pdf.

Forman-Hoffman, V., Richardson, K. K., Yankey, J. W., Hillis, S. L., Wallace, R. B. and Wolinsky, F. D. (2008). Retirement and weight changes among men and women in the Health and Retirement Study. *Journals of Gerontology, Series B: Psychological Sciences and Social Sciences*, 63(3), S146–153.

Fraser, I. (2017). Sisters are doing it for themselves: the retired women who built their own community. *The Telegraph*. 31 May. Available at www.telegraph.co.uk.

Gardner, I. L., Browning, C. and Kendig, H. (2005). Accommodation options in later life: retirement village or community living? *Australasian Journal on Ageing*, 24, 188–195.

Gershuny, J. and Sullivan, O. (2014). Household structure and housework: assessing the contributions of all household members, with a focus on children and youths. *Review of Economics of the Household*, 12(1), 7–27.

Geyer, S., Spreckelsen, O. and von dem Knesebeck, O. (2014). Wealth, income, and health before and after retirement. *Journal of Epidemiology and Community Health*, 68(11), 1080–1087.

Gibbins, D. (1996). *Equity in the Australian Public Service: a change of focus*. Paper presented at the Australian Institute of Criminology Conference, First Australasian Women Police Conference, Sydney. July. Available at www.aic.gov.au/media_library/conferences/poli cewomen/gibbins.pdf.

Global Financial Literacy Excellence Center (2017). *Women and financial literacy: OECD/ INFE evidence, survey and policy responses report*. Available at www.oecd.org/daf/fin/financial-education/TrustFund2013_OECD_INFE_Women_and_Fin_Lit.pdf.

Golladay, C. (2016). Schwab survey finds major differences in how male and female millenials view retirement. Younger women worry more about money than health. *Business Wire*. 15 November. Available at www.businesswire.com/news/home/20161115005264/en/Schwab-Survey.

Gonzales, E., Lee, Y. and Brown, C. (2017). Back to work? Not everyone. Examining the longitudinal relationships between informal caregiving and paid work after formal retirement. *Journals of Gerontology. Series B: Psychological Sciencesand Social Sciences*, 72(3), 532–539.

GOV.UK (2017). *Check your state pension age*. Available at www.gov.uk/state-pension-age.

Grable, J. (2000). Financial risk tolerance and additional factors that affect risk taking in everyday money matters. *Journal of Business and Psychology*, 14(4), 625–630.

Grace, M., Leahy, M. and Doughney, J. (2005). *Response to Striking the Balance: Women, men, work and family*. Available atwww.humanrights.gov.au/sites/default/files/content/sex_dis crimination/publication/strikingbalance/submissions/114.doc.

Grant, B. F., Dawson, D. A., Stinson, F. S., Chou, S. P., Dufour, M. C. and Pickering, R. P. (2004). The 12-month prevalence and trends in DSM-IV alcohol abuse and dependence: United States, 1991–1992 and 2001–2002. *Drug and Alcohol Dependence*, 74(3), 223–234.

Greenfield, E. A. and Marks, N. F. (2003). Volunteering as a moderator of the mental health effects of role-identity absence in older adulthood: Evidence from MIDUS. Poster presented at the annual meeting of the Gerontological Society of America, San Diego, CA.

Greenfield, E. A. and Marks, N. F. (2004). Formal volunteering as a protective factor for older adults' psychological well-being. *Journals of Gerontology, Series B: Psychological Sciences and Social Sciences*, 59(5), S258–264.

Griffin, B., Hesketh, B. and Loh, V. (2012). The influence of subjective life expectancy on retirement transition and planning: a longitudinal study. *Journal of Vocational Behavior*, 81(2), 129–137.

130 References

Grigoryeva, A. (2014). *When gender trumps everything: the division of parent care among siblings* (Working Paper No. 9). Available at www.princeton.edu/csso/working-papers/WP9-Grigoryeva.pdf.

Gustman, A. L. and Steinmeier, T. L. (2005). The social security early entitlement age in a structural model of retirement and wealth. *Journal of Public Economics*, 89(2–3), 441–463.

Hakim, C. (1995). Five feminist myths about women's employment. *British Journal of Sociology*, 46(3), 429–455.

Hakim, C. (2005). Sex differences in work-life balance goals. In D. Houston (ed.), *Work-life balance in the twenty-first century*. London: Palgrave Macmillan, pp. 55–79.

Hakim, C. (2006). Women, careers, and work-life preferences. *British Journal of Guidance & Counselling*, 34(3), 279–294.

Hakim, C. (2011). Women's lifestyle preferences in the 21st century: implications for family policy. In G. Beets, J. Schippers and E. R. Te Velde (eds), *The future of motherhood in western societies: late fertility and its consequences*. Dordrecht: Springer, pp. 177–195.

Harris, C. R., Jenkins, M. and Glaser, D. (2006). Gender differences in risk assessment: why do women take fewer risks than men? *Judgment and Decision Making*, 1(1), 48–63.

Hawkley, L. C. and Cacioppo, J. T. (2007). Aging and loneliness. *Current Directions in Psychological Science*, 16(4), 187–191.

Hawkley, L. C., Hughes, M. E., Waite, L. J., Masi, C. M., Thisted, R. A. and Cacioppo, J. T. (2008). From social structural factors to perceptions of relationship quality and loneliness: the Chicago Health, Aging, and Social Relations Study. *Journals of Gerontology, Series B: Psychological Sciences and Social Sciences*, 63(6), S375–384.

Helldan, A., Lalluka, T., Rahkonnen, O. and Lahelma, E. (2012). Changes in healthy food habits after transition to old age retirement. *European Journal of Public Health*, 22 (4), 582–586.

Henkens, K., van Solinge, H. and Gallo, W. T. (2008). Effects of retirement voluntariness on changes in smoking, drinking and physical activity among Dutch older workers. *European Journal of Public Health*, 18(6), 644–649.

Hermansen, A. (2014). Additional leave as the determinant of retirement timing: Retaining older workers in Norway. *Nordic Journal of Working Life Studies, 4*(4), 89–108.

Hershey, D. A. and Henkens, K. (2014). Impact of different types of retirement transitions on perceived satisfaction with life. *The Gerontologist*, 54(2), 232–244.

Hershfield, H. E., Goldstein, D. G., Sharpe, W. F., Fox, J., Yeykelis, L., Carstensen, L. L. and Bailenson, J. N. (2011). Increasing saving behavior through age-progressed renderings of the future self. *Journal of Marketing Research*, 48, S23–37.

Hess, T. M. and Hinson, J. T. (2006). Age-related variation in the influence of aging stereotypes on memory in adulthood. *Psychology and Aging*, 21, 621–625.

Heybroek, L., Haynes, M. and Baxter, J. (2015). Life satisfaction and retirement in Australia: a longitudinal approach. *Work, Aging and Retirement*, 1(2), 166–180.

Hochschild, A. (1989). *The second shift*. New York: Avon Books.

Holdsworth, L., Hing, N. and Breen, H. (2012). Exploring women's problem gambling: a review of the literature. *International Gambling Studies*, 12(2), 199–213.

Holt, A., Lee, A. H., Jancey, J., Kerr, D. and Howat, P. (2016). Are retirement villages promoting active aging? *Journal of Aging and Physical Activity*, 24(3), 407–411.

Holt-Lunstad, J., Smith, T. B. and Layton, J. B. (2010). Social relationships and mortality risk: a meta-analytic review. *PLoS Medicine*, 7(7), e1000316.

Holt-Lunstad, J., Smith, T. B., Baker, M. and Harris, T. (2015). Loneliness and social isolation as risk factors for mortality: a meta-analytic review. *Perspectives on Psychological Science*, 10(2), 227–237.

Horner, B., McManus, A., Comfort, J. and Freiiah, R. (2012). How prepared is the retirement and residential aged care sector in Western Australia for older non-heterosexual people? *Quality in Primary Care*, 20(4), 263–274.

Housewives are a drain on the economy, new research claims, *Herald Sun*, 10 March 2017.

Hsu, L. M., Chung, J. and Langer, E. (2010). The influence of age-related cues on health and longevity. *Perspectives on Psychological Science*, 5, 632–648.

Hudson, F. (1999). *The adult years: mastering the art of re-invention*. San Francisco, CA: Jossey-Bass.

Hung, A., Yoong, J., & Brown, E. (2012). *Empowering women through financial awareness and education*. Available at www.wikigender.org/wp-content/uploads/files/EmpoweringWomenThroughFinancialAwareness.pdf.

Isaksson, K. and Johansson, G. (2000). Adaptation to continued work and early retirement following downsizing: long-term effects and gender differences. *Journal of Occupational and Organizational Psychology*, 73(2), 241–256.

Jacobs, J. C., Laporte, A., Van Houtven, C. H. and Coyte, P. C. (2014). Caregiving intensity and retirement status in Canada. *Social Science & Medicine*, 102, 74–82.

Jahoda, M. (1997). Manifest and latent functions. In N. Nicholson (ed.), *The Blackwell encyclopedic dictionary of organizational psychology*. Oxford: Blackwell, pp. 317–318.

Jahoda, M., Lazarsfeld, P. and Zeisel, H. (2002). *Marienthal: the sociography of an unemployed community*. Piscataway, NJ: Transaction Publishers.

Janda, M. (2013). Average retirement age rising as Australians live longer, Australian Bureau of Statistics figures show. ABC News. 10 December. Available at www.abc.net.au/news/2013-12-10/figures-show-retirement-age-rising-with-life-expectancy/5146928.

Jaumont-Pascual, N., Monteagudo, M. J., Kleiber, D. A. and Cuenca, J. (2016). Gender differences in meaningful leisure following major later life events. *Journal of Leisure Research, 48*(1), 83–103.

Jean Hailes (2017). *Women's health survey 2017*. South Melbourne: Jean Hailes Foundation. Available at https://jeanhailes.org.au/survey2017/report_2017.pdf.

Jefferson, T. (2009). Women and retirement pensions: a research review. *Feminist Economics*, 15(4), 115–145.

Johnstone, M. and Lee, C. (2009). Young Australian women's aspirations for work and family: individual and sociocultural differences. *Sex Roles*, 61(3–4), 204–220.

Jokela, M., Ferrie, J. E., Gimeno, D., Chandola, T., Shipley, M. J., Head, J. and Kivimäki, M. (2010). From midlife to early old age: health trajectories associated with retirement. *Epidemiology*, 21(3), 284–290.

Jolly, S., Griffith, K., DeCastro, R., Stewart, A., Ubel, P. and Jagsi, R. (2014). Gender differences in time spent on parenting and domestic responsibilities by high-achieving young physician-researchers. *Annals of Internal Medicine*, 160(5), 344–353.

Kahneman, D. and Tversky, A. (1979). Prospect theory: an analysis of decision under risk. *Econometrica*, 47(2), 263–292.

Kang, T. and Hoffman, L. H. (2011). Why would you decide to use an online dating site? Factors that lead to online dating. *Communication Research Reports*, 28(3), 205–213.

Kendig, H., Gong, C. H., Cannon, L. and Browning, C. (2017). Preferences and predictors of aging in place: longitudinal evidence from Melbourne, Australia. *Journal of Housing for the Elderly*, 31(3), 259–271.

Kerry, M. J. and Embretson, S. E. (2018). An experimental evaluation of competing age-predictions of future time perspective between workplace and retirement domains. *Frontiers in Psychology*, 8, 2316.

Kim, J. E. and Moen, P. (2002). Retirement transitions, gender, and psychological well-being: a life-course, ecological model. *Journals of Gerontology, Series B: Psychological Sciences and Social Sciences*, 57, 212–222.

132 References

Kim, S. and Feldman, D. C. (1998). Healthy, wealthy, or wise: predicting actual acceptances of early retirement incentives at three points in time. *Personnel Psychology*, 51(3), 623–642.

King, M. (2005). Seniors discover a new way to connect – online. *Seattle Times*. 4 June. Available at www.seattletimes.com/seattle-news/seniors-discover-new-way-to-connect-8212-online/.

Kiso, H. and Hershey, D. A. (2017). Working adults' metacognitions regarding financial planning for retirement. *Work, Aging and Retirement*, 3(1), 77–88.

Knoll, M. A. Z. (2011). Behavioral and psychological aspects of the retirement decision. *Social Security Bulletin*, 71(4), 15–32.

Koenig, T. L. and Crisp, C. (2008). Ethical issues in practice with older women who misuse substances. *Substance Use & Misuse*, 43(8–9), 1045–1061.

Kopanidis, F. Z., Robinson, L. J. and Reid, M. (2014). State of inertia: psychological preparation of single Australian and UK baby boomer women for retirement housing change. *Journal of Women & Aging*, 26(3), 280–297.

Kubicek, B., Korunka, C., Raymo, J. M. and Hoonakker, P. (2011). Psychological well-being in retirement: the effects of personal and gendered contextual resources. *Journal of Occupational Health Psychology*, 16(2), 230–246.

Kuerbis A. and SaccoP. (2012). The impact of retirement on the drinking patterns of older adults: a review. *Addictive Behaviors*, 37(5), 587–595.

Lahti, J., Laaksonen, M., Lahelma, E. and Rahkonen, O. (2011). Changes in leisure-time physical activity after transition to retirement: a follow-up study. *International Journal of Behavioral Nutrition and Physical Activity*, 8, 36–44.

Lakra, D. C., Ng, R. and Levy, B. R. (2012). Increased longevity from viewing retirement positively. *Ageing & Society*, 32, 1418–1427.

Langer, E. J. (1989). *Mindfulness*. Reading, MA: Addison-Wesley/Addison Wesley Longman.

Langer, E. J. (2009). *Counterclockwise: mindful health and the power of possibility*. New York: Ballantine Books.

Larsen, M. and Pedersen, P. J. (2008). Pathways to early retirement in Denmark, 1984–2000. *International Journal of Manpower*, 29(5), 384–409.

Lee, Y., Tang, F. Kim, K. H. and Albert, S. M. (2015). Exploring the gender differences in the relationships between eldercare and labor force participation in the U.S.: a longitudinal approach. *Canadian Journal on Aging*, 34(1), 14–58.

Leith, L. (2014). Why do women still earn less than men? *Monthly Labor Review*. Available at www.bls.gov/opub/mlr/2014/beyond-bls/why-do-women-still-earn-less-than-men.htm

Levanon, A., England, P. and Allison, P. (2009). Occupational feminization and pay: assessing causal dynamics using 1950–2000 US census data. *Social Forces*, 88(2), 865–891.

Levy, B. R., Pilver, C., Chung, P. H. and Slade, M. D. (2014). Subliminal strengthening: Improving older individuals' physical function over time with an implicit-age-stereotype intervention. *Psychological Science*, 25, 2127–2135.

Levy, B. R., Slade, M. D., Murphy, T. E. and Gill, T. M. (2012). Association between positive age stereotypes and recovery from disability in older persons. *Journal of the American Medical Association*, 308, 1972–1973.

Lewin, K. (1951). Field theory in the social sciences: selected theoretical papers. New York: Harper.

Lievre, A., Jusot, F., Barnay, T., Sermet, C., Brouard, N., Robine, J. M., Brieu, M. A. and Forette, F. (2007). Healthy working life expectancies at age 50 in Europe: a new indicator. *Journal of Nutrition, Health & Aging*, 11(6), 508–514.

Lindsay, C. (2003). A century of labour market change: 1900 to 2000. *Labour Market Trends*. March. 133–144. Available at www.scribd.com/document/39040666/Century-Labour-Market-Change-Mar2003.

Löckenhoff, C. E. (2012). Understanding retirement: the promise of life-span developmental frameworks. *European Journal of Ageing*, 9(3), 227–231.

Löckenhoff, C. E., Terracciano, A. and Costa, P. T. (2009). Five-factor model personality traits and the retirement transition: longitudinal and cross-sectional associations. *Psychology and Aging*, 24(3), 722–728.

Longfellow, Henry Wadsworth, 'The Village Blacksmith', *English Poetry III: From Tennyson to Whitman, 1909–1914*. Vol. XLII. The Harvard Classics. New York: P. F. Collier & Son,.

Lui, H. and Umberson, D. J. (2008). The times they are a changin': marital status and health differentials from 1972 to 2003. *Journal of Health and Social Behavior*, 49(3), 239–253.

Lumsdaine, R. L. and Vermeer, S. J. C. (2015). Retirement timing of women and the role of care responsibilities for grandchildren. *Demography*, 52(2), 433–454.

Lusardi, A. and Mitchell, O. S. (2007). Financial literacy and retirement preparedness: evidence and implications for financial education. *Business Economics*, 42(1), 35–44.

Lusardi, A. and Mitchell, O. S. (2008). Planning and financial literacy: how do women fare? *American Economic Review*, 98(2), 413–417.

Lusardi, A. and Mitchell, O. S. (2011a). Financial literacy and retirement planning in the United States. *Journal of Pension Economics and Finance*, 10(4), 509–525.

Lusardi, A. and Mitchell, O. S. (2011b). Financial literacy around the world: an overview. *Journal of Pension Economics and Finance*, 10(4), 497–508.

Lusardi, A. and Tufano, P. (2009). *Debt literacy, financial experiences, and overindebtedness* (no. 14808). Available at www.nber.org/papers/w14808.pdf.

McGarry, K. (2004). Health and retirement: do changes in health affect retirement expectations? *Journal of Human Resources*, 39(3), 624–648.

Manning, L. K. (2010). Gender and religious differences associated with volunteering in later life. *Journal of Women & Aging*, 22(2), 125–135.

Martin, B. and Xiang, N. (2015). The Australian retirement income system: structure, effects and future. *Work, Aging and Retirement*, 1(2), 133–143.

Matlin, M. W. (2011). *The psychology of women* (7th edn). Belmont, CA: Wadsworth.

Matthews, R. A. and Fisher, G. G. (2013). Family, work, and the retirement process: a review and new directions. In M. Wang (ed.), *The Oxford handbook of retirement*. New York: Oxford University Press, pp. 354–370.

Meleis, A. I., Sawyer, L. M., Im, E., Messias, D. K. H. and Schumacher, K. (2000). Experiencing transitions: an emerging middle-range theory. *Advances in Nursing Science*, 23 (1), 12–28.

Mercado, D. (2017). Here's why you may not trust your financial advisor. CNBC. 18 January. Available at www.cnbc.com/2017/01/18/heres-why-you-may-not-trust-your-financial-advisor.html.

Meschede, T., Cronin, M., Sullivan, L. and Shapiro, T. (2011). *Rising economic insecurity among senior single women*. Available at https://iasp.brandeis.edu/pdfs/2011/LLOL6.pdf.

Metlife Mature Market Institute, David DeLong and Associates and Zogby International (2006). *Living longer, working longer: The changing landscape of the aging workforce. A Metlife study*. Available at www.metlife.com/assets/cao/mmi/publications/studies/mmi-living-longer-working-longer.pdf.

MetLife Mature Market Institute and Scripps Gerontology Center (2011). *The MetLife study of women, retirement, and the extra-long life. Implications for planning*. Available at www.metlife.com/assets/cao/mmi/publications/studies/2011/mmi-women-retirement-extra-long-life.pdf.

Miller, A. and Sassler, S. (2010). Stability and change in the division of labor among cohabiting couples. *Sociological Forum*, 25(4), 677–701.

134 References

Mobily, K. E., Smith, A. K. and Chmielewski, K. (2017). Work, retirement and working out: the construction of exercise and the social world of retired women. *Annals of Leisure Research*, 20(3), 273–295.

Monette, M. (1996). *Canada's changing retirement patterns: findings from the General Social Survey*. Available at http://publications.gc.ca/collections/collection_2016/statcan/CS89-546-1996-eng.pdf.

Moon, M., Glymour, M., Subramanian, S. V., Avendaño, M. and Kawachi, I. (2012). Transition to retirement and risk of cardiovascular disease: prospective analysis of the US health and retirement study. *Social Science & Medicine*, 75(3), 526–530.

Mooney, A., Earl, J. K., Mooney, C. H. and Bateman, H. (2017). Using balanced time perspective to explain well-being and planning in retirement. *Frontiers in Psychology*, 8, 1781.

Mor-Barak, M. (1995). The meaning of work for older adults seeking employment: the generativity factor. *International Journal of Aging & Human Development*, 41(4), 325–344.

Morrow-Howell, N., Hong, S. and Tang, F. (2009). Who benefits from volunteering? Variations in perceived benefits. *The Gerontologist*, 49(1), 91–102.

Munnell, A. H. and Sass, S. A. (2008). *The decline of career employment* (Brief No. 8–14). Chestnut Hill, MA: Center for Retirement Research at Boston College.

Nesteruk, O. and Price, C. A. (2011). Retired women and volunteering: the good, the bad, and the unrecognized. *Journal of Women & Aging*, 23(2), 99–112.

Neville S. and Henrickson, M. (2010). 'Lavender retirement': a questionnaire survey of lesbian, gay and bisexual people's accommodation plans for old age. *International Journal of Nursing Practice*, 16(6), 586–594.

Newkirk, K., Perry-Jenkins, M. and Sayer, A. (2017). Division of household and childcare labor and relationship conflict among low-income new parents. *Sex Roles*, 76(5), 319–333.

Ng, R., Allore, H. G., Monin, J. K. and Levy, B. R. (2016). Retirement as meaningful: positive retirement stereotypes associated with longevity. *Journal of Social Issues*, 72, 69–85.

Nimrod, G. (2007). Expanding, reducing, concentrating, and diffusing: post retirement leisure behavior and life satisfaction. *Leisure Sciences*, 29(1), 91–111.

Nimrod, G. (2008). In support of innovation theory: innovation in activity patterns and life satisfaction among recently retired individuals. *Ageing & Society*, 28(6), 831–846.

Nimrod, G., Janke, M. C. and Kleiber, D. A. (2008). Retirement, activity and subjective well- being in Israel and the United States. *World Leisure Journal*, 50(1), 18–32.

Nimrod, G. and Kleiber, D. A. (2007). Reconsidering change and continuity in later life: toward an innovation theory of successful aging. *International Journal of Aging & Human Development*, 65(1), 1–22.

Number of women working past 70. (2017). *The Guardian*. 23 March. Available at www.theguardian.com/money/2017/mar/22/number-of-women-working-past-70-in-uk-doubles-in-four-years-retirement.

Office for National Statistics (2013). *Full report: women in the labour market*. Available at www.ons.gov.uk/ons/dcp171776_328352.pdf.

Office for National Statistics (2016). *Marriages in England and Wales, 2013*. Available at www.ons.gov.uk/peoplepopulationandcommunity/birthsdeathsandmarriages/marriagecohabitationandcivilpartnerships/bulletins/marriagesinenglandandwalesprovisional/2013.

O'Loughlin, K., Humpel, N. andKendig, H. (2010). Impact of the global financial crisis on employed Australian baby boomers: a national survey. *Australasian Journal on Ageing*, 29(2), 88–91.

Olson, E. (2015). Swindlers target older women on dating websites. *New York Times*. 17 July. Available at www.nytimes.com

Ong, R. and Austen, S. (2017). Women rely on the family home to support them in old age. *The Conversation*. Available at https://theconversation.com/women-rely-on-the-family- home-to-support-them-in-old-age-76703.

Onyx, J. and Benton, P. (1996). Retirement: a problematic concept for older women. *Journal of Women & Aging*, 8(2), 19–34.

Organisation for Economic Co-operation and Development (OECD) (2014). Australia. In *TALIS 2013 results: an international perspective on teaching and learning*. Paris: OECD Publishing. Available athttp://dx.doi.org/10.1787/9789264196261-en.

Organisation for Economic Co-operation and Development (OECD) (2015). Expected years in retirement. In *Pensions at a glance*. Paris: OECD Publishing, pp.164–165. Available atwww.oecd.org/publications/oecd-pensions-at-a-glance-19991363.htm.

Organisation for Economic Co-operation and Development (OECD) (2016). *Ageing and employment policies: statistics on average effective age of retirement* [data file]. Available at www.oecd.org/els/emp/average-effective-age-of-retirement.htm.

Organisation for Economic Co-operation and Development (OECD) (2017a). *Connecting people with jobs: key issues for raising labour market participation in Australia*. Available at www.oecd.org/australia/connecting-people-with-jobs-key-issues-for-raising-labour-market-participation-in-australia-9789264269637-en.htm.

Organisation for Economic Co-operation and Development (OECD) (2017b). *The pursuit of gender equality: an uphill battle*. Paris: OECD Publishing. Available at http://dx.doi.org/10.1787/9789264281318-en.

Osborne, J. W. (2012). Psychological effects of the transition to retirement. *Canadian Journal of Counselling and Psychotherapy*, 46(1), 45–58.

Papageorgiou, C. and Wells, A. (2004). *Depressive rumination: nature, theory and treatment*. Hoboken, NJ: John Wiley.

Paradise, M. B., Naismith, S. L., Davenport, T. A., Hickie, I. B.and Glozier, N. S. (2012). The impact of gender on early ill health retirement in people with heart disease and depression. *Australian and New Zealand Journal of Psychiatry*, 46(3), 249–256.

Park, J. and Park, A. (2016). Longitudinal effects of economic preparation and social activities on life and family relationship satisfaction among retirees. *Asian Social Work and Policy Review*, 10(1), 50–60.

Parkinson, D., Weiss, C., Zara, C., Duncan, A. and Judd, K. (2013). *Living longer on less: women speak on superannuation and retirement*. Melbourne: Women's Health in the North.

Patten, S. (2016). Trust in financial advisers falls. *Financial Review*. 26 May. Available at www.afr.com/business/banking-and-finance/trust-in-financial-advisers-falls-20160525-gp3oqt.

Patulny, R. (2009). The golden years? Social isolation among retired men and women in Australia. *Family Matters*, 83, 39–47.

Paul, K. I. and Batinic, B. (2010). The need for work: Jahoda's latent functions of employment in a representative sample of the German population. *Journal of Organizational Behavior*, 31(1), 45–64.

Petkoska, J. and Earl, J. K. (2009). Understanding the influence of demographic and psychological variables on retirement planning. *Psychology and Aging*, 24(1), 245–251.

Pew Research Center (2009). *Most middle-aged adults are rethinking retirement plans*. 28 May. Available at http://pewresearch.org/pubs/1234/the-threshold-generation.

Pinquart, M. and Schindler, I. (2007). Changes in life satisfaction in the transition to retirement: a latent-class approach. *Psychology and Aging*, 22(3), 442–455.

Pocock, B. and Alexander, M. (1999). The price of feminised jobs: new evidence on the gender pay gap in Australia. *Labour & Industry: A Journal of the Social and Economic Relations of Work*, 10(2), 75–100.

136 References

Potočnik, K., Tordera, N. and Peiró, J. M. (2010). The influence of the early retirement process on satisfaction with early retirement and psychological well-being. *International Journal of Aging & Human Development*, 70(3), 251–273.

Price, C. A. (1998). *Women and retirement: the unexplored transition.* New York: Garland.

Price, C. A. (2003). Professional women's retirement adjustment: the experience of reestablishing order. *Journal of Aging Studies*, 17(3), 341–355.

Price, C. A. and Joo, E. (2005). Exploring the relationship between marital status and women's retirement satisfaction. *International Journal of Aging & Human Development*, 61(1), 37–55.

Price, C. A. and Nesteruk, O. (2015). What to expect when you retire: by women for women. *Marriage & Family Review*, 51(5), 418–440.

Procter, I. and Padfield, M. (1999). Work orientations and women's work: a critique of Hakim's theory of the heterogeneity of women. *Gender, Work & Organization*, 6(3), 152–162.

Pushkar, D., Chaikelson, J., Conway, M., Etezadi, J., Giannopolous, C., Li, K. and Wrosch, C. (2010). Testing continuity and activity variables as predictors of positive and negative affect in retirement. *Journals of Gerontology, Series B: Psychological Sciences and Social Sciences*, 65B(1), 42–49.

Quinn, J. and Cribb, R. (2013). Love fraud costs woman $1.3 million. *Toronto Star.* 30 November. Available at www.pressreader.com/canada/toronto-star/20131130/281487864142676.

Raymo, J. M., Warren, J. R., Sweeney, M. M., Hauser, R. M. and Ho, J.-H. (2011). Precarious employment, bad jobs, labor unions, and early retirement. *Journals of Gerontology, Series B: Psychological Sciences and Social Sciences*, 66B(2), 249–259.

Reinitz, J. (2012). Web scammers fleecing people looking for love. *The Courier.* 19 May. http://wcfcourier.com.

Reitzes, D. C. and Mutran, E. J. (2004). The transition to retirement: stages and factors that influence retirement adjustment. *International Journal of Aging & Human Development*, 59(1), 63–84.

Reitzes, D. C. and Mutran, E. J. (2006). Lingering identities in retirement. *Sociological Quarterly*, 47(2), 333–359.

Reitzes, D. C., Mutran, E. J. and Fernandez, M. E. (1996). Preretirement influences on postretirement self-esteem. *Journals of Gerontology, Series B: Psychological Sciences and Social Sciences*, 51(5), S242–249.

Rice, N. E., Lang, I. A., Henley, W. and Melzer, D. (2011). Common health predictors of early retirement: findings from the English Longitudinal Study of Ageing. *Age and Ageing*, 40(1), 54–61.

Robinson, O. C., Demetre, J. D. and Corney, R. (2010). Personality and retirement: exploring the links between the Big Five personality traits, reasons for retirement and the experience of being retired. *Personality and Individual Differences*, 48(7), 792–797.

Robison, J. T. and Moen, P. (2000). A life-course perspective on housing expectations and shifts in late midlife. *Research on Aging*, 22, 499–532.

Rohwedder, S. and Willis, R. J. (2010). Mental retirement. *Journal of Economic Perspectives*, 24 (1), 119–138.

Rosenthal, D. and Moore, S. (2012a). *New age nanas.* Unpublished raw data.

Rosenthal, D. A. and Moore, S. M. (2012b). *New age nanas: being a grandmother in the 20th century.* Newport: Big Sky Publishing.

Rotolo, T. and Wilson, J. (2007). Sex segregation in volunteer work. *Sociological Quarterly*, 48(3), 559–585.

Ryff, C. D. and Keyes, C. L. (1995). The structure of psychological well-being revisited. *Journal of Personality and Social Psychology*, 69(4), 719–727.

References **137**

Sahlgren, G. H. (2013). *Work longer, live healthier* (Discussion Paper No. 46). Available at https://iea.org.uk/wp-content/uploads/2016/07/Work%20Longer,%20Live_Healthier.pdf.

Sapienza, P., Zingales, L. and Maestripieri, D. (2009). Gender differences in financial risk aversion and career choices are affected by testosterone. *Proceedings of the National Academy of Sciences of the United States of America*, 106(36), 15268–15273.

Sargent-Cox, K. A., Anstey, K. J. and Luszcz, M. A. (2012). The relationship between change in self-perceptions of aging and physical functioning in older adults. *Psychology and Aging*, 27, 750–760.

Sass, S. A., Monk, C. and Haverstick, K. (2010). *Workers' response to the market crash: save more, work more?* Available at http://crr.bc.edu/wp-content/uploads/2010/02/IB_10-3.pdf.

Scherger, S., Nazroo, J. and Higgs, P. (2011). Leisure activities and retirement: do structures of inequality change in old age? *Ageing & Society*, 31(1), 146–172.

Schieman, S. and Taylor, J. (2001). Statuses, roles and sense of mattering. *Sociological Perspectives*, 44(4), 469–484.

Schlossberg, N. (2004). *Retire smart, retire happy: finding your true path in life*. Washington, DC: American Psychological Association.

Schmidt, J. A. and Lee, K. (2008). Voluntary retirement and organizational turnover intentions: the differential associations with work and non-work commitment constructs. *Journal of Business and Psychology*, 22(4), 297–309.

Scottish Widows (2016). *Women and retirement report 2016. One gender, different lives.* Available at http://reference.scottishwidows.co.uk/literature/doc/2016-women-retirement-report.

Selenka, E., Batinic, B. and Paul, K. (2011). Does latent deprivation lead to psychological distress? Investigating Jahoda's model in a four-wave study. *Journal of Occupational and Organizational Psychology*, 84(4), 723–740.

Seligman, M. E. (2012). *Flourish: a visionary new understanding of happiness and well-being*. New York: Simon and Schuster.

Seligman, M. E. and Csikszentmihalyi, M. (2000). Positive psychology: an introduction. *American Psychologist*, 55(1), 5–14.

Shacklock, K., Brunetto, Y. and Nelson, S. (2009). The different variables that affect older males' and females' intentions to continue working. *Asia Pacific Journal of Human Resources*, 47(1), 79–101.

Shaffer, H. J. and Korn, D. A. (2002). Gambling and related mental disorders: a public health analysis. *Annual Review of Public Health*, 23, 171–212.

Shakespeare, William, *The Tragedy of King Lear*. New York: University Society (1901), Act 1, Scene 1, p. 26. Available at https://archive.org/details/kinglear00shak.

Shillington, R. (2012). *An analysis of the economic circumstances of Canadian seniors*. Available at www.broadbentinstitute.ca/an_analysis_of_the_economic_circumstances_of_canadian_seniors.

Silver, M. P. (2010). Women's retirement and self-assessed well-being: an analysis of three measures of well-being among recent and long-term retirees relative to homemakers. *Women & Health*, 50(1), 1–19.

Simmons, B. A. and Betschild, M. J. (2001). Women's retirement, work and life paths: changes, disruptions and discontinuities. *Journal of Women & Aging*, 13(4), 53–70.

Sjosten, N. M., Kivimaki, M., Singh-Manoux, A. and Vahtera, J. (2012). Change in physical activity and weight in relation to retirement: the French GAZEL Cohort Study. *BMJ Open*, 2(1), e000522.

Slevin, K. F. and Wingrove, C. R. (1995). Women in retirement: a review and critique of empirical research since 1976. *Social Inquiry*, 65(1), 1–21.

Snow, C. B. and Snow, J. K. (2016). The Equal Pay Act of 1963. *Utah Bar Journal*, 29, 14–16.

138 References

Social Security (n.d.). *Retirement benefits by year of birth.* Available at www.ssa.gov/planners/retire/agereduction.html.

Social Security Administration (2016). *Marital status and poverty.* Available at www.ssa.gov/retirementpolicy/fact-sheets/marital-status-poverty.html.

Starts at 60 (2017). *These are the real signs of old age.* Available at https://startsat60.com/health/these-are-the-real-signs-of-old-age.

Statistics Canada (2013). *Marital status: overview, 2011.* Available at www.statcan.gc.ca/pub/91-209-x/2013001/article/11788-eng.htm.

Stats NZ (2017). *Marriages, civil unions, and divorces: year ended December 2016.* Available at www.stats.govt.nz/information-releases/marriages-civil-unions-and-divorces-year-ended-december-2016.

Steffens, N. K., Cruwys, T., Haslam, C., Jetten, J. and Haslam, S. A. (2016). Social group memberships in retirement are associated with reduced risk of premature death: evidence from a longitudinal cohort study. *BMJ Open*, 6(2), e010164.

Steptoe, A., Shankar, A., Demakakos, P. and Wardle, J. (2013) Social isolation, loneliness, and all-cause mortality in older men and women. *Proceedings of the National Academy of Sciences of the United States of America*, 110, 5797–5801.

Stich, S. (n.d.). *Five fun alternatives to retiring at home.* Available at https://grandparents.com/money-and-work/retirement/retirement-ideas.

Stritof, S. (2017). *Estimated median age of first marriage by gender: 1890 to 2015. Couples are waiting longer to get married every year.* Available at www.thespruce.com/estimated-median-age-marriage-2303878.

Strough, J., Bruine de Bruin, W., Parker, A. M., Lemaster, P., Pichayayothin, N. and Delaney, R. (2016). Hour glass half full or half empty? Future time perspective and pre-occupation with negative events across the life span. *Psychology and Aging*, 31, 558–573.

Sullivan, O. (2000). The division of domestic labour: twenty years of change? *Sociology*, 34(3), 437–456.

Super, D. E. (1990). A life-span, life-space approach to career development. In D. Brown and L. Brooks (eds), *Career choice and development* (2nd edn). San Francisco, CA: Jossey-Bass, pp. 197–261.

Svensson, I., Lundholm, E., De Luna, X. and Malmberg, G. (2015). Family life course and the timing of women's retirement: a sequence analysis approach. *Population, Space and Place*, 21(8), 856–871.

Szinovacz M. E. and Davey, A. (2005). Predictors of perceptions of involuntary retirement. *Gerontologist*, 45(1), 36–47.

Tamborini, C. R. (2007). The never-married in old age: projections and concerns for the near future. *Social Security Bulletin*, 67(2), 25–40.

Teachers Insurances and Annuity Association (TIAA) (2016). *Voices of experience survey.* Available at www.tiaa.org/public/pdf/C30785_voices_of_experience_survey_findings_final.pdf.

Tennyson, Alfred 1st Baron (1900). *The lotos-eaters, Ulysses, Ode on the death of the Duke of Wellington, Maud, The coming of Arthur, The passing of Arthur*, with Introduction and notes by F. J. Rowe and W. T. Webb, London, Lond. &c.

Tibbitts, C. (1954). Retirement problems in American society. *American Journal of Sociology*, 59(4), 301–308.

Touvier, M., Bertrais, S., Charreire, H., Vergnaud, A. C., Hercberg, S. and Oppert, J. M. (2010). Changes in leisure-time physical activity and sedentary behaviour at retirement: a prospective study in middle-aged French subjects. *International Journal of Behavioral Nutrition and Physical Activity*, 7, 14.

Tversky, A. and Kahneman, D. (1974). Judgments under uncertainty: heuristics and biases. *Science*, 185(4157), 1124–1131.

US Bureau of Labor Statistics (2014). *Women in the labor force: a databook* (Report No. 1052). Available at www.bls.gov/opub/reports/womens-databook/archive/women-in-the-labor-force-a-databook-2014.pdf.

US Equal Employment Opportunity Commission (2008). *Facts about age discrimination.* Available at https://www.eeoc.gov/facts/age.html.

UK Office for National Statistics (2013). *Full report: Women in the labour market.* Available at http://webarchive.nationalarchives.gov.uk/20160105160709/http://www.ons.gov.uk/ons/dcp171776_328352.pdf.

United States Department of Labor (2000). *The economics daily: changes in women's labor force participation in the 20th century.* Available at www.bls.gov/opub/ted2000/feb/wk3/art03.htm.

United States Department of Labor (2016). *Data and statistics. women in the labor force.* Available at www.dol.gov/wb/stats/stats_data.htm.

Van Dalen, H. P., Henkens, K. and Schippers, J. (2010) How do employers cope with an ageing workforce? Views from employers and employees. *Demographic Research,* 22(32), 1015–1036.

Van den Bogaard, L. (2017). Leaving quietly? A quantitative study of retirement rituals and how they affect life satisfaction. *Work, Aging and Retirement,* 3(1), 55–65.

Van den Hounaard, D. K. (2015). Constructing the boundaries of retirement for baby-boomer women: like turning off the tap, or is it? *Qualitative Sociology Review,* 11(3), 41–58.

Van der Heide, I., van Rijn, R. M., Robroek, S. J. W., Burdorf, A. and Proper, K. I. (2013). Is retirement good for your health? A systematic review of longitudinal studies. *BMC Public Health,* 13(13), 1180–1191.

Van Rijn, R. M., Robroek, S. J. W., Brouwer, S. and Burdorf, A. (2014). Influence of poor health on exit from paid employment: A systematic review. *Occupational and Environmental Medicine,* 71(4), 295–301.

Van Rooij, M., Lusardi, A. and Alessie, R. (2011). Financial literacy and stock market participation. *Journal of Financial Economics,* 101(2), 449–472.

Van Solinge, H. and Henkens, K. (2005). Couples' adjustment to retirement: a multifactor panel study. *Journals of Gerontology, Series B: Psychological Sciences and Social Sciences,* 60(1), S11–20.

Van Solinge, H. and Henkens, K. (2007). Involuntary retirement: the role of restrictive circumstances, timing, and social embeddedness. *Journals of Gerontology, Series B: Psychological Sciences and Social Sciences,* 62(5), S295–303.

Van Solinge, H. and Henkens, K. (2008). Adjustment to and satisfaction with retirement: two of a kind? *Psychology and Aging,* 23(2), 422–434.

Van Solinge, H. and Henkens, K. (2014). Work-related factors as predictors in the retirement decision-making process of older workers in the Netherlands. *Ageing & Society,* 34 (9), 1551–1574.

Vanderweerd, C., Myers, J., Coulter, M., Yalcin, A. and Corvin, J. (2016). Positives and negatives of online dating according to women 50+. *Journal of Women & Aging,* 28(3), 259–270.

Vermeer, N., Mastrogiacomo, M. andvan Soest, A. (2015). *Demanding occupations and the retirement age* (No. 9462).Available at http://ftp.iza.org/dp9462.pdf.

Voltaire (1888). *Voltaire's Candide or The Optimist and Rasselas Prince of Abissinia,* trans. Samuel Johnson. 3rd edn. London: George Routledge and Sons.

Von Bonsdorff, M. E. and Ilmarinen, J. (2013). Continuity theory and retirement. In M. Wang (ed.), *The Oxford handbook of retirement.* New York: Oxford University Press, pp. 73–87.

140 References

Vu, J. and Doughney, J. (2009). Women and superannuation: work until you drop? *Journal of Business Systems, Governance and Ethics*, 4(1), 41–54.

Wade, L. (2016). The invisible workload that drags women down. *Time*. 29 December. Available at http://time.com/money/4561314/women-work-home-gender-gap/.

Walzer, S. (1998). *Thinking about the baby: gender and transitions into parenthood*. Philadelphia, PA: Temple University Press.

Wang, M. (2007). Profiling retirees in the retirement transition and adjustment process: examining the longitudinal change patterns of retirees' psychological wellbeing. *Journal of Applied Psychology*, 92(2), 455–474.

Wang, M. and Hesketh, B. (2012). *Achieving wellbeing in retirement: recommendations from 20 years of research*. Available at www.siop.org/SIOP-SHRM/SIOP-Achieving_Well-Being_in_Retirement_final.pdf.

Wang, M. and Shi, J. (2014). Psychological research on retirement. *Annual Review of Psychology*, 65, 209–233.

Wang, M. and Shultz, K. S. (2010). Employee retirement: a review and recommendations for future investigation. *Journal of Management*, 36(1), 172–206.

Wang, M., Henkens, K. and van Solinge, H. (2011). A review of theoretical and empirical advancements. *American Psychologist*, 66(3), 204–213.

Warren, D. (2015a). Why single women are more likely to retire poor. *The Conversation*. 27 November. Available at http://theconversation.com/why-single-women-are-more-likely-to-retire-poor-51126.

Warren, D. A. (2015b). Retirement decisions of couples in Australia: the impact of spousal characteristics and preferences. *Journal of the Economics of Ageing*, 6, 149–162.

Wetzel, M., Huxhold, O. and Tesch-Römer, C. (2016). Transition into retirement affects life satisfaction: short- and long-term development depends on last labor market status and education. *Social Indicators Research*, 125(3), 991–1009.

Wilkins, R. (2016). *The Household, Income and Labour Dynamics in Australia Survey: Selected Findings from Waves 1 to 14. The 11th Annual Statistical Report of the HILDA Survey*. Available at http://melbourneinstitute.unimelb.edu.au/hilda/publications/hilda-statistical-reports.

Wilson, T. D. and Gilbert, D. T. (2003). Affective forecasting. In M. P. Zanna (ed.), *Advances in Experimental Social Psychology*. San Diego, CA: Academic Press, pp. 345–411.

Wink, P. and James, J. B. (2006). Conclusion: is the third age the crown of life? In J. B. James and P. Wink (eds), *Annual review of gerontology and geriatrics, Volume 26, 2006: The crown of life: Dynamics of the early postretirement period*. New York: Springer Publishing Co, pp. 305–325.

Wolcott, I. (1998). *Families in later life: dimensions of retirement* (Working Paper No. 14). Available at https://aifs.gov.au/publications/families-later-life/contexts-retirement-private-and-public-dimensions.

Women's Health Australia (2015). *Australian longitudinal study on women's health Sixth survey for the women of the 1946–51 cohort*. Available at www.alswh.org.au/images/content/pdf/Surveys_and_Databooks/Surveys/2010Mid6Survey.pdf.

Workplace Gender Equality Agency (2016). *Superannuation & gender pay gaps by age group*. Available at www.wgea.gov.au/sites/default/files/Gender_pay_and_superannuation_gaps_by_age_group.pdf.

Workplace Gender Equality Agency (2017). *Gender workplace statistics at a glance*. Available at: www.wgea.gov.au/sites/default/files/Stats%20at%20a%20Glance%20FEB2017.pdf.

World Bank (2012). Gender differences in employment and why they matter. In *World Development Report 2012: Gender Equality and Development*. Washington, DC: World Bank: pp. 198–253. Available at http://documents.worldbank.org/curated/en/492221468136792185/Main-report.

World Health Organization (WHO) (2011). *Global health and aging.* Available at www.who.int/ageing/publications/global_health.pdf?ua=1.

World Health Organization (WHO) (2012). *Are you ready? What you need to know about ageing.* Available at www.who.int/world-health-day/2012/toolkit/background/en/.

Wu, C., Odden, M. C., Fisher, G. G. and Stawski, R. S. (2016). The association of retirement age with mortality: a population-based longitudinal study among older adults in the United States. *Journal of Epidemiology and Community Health*, 70(9), 917–923.

Yogev, S. (2017). *6 links between retirement and alcohol abuse.* Available at https://www.nextavenue.org/retirement-alcohol-abuse/.

Yon, Y., Mikton, C., Gassoumis, Z. and Wilber, K. (2017). Elder abuse prevalence in community settings: a systematic review and meta-analysis. *The Lancet Global Health*, 5(2), e147–e156.

Young, M., Wallace, J. E. and Polachek, A. J. (2015). Gender differences in perceived domestic task equity: a study of professionals. *Journal of Family Issues*, 36(13), 1751–1781.

Yunus, M. (2017). *A world of three zeroes.* Melbourne: Scribe.

Zaniboni, S., Sarchielli, G. and Fraccaroli, F. (2010). How are psychosocial factors related to retirement intentions? *International Journal of Manpower*, 31(3), 271–285.

Zaninotto, P., Breeze, E., McMunn, A. and Nazroo, J. (2013). Formal volunteering as a protective factor for older adults' psychological well-being. *Journals of Gerontology, Series B, Psychological Sciences and Social Sciences*, 59(5), S258–264.

Zantinge, E. M., van den Berg, M., Smit, H. A. and Picavet, H. S. J. (2014). Retirement and a healthy lifestyle: opportunity or pitfall? A narrative review of the literature. *European Journal of Public Health*, 24(1), 433–439.

Zhu, R. (2016). Retirement and its consequences for women's health in Australia. *Social Science & Medicine*, 163, 117–125.

Zimbardo, P. G. and Boyd, J. N. (1999). Putting time in perspective: a valid, reliable individual-differences metric. *Journal of Personality and Social Psychology*, 77, 1271–1288.

Zimbardo, P. G. and Boyd, J. N. (2008). *The time paradox: the new psychology of time that will change your life.* New York: Free Press.

INDEX

401(k) plans 59

activity 18–19
adapting to retirement 68–9; health and 90–2
adaptive group 23–4
adolescent identity crisis 5
adventurers 12–13
affective forecasting 54
age discrimination 50
ageing 83–4
ageism 84, 113
ages and stages 5–6, 72
Age UK 120
alcohol misuse 107–8
Almenberg, J. 40–1
American Association for Retired Persons (AARP) 39, 120
'Analysis of the Economic Circumstances of Canadian Seniors' (Shillington) 43
anchoring effect 54
appearance 115
Asebedo, S. D. 114
assets 33–4
attachment to workplace 74–5
Austen, S. 33
Australia: equal pay acts 2; health studies 87–8; Internet use 101; social security system 44; Victoria police force 120
Australian Bureau of Statistics (ABS) studies 12, 34, 56, 105
Australian Human Rights Commission 31
Australian Institute of Family Studies 35

Australian Longitudinal Study on Women's Health 24, 37–8
Australian Securities and Investments Commission 40

baby-boomers 3, 12, 52, 59
Bamber, M. 69
Bamburger, P. A. 107–8
Barbosa. L. M. 93, 95
Barnes, H. 75–6
Barnes-Farrell, J. L. 58
Batinic, B. 19
Baxter, J. 24
Beehr, T. A. 52–4
Behncke, S. 84–5
Bennetts, L. 43, 44
Betschild, M. J. 4
Bevan 107
Bianchi, S. M. 20
biographical disruption 107
Blair-Loy, M. 21
blood pressure 115
Borrero, L. 4, 11, 75
Boyd, J. N. 64
British Household Panel Survey 87
Bronfenbrenner, U. 6–7
Browning, C. J. 68
Bucher-Koenen, T. 40, 41, 47
Buhlmann, F. 22
bullying 58, 65
business owners 55
Byles, J. 12

Index **143**

Calvo, E. 85
Canada: care provision study 103–4; poverty rate for women 43
care provision 11, 13–14, 29, 48, 57, 102–5; to elderly parents 72, 79, 102, 103; gender and 103–5; 'unretirement' 104; as volunteer work 100
Carstensen, L. L. 6
CEOS, women 32
Chesters, J. 24
choice 23–4; constraint vs. 59–61; Preference Theory 23–7; socio-economic group and 24
Clinton, Hillary 26
Coan, V. 95
cognitive biases and heuristics 54
cognitive decline 55, 62, 85
co-living housing 107
Collard, S. 41–2
collective purpose 18, 19
Collinson, C. 117–18
comfort zone 72
Committee on Women's Rights and Gender Equality (European Parliament) 21
Commonwealth Public Service, Australia 2
conscientiousness 56
conservative nations 22
continuers 12
continuity 1
continuity theory 110–11
Crisp, C. 109
Crisp, D. A. 106
critical incidents 69
Culberson, J. W. 109
cultural expectations 52
Cussen, M. P. 70, 73

Damaske, S. 25
Damman, M. 71
Darzins, P. 46
dating sites 101–2
Dave, D. 85
Davey, A. 77
David DeLong and Associates 56
decision-making 50–66
dementia 84
depression 17, 71, 92, 109, 114
Desmette, D. 52
disabled spouses 57
discrimination 32
disenchantment phase 71–2
disruptions and trajectories 27–30, 38, 48; 'Motherhood Penalty' 35
divorce 28, 43; financial planning and 38–9
'do it yourself' approach 39

domestic violence 43
domestic work 10–11; gendered division of labor 20–1; 'second shift' 3, 20–1; structured 19
'double shift' 3, 20–1
Doughney, J. 47, 48
Dow, B. 103
downshifting 4
Duberley, J. 4, 7, 87

Earl, J. K. 64, 110
easy gliders 13
eating habits 88–9
ecological systems theory 6–7
economic conditions 58–9
'Economic Security for Women in Retirement' report 35
Edgar, Don 113
Edgar, Patricia 113
education 1–2, 56
Ekerdt, D. J. 9, 10
Elder Economic Security Index 44
elder financial abuse 46, 101–2
elective belonging 107
Electricité de France-Gaz de France (EDF-GDF) 88
Elizabeth II 66
Ellis, Kate 27
employer-based supports 120
Employment Protection Act (1975, United Kingdom) 2
English Longitudinal Study on Ageing 84–5, 110–11
Equal Pay Act (American, 1963) 2
equal pay acts 2
Erikson, Erik 5–6, 72
ethic of care 100
eudemonic approach 7
European Institute for Gender Equality 21
European Social Survey 22
European Union (EU) 22
Eurostat study 101
Everingham, C. 4, 11, 12
exosystem 7
'expander' category 111
experiences of retirement 97–111; care provision 102–5; continuity and change in retirement activities 110–11; Internet/social media use 100–2; leisure activities 98–9; maladaptive behaviours 107–10; relocation as option 105–7

family factors: care provision 11, 13–14, 29, 48, 72, 78–9, 100; post-retirement changes in relationships 78–9; retirement

144 Index

decision-making 53, 56–8; support from family 71–2; tragedies 57–8
farewell events 68, 94
Feldman, D. C. 52–4
feminist viewpoint 24–5
financial planners 63
financial security 14, 31–49, 117–18; assets 33–4; effects of financial inequity on women 43–5; financial literacy 39–41; gender pay gap 32–3; gender wealth gap 33–4; partner's income 34–5, 36; personal superannuation 31; planning for 38–9; policy responses 47; preparation for 36–8; retirement income 34–5; risk-taking 41–2; savings 31, 35–6; sexually transmitted debt 42–3; three pillars of resources 31–2, 34, 55; working longer to counter 38
financial swindles 45–6, 101–2
Finch, N. 55–6
Finnish study 88
Fisher, G. G. 34, 53–4, 90
flexibility 12, 23, 118, 119
Floyd, F. J. 60
France, studies 87; GAZEL Cohort Study 88
Frech, A. 25
freedom 70, 77, 97–8
French, Marilyn 28
future generations 121

Gaillard, M. 52
gambling 42, 109–10
Gardner, I. L. 106
gateway model 11
GAZEL Cohort Study (France) 88
gender: care provision and 103–5; health and 84–5; identity transition and 75–6; occupational divide 25–7; pay gap 32–3; wealth gap 33–4
gender roles 2, 75–6, 122; cross-national comparison 22; public attitudes 25
generativity 5–6, 72
Germany, studies 40, 89
Gerontological Society of America 95
Geyer, S. 89
'giving back' 100, 104
global financial crisis of 2008 58–9, 63
Global Financial Literacy Excellence Center 40
Gonzales, E. 104
government and workplace policies 21–2
Grable, J. 41
Grace, M. 47
grandchildren, caring for 11, 13–14, 29, 57, 102–3

Grant, B. F. 107
grief counselling 72
Griffin, B. 53
Gustman, A. L. 57

hair salon study 115
Hakim, Catherine 23–5
health 13, 44–5, 71, 83–96, 119; adjustment to retirement 90–2; ageing and 83–4; cognitive decline 55, 85; factors that influence 84–6; gender and 84–5, 95–6; later retirement at 85; lifestyle activities and 86–9; planning for retirement and 55, 60, 62; pros and cons of retirement 89–90; relocation and 105; satisfaction, predictors of 92–4; social connections and 80; trajectories 68; women's 95–6
Healthy Working Life Expectancy 3
Helldan 88
Hemingway, Ernest 9
Henkins, K. 60
Hershey, D. A. 60, 62
Hershfield, H. E. 48
Heybroek, L. 91–2
Hoffman, L. H. 102
Holdsworth, L. 109–10
home-based offices 17
homelessness 45
honeymoon phase (of retirement) 5, 70–1
Household, Income and Labour Dynamics in Australia (HILDA) Survey 33, 43, 53, 87
housing 89; as asset 33–4, 42–3; co-living housing 107; fear of loss of 44–5; non-private dwellings 105; park homes/mobile homes 106–7; relocation as option 105–7
Hung, A. 40, 48

identity 94; continuity 75–6; disruption 74–5; gender and 75–6; multifaceted 75; reorienting of 73–4
identity, sense of 56
industrialised countries 2
inflation 39
influences on decision making 6–7
innovation 111
intended age of retirement 30, 53–4
interest 39, 40
Internet/social media 46, 80–1, 100–2, 121
invisible work 20–1
involved spectators 13
isolation 17, 65, 119; marital status and 76–8; mortality risk and 89; sources of support 120

Israeli retirees 111
Italian workers 56

Jahoda, M. 17–18
Jaumont-Pascual, N. 100, 110, 111
Jefferson, T. 48
Johnstone, M. 24
Jolly, S. 20

Kang, T. 102
Kim, J. E. 114
King Lear (Shakespeare) 9
Kiso, H. 62
Knoll, M. A. Z. 52, 54
Koenig, T. L. 109
Kopanidis, F. Z. 105
Korn, D. A. 109
Kruger, T. M. 4, 11, 75
Kubicek, B. 7, 95
Kuerbis, A. 108

Lahti, J. 110
Lakra, D. C. 113
Langer, Ellen 114–15
Lee, Y. 24
legal changes 2
leisure gap 20–1
leisure pursuits 11, 21, 56, 73, 98–9
lesbian, gay and bisexual (LGBT)
    people 106
Levy, B. R. 113
liberal nations 22
life expectancy 3, 4, 14, 31, 48, 78, 84;
    subjective life expectancy (SLE) 53
lifespan developmental journey 1, 8
lifestyle activities, health and 86–9
lifestyle planning 63
liminality 69
links to former workplace 56, 62
literacy, financial 39–41
Lockenhoff, C. E. 6
loneliness 17, 65, 70–1, 76–7, 80–1, 89,
    109–10, 119–20
loss aversion 54
Lumsdaine, R. L. 57
Lusardi, A. 39

macrosystem 6–7
maladaptive behaviours 107–10
male models of retirement 4
Marienthal, Austria, study 17–19
marriage 4, 27; age at 2–3; protection from
    poverty 44; social connection and 76–8;
    women banned from occupations 1, 2
McGarry, K. 55

Meleis, A. I. 68–9
men: adjustment to retirement 7–8, 19, 75;
    unpaid domestic work 20
mental health 7, 90; depression 17, 71, 92,
    109, 114; post-retirement depression 17;
    sources of support 120–1
Mentally Healthy Retirement 120–1
mentoring 120
mesosystem 7
MetLife studies (United States) 37, 38, 56
Meyer, C. 103
microsystem 6–7
millennials, United States 47
mindfulness 114–15
Mindfulness (Langer) 114–15
Mini-Mental State Examination 85
Mitchell, O. S. 39
Mobily, K. E. 98–9
Moen, P. 105, 114
Moon, M. 85–6
Mor-Barak, M. 6
'Motherhood Penalty' 35
multilevel models 6–7
Mutran, E. J. 74, 76

National Council on Aging (United
    States) 120
national data 22
National Longitudinal Survey of Youth
    (United States) 25
Nesteruk, O. 63–4, 71, 100
Netherlands, studies 29, 30, 71, 94; financial
    literacy 40
neuroticism 61
Ng, R. 113
Nimrod, G. 111
not-for-profit organisations 107

obesity 87, 89
O'Brien, Anna Belle Clement 26
occupational segregation 25–7
Office for National Statistics (UK) 21
O'Loughlin, K. 59
Ong, R. 33
Organisation for Economic Co-operation
    and Development (OECD) 25, 33, 51,
    84; International Network on Financial
    Education 39
Osborne, J. W. 94
outcomes, focus on 7
outplacement 120

paid work 10–11
park homes/mobile homes 106–7
Parry, J. 75–6

146 Index

partnered women 14; co-ordinating retirements 53, 56–7; reliance on partner after retirement 35–7; retirement satisfaction and 76–8. *See also* marriage
part-time work 21–3, 69; Preference Theory 23–4; 'unretirement' 104
passive disconnected women 14
pathways to retirement 11–12
Patulny, R. 80
Paul, K. I. 19
pension asset test 33
Pension Policy Institute (United Kingdom) 35
pensions: employer-funded 51; self-funded 51; state 31–2, 51
pension/superannuation systems 31; employer-contributed 34; state pensions 31–2
personality characteristics 13, 41, 42, 56; neuroticism 61
physical activity 88, 98–9, 106, 110
physically active women 13
pink-collar work 25–7
planning for retirement 38–9, 50–66; age categories 53–4; assessing when to retire 53–4; choice vs. constraint 59–61; decision-making process 51–4; economic conditions 58–9; flexibility in changing plans 64–5; imagining future 52; individual and demographic factors 55–6; intended age of retirement 30, 53–4; lifestyle planning 63; making the plan 61–5; psychological 113; push-pull factors 54, 58; satisfaction levels 59–62; three-phase model 52–4; timing of retirement 55–9, 94, 96; women who never retire 65–6; work factors 58
positive approaches 112–22; making the most of retirement 117–19; positive psychology 113–15; sources of advice 119–20; temporal focus and satisfaction 115–17
'possibility years' 112
post-retirement jobs 104
post-retirement changes in family relationships 78–9
Potočnik, K. 58
poverty 31, 43–4; gambling and 110
predictors of satisfaction 92–4
Preference Theory 23–5
pregnancy 2, 3
prescription drugs 108–9
'present hedonistic' time perspective 64
Price, C. A. 63–4, 71, 75, 95–6, 100
protective strategies 17
proto-retirement 98

psychological planning 113
psychosocial journey from worker to retiree 67–82, 113; adapting to retirement 68–9; critical incidents 69; disenchantment phase 71–2; honeymoon phase 70–1; moving on 81–2; post-retirement changes in family relationships 78–9; renegotiating social relationships 76–81; reorientation phase 72–3; reorienting of identity 73–6; retirement as life transition 67–8
psychosocial maturity 5–6
public protection 64
Pushkar, D. 111
push-pull factors 54, 58

qualitative studies 10
quality of life 93
Queensland, Australia, study 24

redundancy 10, 38, 50, 59–60, 62–3, 69, 94, 121
Reitzes, D. C. 74, 76
relocation 105–7
reorientation phase 72–3
Retired Peer Support Officers (RPSOs) 120
retirement: defining 9–11, 28; early 29, 33–4, 92; expectations 3, 52, 55; operationalisation of 10; as process 119; research 4–5
'retirement blues' 71
retirement frameworks 5–8
retirement income 34–5
retirement timing 55–9, 94, 96
retirement villages 105–6
retreaters 13
reverse ageing study 114–15
risk diversification 39–40
risk/return trade-off 40
risk-taking 41–2
rites of passage 68, 94
Robinson, O. C. 60–1
Robison, J. T. 105
Rohwedder, S. 85
role expansion 75
Russian Federation 40
Ryff, Carol 7

Sacco, P. 108
Sahlgren, G. H. 83, 92
salaried work 1
Sapienza, P. 42
Sass, S. A. 59
satisfaction levels 59–61, 59–62, 70; health and 92–4; positive approach and 114; temporal focus and 115–17

Save-Soderbergh, J. 40–1
savings 31, 35–6
scams 45–6, 101–2
Scherger, S. 110–11
Schlossberg, N. 68
Schlossberg, Nancy 12–13
Scottish Widows study 36–9
searchers 13
Seay, M. C. 114
'second shift' 3, 20–1
second-wave feminism 3
Selenka, E. 19
self-absorption 72
self-esteem 96
self-help literature 98, 119
self-insurance 64
self-protection 64
Seligman, Martin 114, 115
semi-retirement 56
Senate, Australian 47
Senior Financial Security Index 44
Sex Discrimination Act (1975, United Kingdom) 2
sexually transmitted debt 42–3
Shaffer, H. J. 109
Shakespeare, William 9
Shi, J. 5, 6, 7, 8, 10
Silver, M. P. 94
Simmons, B. A. 4
single women 14, 24, 77–8
Sjosten, N. M. 88
Skype 101
sleep, restful 68
Slevin, K. F. 92
slot machines 109
social change 1–5
social contact 17
social isolation *See* isolation
social life 51, 62, 64, 65, 73; contact with former workplace 56, 94; replacements for workplace socialising 79–81
socially active/generative retirees 13
social networks 73, 75, 76–8, 101–2, 108, 110
Social Security benefits (United States) 35, 52
social security system: Australia 44
socio-democratic nations 22
socio-economic status 24–5
Socioemotional Selectivity Theory 6
Spanish studies 58, 111
stages of life 5–6, 9
standard of living 19
Standard & Poor's 500 Index 32
state pensions 31–2; eligibility age 51

status provision 18
statutory retirement age 50
stay-at-home mums 23; as drain on economy 25
Steffens, N. K. 80
Steinmeier, T. L. 57
stereotypes of retirement 9, 84, 112
stigmatisation for working 2
stress at job 60; lingering effects 108
stressful or otherwise unsafe workplaces 120
subjective life expectancy (SLE) 53
substance abuse 108–9
Sullivan, O. 20
superannuation 48–9
SuperFriend 120
Svensson, I. 10, 29–30
Swedish study 29–30
Szinovacz, M. E. 77

taxation 35
Teachers Insurance and Annuity Association (TIAA) study 97
technology 121–2
temporal focus 115–17
testosterone 42
time 70
time horizons 6
time perspective 64
time structures 17
timing of retirement 55–9, 94, 96
togetherness 77
total remuneration 32
Touvier, M. 88
transformative model 12
transitional model 11
transitions 1, 67–8, 118, 121; gradual retirement 67–8; stages of 69–76; theoretical perspectives 68–9
trust 63, 102
TV watching 88
types of retirement 12–14

unemployment: future generations and 121
unemployment, forced 19
United Kingdom: equal pay act 2; health studies 86, 87; preparation for retirement 37; research on life satisfaction 60–1
United States 111; 401(k) plans 59; alcohol misuse 107–8; financial literacy 40; financial security 35; millennials 47; poverty rate for women 43; Standard & Poor's 500 Index 32; wellbeing study 95
unpaid work 1, 22–3
'unretirement' 104
unsatisfied women 14

US Census Department data 43–4
US Health and Retirement Study 57, 85–6, 104

van den Bogaard, L. 94
van der Heide, I. 90
van Duijn, R. 71
Vermeer, S. J. C. 57
Victoria police force 120
voluntary retirement 60–1
voluntary work 9–10
volunteering 10, 18, 56, 70, 81, 99–100
voting rights 2
Vu, J. 47, 48

wages 1; gender pay gap 32–3, 110; pink-collar work 26; total remuneration 32
Wang, M. 5, 6, 7, 8, 10, 91
Warren, D. 53
welfare provisions 21
wellbeing 93, 113, 114–15
Wellbeing, Health, Retirement and the Lifecourse project (WHERL) 35
wellbeing outcomes 6, 7–8
Wider Opportunities for Women (WOW) study 44
widows 119; Scottish Widows study 36–9
Willis, R. J. 85
Wingrove, C. R. 92

Wisconsin Longitudinal Study 7
The Women's Room (French) 28
women who never retire 65–6
work 16–30; disruptions and trajectories 27–30; functions of 16–19; issues affecting women's 19–23; latent function 17–19; latent functions of 56; manifest function 16; part-time 21–4; pink-collar work and gender occupational divide 25–7; Preference Theory 23–7; 'second shift' 3, 20–1
'workaholics' 6
work histories 10–11
work participation rates 2
world wars 2
Wu, C. 85

Yogev, S. 108
younger age groups, views of older people 52
Yunus, Muhammad 121

Zaniboni, S. 56
Zantinge, E. M. 89
Zhu, R. 87–8
Zimbardo, P. G. 64
Ziska, M. 109
Zogby International 56